A Common Strangeness

VERBAL ARTS :: STUDIES IN POETICS
....
SERIES EDITORS :: Lazar Fleishman & Haun Saussy

A Common Strangeness

CONTEMPORARY POETRY,
CROSS-CULTURAL ENCOUNTER,
COMPARATIVE LITERATURE

Jacob Edmond

FORDHAM UNIVERSITY PRESS *New York* 2012

THIS BOOK IS MADE POSSIBLE BY A COLLABORATIVE GRANT
FROM THE ANDREW W. MELLON FOUNDATION.

Fordham University Press is grateful to the University
of Otago for a generous subvention to help with
publication costs associated with this book.

Fordham University Press has no responsibility for the
persistence or accuracy of URLs for external or third-
party Internet websites referred to in this publication
and does not guarantee that any content on such
websites is, or will remain, accurate or appropriate.

Fordham University Press also publishes its books
in a variety of electronic formats. Some content that
appears in print may not be available in electronic
books.

Library of Congress Cataloging-in-Publication Data

Edmond, Jacob.
A common strangeness : contemporary poetry, cross-
cultural encounter, comparative literature / Jacob
Edmond. — 1st ed.
p. cm.
Includes bibliographical references and index.
ISBN 978-0-8232-4259-7 (cloth : alk. paper)
ISBN 978-0-8232-4260-3 (pbk. : alk. paper)
1. Poetry, Modern—20th century—History and
criticism. 2. Comparative literature. 3. Literature and
globalization. I. Title.
PN1270.5.E36 2012
809.1'04—dc23

                   2011050654

Printed in the United States of America

14 13 12   5 4 3 2 1

First edition

CONTENTS

ACKNOWLEDGMENTS

I began work on this book while based at the Davis Center for Russian and Eurasian Studies at Harvard University as a Fulbright Visiting Scholar. I thank Fulbright New Zealand and the Davis Center—in particular, Timothy Colton and Lisbeth Tarlow—for providing me with the opportunity to research and write in a stimulating interdisciplinary environment. I am especially grateful to Stephanie Sandler, who welcomed me into the intellectual life of the university. Her scholarship and her engagement with my work are ongoing sources of inspiration. I am also very grateful to the graduate students and other faculty in the Departments of Slavic Languages and Literatures, East Asian Languages and Civilizations, English, and Comparative Literature, and especially to Svetlana Boym. Her invitation to contribute to a special issue of *Poetics Today* on estrangement led me to draft an initial chapter of this book and to begin to map its conceptual framework.

I wrote the rest of this book while based at the University of Otago. I am grateful to my colleagues there, especially those in the Department of English, the Russian Studies Research Cluster, the Asia-New Zealand Research Cluster, and the Cross-Cultural and Comparative Studies research group, for providing a supportive and challenging scholarly milieu in which to test and develop my ideas. My departmental chair, Lyn Tribble, provided extraordinary institutional and intellectual support for which I am deeply grateful. Wendy Parkins also gave me incisive feedback on a draft of chapter 1. Many other colleagues have offered help, suggestions, and encouragement in ways too numerous to list here but for which I am no less grateful.

Once at the University of Otago, I was the recipient of a Fast-Start Grant from the Marsden Fund, administered by the Royal Society of

New Zealand. This grant allowed me to carry out much of the research for and writing of this book. I am also grateful for the generous financial support of the University of Otago and for the assistance of various bodies within the university, including the Department of English, the Centre for Research on National Identity, and the Asia-New Zealand and Russian Studies Research Clusters.

Numerous people generously assisted me in researching this book. I would like especially to thank Maghiel van Crevel and Bonnie McDougall for their extensive help with locating primary sources and for their feedback on drafts. I am also grateful to Bonnie for permission to cite from her unpublished correspondence with me and from her letters and papers, including those held in the Bei Dao Archive at the Chinese University of Hong Kong. I likewise thank Anders Hansson for permission to cite from one of his letters held in this archive, and Alexander Kan and Michael Molnar for permission to quote from their letters to Lyn Hejinian. I am also grateful to Leo Ma and the staff of the New Asia College Library and the Research Centre for Translation in the Institute of Chinese Studies at the Chinese University of Hong Kong; the staff and curators at the Jane Voorhees Zimmerli Art Museum at Rutgers, The State University of New Jersey, especially Jane Sharp and Julia Tulovsky; the librarians at the University of Auckland special collections; the staff of the Memorial archives in Moscow and St. Petersburg; and the librarians at the University of California San Diego Mandeville Special Collections, especially Lynda Claassen and Robert Melton, and the Friends of the UCSD Libraries.

Many others have offered feedback on drafts or oral presentations or pointers and encouragement for further research, or have in other ways assisted me in my work on this book, including Cosima Bruno, Rey Chow, Katerina Clark, David Damrosch, Michael Davidson, David Herd, Michel Hockx, Ilya Kutik, Brian Moloughney, Mary Nicholas, Stephen Owen, Benjamin Paloff, Evgeny Pavlov, Marjorie Perloff, Ellen Rutten, Lisa Samuels, Stephanie Sandler, Ann Vickery, Donald Wesling, Erika Wolf, and Michelle Yeh. Christopher Bush, Craig Dworkin, Edward Gunn, Eric Hayot, Michael Heim, Gerald Janecek, and Barrett Watten in particular offered incisive feedback on drafts of chapters of this book in ways that have proved crucial.

My work on three of the authors discussed here—Yang Lian, Lyn Hejinian, and Arkadii Dragomoshchenko—began with my PhD dissertation written at the University of Auckland under the guidance of Hilary Chung, Michael Hanne, Ian Lilly, and Michele Leggott, and with the generous financial support of the university and a Top Achiever Doctoral Scholarship, funded by the New Zealand government through what was then the Foundation for Research, Science, and Technology. While *A Common Strangeness* contains almost nothing that comes directly from my dissertation, I am grateful to my academic advisors, other faculty, and graduate students in the Department of Comparative Literature, the School of European Languages and Literatures, the Department of English, and the School of Asian Studies for helping me lay the intellectual foundations for this book. Hilary Chung in particular went beyond the call of duty in providing extensive support for and feedback on my dissertation and subsequently collaborated with me on a book of translations of Yang Lian's Auckland work, *Unreal City: A Chinese Poet in Auckland* (Auckland University Press, 2006). Chapter 1 owes a great deal to the conversations that arose from our work on that book.

I am deeply indebted to each of the six poets on whom this study focuses. They have all in various ways generously supported my work, while respecting my critical independence. I thank Yang Lian for his infectious enthusiasm for my work and for poetry at large, and for his permission to cite from his correspondence with me here. I thank Arkadii Dragomoshchenko for assisting me in innumerable ways since he first introduced me to literary life in St. Petersburg in the summer of 2000, and for his permission to reproduce his published writings and unpublished letters and manuscripts here. Lyn Hejinian has likewise generously granted permission to quote from her published and unpublished writings and letters, as well as her translations of Dragomoshchenko's work. I likewise thank Charles Bernstein and Susan Bee for permission to reproduce their work here. I thank Zhao Zhenkai (Bei Dao) for his generosity in granting me permission to quote three of his poems in full in Chinese. The English translations "The Answer," "Hello, Baihua Mountain," and "A perpetual stranger . . . " are taken from Bei Dao's *The August Sleepwalker*, translated by Bonnie S. McDougall, published by Anvil Press Poetry in 1988 and by New Directions in 1990 (copyright © 1988 by Bei Dao; translation copyright © 1988, 1990 by Bonnie S. McDougall). The translations are reprinted by permission of Anvil Press Poetry and New Directions Publishing Corporation. I also thank Peter Jay of Anvil Press for permission to cite from his correspondence with Bonnie McDougall regarding the publication of Bei Dao's work.

To my great sadness, during the writing of this book, Dmitri Prigov passed away. I thank him for his support for my work, and I thank his family, friends, and associates for assisting me with my work after his death. In particular, I thank Nadia Bourova, Andrei Prigov, Natalia Mali, and the Estate of Dmitri Prigov for generously granting gratis permission to reproduce his work here. For their assistance in sourcing the images of Prigov's work reproduced here, I also thank Katharina Eloshvili of Krings-Ernst Galerie in Cologne, Ekaterina Kochetkova of the Moscow Museum of Modern Art, Vitaly Patsyukov and Maria Punina of the National Centre for Contemporary Arts in Moscow, and Barbara Barsch, Irina Bogomolova, Ev Fischer, Boris Raev, and Yuri Traisman.

Some of the material in this book has appeared elsewhere. Chapter 1 is a revised version of "The Flâneur in Exile," published in *Comparative Literature* 62, no. 4 (Fall 2010). Chapter 3 appeared in an earlier form in *Poetics Today* 27, no. 1 (Spring 2006). A part of chapter 2 was published as "Arkady Dragomoshchenko's Correspondences" in the *Slavic and East European Journal* 55, no. 4 (Winter 2011). I am grateful to the journals and presses for their assistance and for permission to reproduce my work here. I also thank the journals' editors, Meir Sternberg, George Rowe, and Gerald Janecek, and their anonymous reviewers. I presented drafts of parts of this book at Harvard University, the University of Otago, the University of Auckland, UCLA, UC Berkeley, the University of Kent, the School of Oriental and African Studies, and University College London, and at numerous conferences. I thank the audiences for their feedback and questions.

I am very grateful to Haun Saussy and Lazar Fleishman for their belief in my project and their championing of it through their series. Haun in particular has been a source of ongoing inspiration, both through his own work and through his support for mine. I also thank the editorial team at Fordham University Press, particularly Helen Tartar, Thomas Lay, and Tim Roberts. I am especially grateful to Helen for her enthusiasm for and commitment to my work.

Several people contributed their editorial skills to this book. I thank Lisa Marr for her tireless work in proofreading and source checking, and Emma Neale for her expert editorial eye, which helped shape and clarify my prose. I am grateful to Karen McLean and Poppy Haynes for their assistance with proofreading and formatting, and to Edward Batchelder for his copyediting. I thank Joanna Forsberg for her photography, and her and Lynette Jones for their assistance in the preparation of image files. I am indebted to Mary Newberry for her work on the index.

This book would not have been possible without the support of my family. I thank my parents, Murray Edmond and Mary Paul, and my aunt Charlotte Paul for their intellectual and emotional support, and my children, Nīkau and Kāhu Edmond-Smaill, for their inspirational enthusiasm for language, books, and writing. Last but not least, I thank my wife, Esther Smaill. She has supported and sustained me and my work in countless ways. This book is dedicated to her.

Introduction

The transition from the general to the particular always has stimulating surprises in store, when the interlocutor without contours, ghostly, takes shape before you, gradually or at a single blow, and becomes the *Mitmensch*, the co-man, with all his depth, his tics, anomalies, and incoherences.

—PRIMO LEVI, *The Periodic Table*

... the common strangeness that does not allow us to speak of our friends but only to speak to them ...

—MAURICE BLANCHOT, *Friendship*

There is no third alternative. Yet that is precisely the one that must be chosen.

—VIKTOR SHKLOVSKY, *Third Factory*

In 1984, in what was to become a foundational text for attempts to understand our current era of globalization, Fredric Jameson cited the then-little-known San Francisco Language writer Bob Perelman and his poem "China," alongside canonical figures from Samuel Beckett to Andy Warhol.[1] For Jameson, Perelman's short, disjunctive poem was exemplary of the "cultural logic of late capitalism." This was precisely because it had "little enough to do with that referent called China." As a unified, collective "subject of history," China was for Jameson antithetical both to the breakdown of the subject in postmodern culture and to the fragmentation of late capitalism as a whole.

Almost three decades later, much has changed. Today it would be hard to imagine a discussion of "multinational capitalism" (to use Jameson's other, more neutral term) that dismissed the relevance of China. Literary and cultural studies have likewise taken a transnational—and increasingly Asian—turn. This turn throws into relief the narrowness of Jameson's assumed Western and US frame of reference, especially when compared to the poem's planetary perspective. (The poem begins: "We live on the third world from the sun. Number three.")[2] We can now see that Jameson was writing at the beginning of a period of global change. This shift included the transformation of China after the end of the Cultural Revolution in 1976 ("the unexpected emergence, between the two super-powers, of 'number three,'" as Jameson described China in 1984)[3]; Gorbachev's accession to power in 1985 and the ensuing glasnost reforms; the Chinese government crackdown on June 4, 1989; the fall of the Berlin Wall and communist regimes in Eastern and Central Europe the same year; the collapse of the Soviet Union and the end of the Cold War in 1991; and the explosive capitalist expansion ushered in by Deng Xiaoping's 1992 boost to free market reforms. How have these economic and geopolitical events transformed the way we think about literature and culture on a global scale? How have avant-garde poets like Perelman and their readers like Jameson participated in and responded to these historic changes? What might their responses tell us about how we have come to understand our own era as both more global and more diverse? What might they reveal about the historical and rhetorical structures that produce these poles of sameness and difference? What is the history—and what is the poetry—of this common strangeness?

One response to these questions might simply dismiss the relevance of poetry and poetics to the economic, geopolitical, and social changes of the last few decades. The accepted wisdom after all is that the end of the Cold War and the rise of the free market in countries such as China and Russia were the death knell of poetry as a leading intellectual and social force, leaving it confined to the margins, as it had already long been in countries such as the United States.[4] Even there, poetry arguably became more marginal after 1989. It no longer attracted the red baiting that—from Allen Ginsberg in the 1950s to Perelman and his fellow Language writers in the 1980s—gave it at least some political edge and cultural resonance.[5] Add to this poetry's reliance on linguistic particularity—idiom, form, *le mot juste*— and the transformation of modernism's once radically estranging techniques into the commonplace condition of fragmentation in an era of multinational capitalism, and poetry's irrelevance today seems assured.

To the contrary, this book argues that poets from China, Russia, and the United States have responded to the world historical changes in which their countries played such key roles in ways that attest to the art form's resilience and even renaissance. It identifies in these poetic responses a common concern with strangeness in textual practice, cross-cultural encounter, and transnational affiliation. On its own this claim would barely make a ripple in the fields of literary and cultural studies. But *A Common Strangeness* engages broader issues: it shows how the poetics of strangeness—just as much as history, geopolitics, and economics—have shaped conceptions of the global.

A Common Strangeness homes in on an alternative to the binary of sameness and strangeness that limits our understanding of many aspects of our own age, from geopolitics to poetics. Rather than building my study around an East/West or local/global opposition, I triangulate between Russian, Chinese, and US examples to highlight the multilateral cross-cultural referents and personal encounters that are neither local nor global, but that reveal the historical origins and contingencies of this dichotomy. During the period of confusing and contradictory flux when the old Cold War binaries unraveled but the new local/global dichotomies were yet to coalesce into conceptual commonplaces, avant-garde writers sought to reimagine the world. They did so by intertwining linguistic strangeness and multiple cross-cultural engagements in ways that offer new possibilities for reconceiving literary and cultural studies. Recognizing these possibilities requires extending literary and cultural studies beyond even two languages or regions of the globe, and outside familiar contours of transnational affiliation and influence. It means exploring how referents such as "China" function not merely as arbitrary signifiers of a global reality nor just as markers of cultural difference, but as multilayered figures in cross-cultural encounters and readings—such as Perelman's use of a Chinese language primer as the impetus for his poem, or Jameson's 1985 trip to China, which shaped his attempts to theorize our era of globalization. These cross-cultural readings are of course always particularly located and frequently globally oriented—they attempt to imagine the world or the globe as a whole. Yet they are also embedded in a messy, complex reality of interactions that a dichotomy such as local-or-global elides.

Global theory, comparative literature, and modernist poetics all orbit around the mutually constituting and reinforcing poles of linguistic and cultural sameness and difference. This binary reflects deep-seated habits of thought that continue to shape our understanding of literature and culture at the very moment when they seem to have outlived their usefulness. Deriving from Eurocentric and colonial attitudes and

Cold War politics, the binary opposition of commonness and strangeness infects our very attempts to move beyond such modes of thinking and to grasp the complexity of our current situation. Therefore while *A Common Strangeness* participates in the transnational turn that literary and cultural studies have taken over the past two decades, it also shows that this turn remains incomplete: many fields of intellectual endeavor, such as area studies and comparative literature, are still shaped by the history and conceptual and political structures of the Cold War.[6] This claim might seem less surprising if we consider, for example, that Jameson's theory of culture in an era of multinational or global capitalism (published in full only in 1991) depended on his appeal, via Perelman's poem, to China as the communist counterexample that proved the general rule. Beyond the fields of literary and cultural studies, Cold War institutions, mindsets, symbolism, and rhetoric constrain efforts to construct a more complex picture of recent world history and continue to cast a long shadow over international affairs: from the UN Security Council and the Korean Peninsula, to the domestic political discourse of countries such as Russia, China, and the United States.[7] They do so in ways that can seem strikingly at odds with new global economic and geopolitical realities.

The responses of Russian, Chinese, and US poets, critics, and theorists to the historical changes at the end of the Cold War reflect a transition from the them-and-us oppositional structures of the late–Cold War period to the appositional, transnational, and multiculturalist poetics of our current era.[8] But they also show an underlying conceptual continuity. Jameson's essay was just one of a number of influential texts that cited contemporary avant-garde poetries from the three countries as examples of a profound shift in international culture associated with the rise of globalization and with postmodernism, as it was termed in the 1980s and early 1990s. Despite this fresh sense of globalism, these poetries were largely discussed in isolation or read through a dichotomizing, Cold War–inflected view of culture, politics, modernism, and modernity in which Western, typically US, postmodernism was contrasted with—estranged from—its Russian or Chinese variant.[9] Where in the past the distinction might have been made between East and West, it increasingly came to be drawn between local heterogeneity and global homogeneity. Still, the dichotomy remained.

Comparative literature in the wake of the "transnational turn" in literary and cultural studies seems equally caught in a binary of

commonness and strangeness that resembles the Cold War dichot-
omy of them and us, and the post–Cold War opposition of the local
and the global.[10] Increasingly popular in recent years, transnational
and comparative studies have tended to adopt one of two binary ap-
proaches. On the one hand, exploiting the extremely fruitful line of
inquiry opened up by Edward Said's *Orientalism*, scholars have en-
gaged the them/us polarities of cross-cultural representations from
the perspective of one nation, or at best as a dialogue between two
nations or regions, as, for example, between China and the United
States, or between the West and East Asia.[11] On the other hand, they
have explored the tension between generalized, free-floating concep-
tions of world literature, global modernity, postmodernity, or super-
modernity, and an antithetical local.[12] The former approach addresses
the problem by emphasizing the ideological underpinnings that shape
how one culture reads another, and the latter emphasizes the resis-
tance of local particularity to global theory. Both dichotomizing ap-
proaches evince the institutional structures of national literary and
area studies as they were consolidated in the Cold War period. But
they also reflect the way recent theorists of comparative literature
have been preoccupied with how to compare when any global unit
for comparison comes tainted by the discipline's Eurocentric legacy
and threatens to subordinate heterogeneous texts to a homogenous
norm.[13] Locked in this theoretical bind, which is a product both of
modernity at large and of our post–Cold War moment, comparative
literature today seems caught in an endless oscillation between same-
ness and difference.[14]

To address this persistent dichotomy, *A Common Strangeness* turns
to six avant-garde poets: Bei Dao 北岛 (pseudonym of Zhao Zhen-
kai 赵振开; 1949–) and Yang Lian 杨炼 (1955–) from China; Arka-
dii Dragomoshchenko (1946–) and Dmitri Prigov (1940–2007) from
Russia; and Charles Bernstein (1950–) and Lyn Hejinian (1941–)
from the United States. But it does so not in order to make a new
global claim based on an expanded range of particularized local ex-
amples. Such shifts in scale, as necessary as they are to grasping the
complexity of our era, leave untouched the entrapping alternation be-
tween the general and the particular, sameness and difference.[15] It is
not easy to move from the bewildering abstraction of billions to the
particularity of a single person and text without succumbing to this
binary logic.[16] Yet in engaging with the fluctuating terms of this bi-
nary at the end of the Cold War, these six poets confronted precisely

this difficulty. Their responses provide largely neglected tools for addressing the same problem today. These poets' attentiveness to poetics, to how we construct an image of the world in language, not only leads to an acute awareness of the rhetorical structure of sameness and strangeness but also offers ways of writing—and so thinking—our world differently. By considering and emulating these responses, in all their irreducible, multilateral complexity, this book seeks insights into how we have come to see the world in such a dichotomous way and how we might see it otherwise.

During the late twentieth century, avant-garde poetry took a transnational turn that was caught between poetic, personal, and collective assertions of strangeness and commonness and that shared with comparative literature a desire to avoid either radical nominalism or abstracted globalism.[17] Building on the search for a poetics that traverses the boundaries of nation and culture, which had been a major driver of avant-garde poetry for the past one hundred years, many writers had a powerful if ill-defined dream of an imagined transnational poetic community whose shared sense of location was based, paradoxically, on its dislocation. Dislocation here means not just separation or estrangement from home and nation, but an aesthetic that questions the solidity of the relationship between word and world through writing that foregrounds its own strangeness.[18] These forms of textual strangeness derived from diverse modernist and avant-garde practices and were intertwined with imaginings of other places and times, but poets gave them increasing emphasis in response to the period of change at the end of the twentieth century. They articulated renewed international affiliations and a heightened sense of location and difference.[19] Like many transnational movements, they adopted an ambivalent position between participating in and resisting globalization and its homogenizing forms.[20]

In US poetry after the Second World War, poets such as Charles Olson and Jerome Rothenberg developed transcultural poetics that drew on but distinguished themselves from Ezra Pound's authoritarian vision—though arguably not realization—of a transnational cultural essence.[21] At the end of the Cold War, in response to the collapse of any viable alternative to the capitalist status quo, US poets working in the avant-garde tradition, such as Hejinian and Bernstein, gave greater attention and new articulation to the problem of developing a nonappropriative, antinational, antihomogenizing, appositional, and multicultural poetics. They not only moved away from the oppositional poetics of the Cold War, in which Perelman's "China" and Rothenberg's and Olson's earlier use of other cultures and translations can be located, but also provided a new, retrospective way of understanding the avant-garde poetic tradition, from Pound to Perelman.[22] No longer seen as oppositional resistance to capitalist commoditization, avant-garde poetry came to be viewed as an appositional, polyvocal, and transcultural response to an increasingly multipolar world. This response has in turn been extended by the next generation of English-language avant-garde writers from Caroline Bergvall to Juliana Spahr.[23]

By the 1970s and 1980s, avant-garde artists and writers in the socialist world generally saw Marxist ideas as irrelevant at best, yet there too those decades marked a shift in avant-garde poetics. In China, the latter half of the Cultural Revolution saw the renewal of avant-garde poetry by writers such as Mang Ke 芒克, Duoduo 多多, and Bei Dao, who turned to the example of earlier modernists, Chinese and foreign alike. They found in these predecessors estranging forms with which they sought to counter the rhetorical norms of official ideology. Yet they equally aimed to construct a transnational and translational vision of poetry outside the restrictive boundaries of Chinese nationalism. The exile of prominent mainland Chinese writers, including Gao Xingjian 高行健, Duoduo, Yang Lian, and Bei Dao, after June 4, 1989, exacerbated their sense of social estrangement and increased their global profile and transnational outlook.[24]

Meanwhile in Russia in the 1970s and early 1980s, writers and artists such as Dragomoshchenko, Prigov, Lev Rubinshtein, Vitaly Komar, and Aleksandr Melamid turned to recent developments in Western art and thought. They adapted conceptualism and poststructuralism to the radically different Russian context as a foil to the literature and art of both official and unofficial Soviet cultures. Opposing the suffocating insularity of each culture, their dialogue with Western art and theory imagined a transnational avant-garde community. Yet they also stressed the particularity of the Soviet context, their relation to Russian predecessors (from Pushkin to modernists such as Malevich and Khlebnikov), and their singular responses. Their dialogue with the West took on renewed urgency in the late 1980s when the literary field was transformed through the collapse of strict censorship and the institutions of Soviet samizdat culture, the move to a free market economy, and new possibilities for emigration and travel. In response, Prigov and Dragomoshchenko in particular (and in their wake younger poets such as Aleksandr Skidan and Dmitri Golynko-Vol'fson) came to rethink their national literature and avant-garde practices in relation to a new, more global context.[25]

Combining linguistic strangeness with appeals to foreignness and transnational affiliation, these Russian, Chinese, and US writers responded to these changes by drawing on the concept of estrangement as it had developed in twentieth-century literary theory and practice. Through estrangement, they negotiated a period of historical change and the binary of sameness and difference that undergirds Cold War and transcultural poetics, comparative and world literature, and global theory. Yet in doing so, they also destabilized this binary by exploiting estrangement's multiple and often contradictory cross-cultural, historical, structural, and phenomenological oppositions.

In their efforts to come to terms with geopolitical and poetic change, these writers frequently conflated their cross-cultural engagements with estrangement as an artistic device. For centuries, writers have turned to foreign languages and cultures in a persistent literary-historical dynamic of sameness and difference. By employing foreign words and forms, they have alternately sought to define, celebrate, or criticize their native tradition, or even to highlight its internal heterogeneity. They have done so in a proliferate range of ways: from the adoption of Sanskrit prosody in Medieval Chinese poetry, and Italian and French verse forms in Medieval and Early Modern England, to Rothenberg's use of non-Western oral traditions to reform the canon of Western poetry in the mid-twentieth-century United States.[26] Although appeals to foreignness might appear to be quite distinct from concepts of estrangement such as Shklovsky's *ostranenie* and Brecht's *Verfremdung*, they in fact play a constitutive role in seemingly universalist modernist theories. Shklovsky frequently conflated estrangement as a literary device with estrangement as foreignness, describing the power of *ostranenie* to restore the "sensation of holding a pen . . . or speaking a foreign tongue for the very first time."[27] Brecht likewise tied estrangement to foreignness and to China in particular, reflecting the ethnicizing or feminizing of linguistic strangeness that is common among many twentieth-century literary theorists.[28] (These even include writers such as Derrida and Foucault, who argue that the depiction of the East as the locus of otherness is one means by which heterogeneity and difference are excluded from Western metaphysics, epistemology, and conceptions of identity.)[29] Responding to this conflation of poetic and cultural estrangement, avant-garde poets at the end of the twentieth century filtered their complex cross-cultural encounters through the binary of sameness and difference.

Yet these writers also used the internal contradictions and cultural and historical contingencies inherent to theories of estrangement to question the binaries that these theories would seem to reinforce. In Shklovsky's formulation, *ostranenie*, or estrangement, is both formalist and phenomenological; both a literary technique for highlighting linguistic signs and conventions, and a device for allowing the individual to see through conventions of art and everyday life to the real object, which is apprehended again as if for the first time.[30] In ways that have been fundamental to many twentieth-century avant-garde practices, Shklovsky emphasized the divide between art and life, between language and reality, between text and person, but also attempted to bridge that divide—to "make a stone feel stony" again.[31] Brecht's *Verfremdung* maintained Shklovsky's dialectical if not contradictory structure, though he emphasized to a much greater extent the development of the audience's awareness of the sociopolitical conventions and institutions that govern our world. As Shklovsky's fellow Formalist Yuri Tynianov also highlighted, estrangement is not an inherent linguistic or artistic property with a set form and function. Instead, like the conventions it seeks to counter, estrangement is historically—as well as culturally—contingent.[32] A literary device's position on the continuum between the conventional and the strange shifts over time, just as a foreign form, like the sonnet, may become assimilated into a tradition. The writers examined here employ diverse modernist estranging techniques in historical circumstances that themselves bear down on the relationship between the everyday and the strange, and that variously shape the personal, political, and cultural resonances of estranging forms. For example, everyday life became oppressively strange in China during the Cultural Revolution, while in 1920s Russia, Shklovsky's *ostranenie* changed from "an artistic device into a technique for survival"—the "third alternative" when "there is no third alternative" between toeing the official line and remaining silent.[33]

The theory and practice of estrangement in the twentieth century has highlighted the relationship between the linguistic structures and conventions that enable—but also constrain—meaning making and the personal experiences, estranging devices, and historical contingencies that belie (while relying on and shaping) those conventions. Modernist conceptions of estrangement inform in often unacknowledged ways the suspicious modes of reading that dominate literary and cultural studies today, and that are particularly noticeable in the recent comparative and transnational turn. Working within these suspicious modes, scholars depend on the poles of the ordinary and the extraordinary, the same and the strange, whether they seek to uncover the hidden structures, meanings, and ideologies beneath the surface of a text, or to defend its unassailable singularity.[34]

In its original avant-garde formulations, however, estrangement enfolds phenomenological, hermeneutic, and historical accounts into a structural one. It therefore emphasizes the historical contingencies, personal experiences, and cross-cultural encounters that complicate literary and cultural analysis built on a structural or comparative binary of sameness and difference, everydayness and strangeness, them and us, local and global, particular and universal. By exploring both the estranging practices and the lyric staging of the coming into being of intersubjectivity in contemporary avant-garde poetry, *A Common Strangeness* traces the pathways whereby the local and the global, East and West, are constructed. It asks what places, histories, and individuals are elided when, for example, a single writer comes to stand for "post-Soviet subjectivity" (in the case of Dragomoshchenko), or for "world poetry" (in the case of Bei Dao).

Maurice Blanchot writes of "the common strangeness" (*l'étrangeté commune*) that precedes the coming into being of subject and object, the same and the other, the moment when self-strangeness is recognized. According to Blanchot, this "common strangeness" demands that we do not "speak *of* . . . but only . . . speak *to*": that we do not represent others but recognize and respond to their unrepresentable otherness, their strangeness—their "infinite distance."[35] For Blanchot, this response is the task of poetry.[36] Blanchot follows the tradition that extends from the biblical imperative to "love thy neighbor as thyself" to Levinas's "*being-for-the-other.*"[37] He proposes the "common strangeness" of our response to the other as a way to resolve the dialectic relation between self and other, home and not-home, sameness and difference. By contrast, this book proposes a third alternative. It investigates the oscillation between collective description and dialogue, between the common and the co-man, between speaking *of* others—of exile literature, modernism, or world literature—and speaking *to* them: responding to how we can know or write about each other in the first place. Yet in exploring how contemporary poetry deploys and unsettles representations of personal, cultural, linguistic, and national difference, it refuses to be limited by the conceptual binary upon which even such theories of responsibility to the other are based.

Instead of maintaining the binary between speaking *of* and speaking *to*, *A Common Strangeness* draws on the writers' own complications of the opposition. In writing *of* these poets working in the period of transition from the late–Cold War world to our current era of globalization, I recognize a striking common commitment to forms of strangeness. Recognizing this strangeness also means taking seriously the task of speaking *to* their work and its challenge to conventional historiography, interpretation, representation, and identity. Yet this strangeness takes the form of encounters involving many kinds of collective representation and individual address irreducible to writing either *of* or *to* another. These textual, personal, and cross-cultural encounters—found in poems, letters, translations, friendships, readings—occupy the space between the dialectic of commonness and strangeness and the dichotomies of the national and the international, the individual and the collective, the local and the global.

A Common Strangeness brings such encounters together not as clues to an imagined universal, nor as examples of incomparable difference, but as illustrations of the often violently superimposed singularities through which the poles of sameness and difference are constructed and sometimes challenged. Chapter 1 addresses how this process of superimposition might be theorized through a discussion of Yang Lian. In his prose and poetry written in exile in Auckland, New Zealand, after June 4, 1989, Yang superimposes Beijing onto Auckland through depictions of a walker in a city. These depictions invite comparison with the nineteenth-century French figure of the flâneur, and with that figure's most influential exponents and theorists, Charles Baudelaire and Walter Benjamin. The figure and Benjamin's related concept of "constellation" suggest a mode of cross-cultural comparison that juxtaposes elements from disparate places and times, rather than producing either isolated particulars or a totalizing whole. This mode reflects a historical-materialist attention to repressed forms of textual and cultural heterogeneity and to the way particulars resist overarching narratives.[38] In reading the flâneur outside Europe and in exile, however, I distinguish the historical materialist's implicit commitment to the binary of the local and the global, the particular and the general—reflected in Benjamin's Eurocentric focus on Paris as "the capital of the nineteenth century"—from Yang's late

twentieth-century poetics and from the model that this book seeks
to develop. Taken together, Baudelaire, Benjamin, and Yang reveal
how notions of modernity in the West and East Asia result from mu-
tually transforming cross-cultural reading and misreading. Reading
each through the other in turn produces a mutually informing and es-
tranging dialogue that cannot be reduced to either a local or a global
form. Drawing on both Yang's figure of the eclipse and Benjamin's
astronomical figure of constellation, I develop the concept of "super-
imposition." Superimposition denotes a mode of writing and think-
ing that acknowledges how reading a text through an overarching
schema necessarily obscures elements of its singularity—even when,
as in Benjamin's case, that schema in principle eschews hierarchical or
totalizing structures. The concept equally recognizes that singularity
is never wholly singular, but always the product of overlaid encoun-
ters and exchanges.

Each subsequent chapter addresses a single writer in a nexus of
cross-cultural engagements and relates to the others in a constel-
lated system of interconnections. Though there are many personal
and literary points of contact among the six poets, none have had
such a close relationship as Arkadii Dragomoshchenko and Lyn He-
jinian.[39] Chapters 2 and 3 examine their encounter from both direc-
tions. Their correspondence, translations, collaborations, and friend-
ship span the period from the heightened tensions between their two
countries in the early 1980s, through perestroika, to the collapse of
the Soviet Union. In different ways, both writers emphasize and en-
twine various kinds of strangeness: they lace together forms of textual
strangeness with their personal experience of strangeness in encoun-
tering each other; with the cultural and geopolitical sense of estrange-
ment enforced by the Cold War divide; and with the further sense of
strangeness induced by the destabilizing of the political and represen-
tational terms of that divide in the late 1980s and early 1990s. Drago-
moshchenko's letters and poems written for Hejinian address the
frames through which we read a text from another culture—as a win-
dow on another world, or for correspondences with our own. Read-
ings of Dragomoshchenko's work have repeatedly been constrained
by those frames, especially as they derive from Cold War oppositions.
Yet his writing questions such frames by combining the interper-
sonal exchange of letter writing with the modernist complication—
as exemplified by Baudelaire's "Correspondances"—of romanticism's
stress on correspondence between language and the world. Hejinian

negotiates a transformative moment in geopolitics, poetics, and conceptions of personhood (which she distinguishes from essentialized notions of identity, subjectivity, and selfhood) by linking one of the most influential critical terms in modernist poetics, Shklovsky's concept of *ostranenie*, with her literal travels to Russia, and with her vision of a transnational Russian and US avant-garde that would transcend the crumbling Cold War divide.

Where the first three chapters examine writers working in response to direct personal encounters shaped by the late–Cold War period and the subsequent rise of globalization, the chapters that follow consider attempts at this same moment of change to use poetry to rethink literature and culture on a transnational or global scale. Chapter 4 occupies a transitional position. It examines how, by appealing to the world and to world literature, Bei Dao responded to the pressures he experienced at the time of the Cultural Revolution and during China's subsequent reform of its political, economic, and cultural relationship with the rest of the world. It also explores how and why his work from this period was retrospectively inserted into a post-1989 debate about translation, world literature, and globalization in the United States. Bei Dao's writing invites but also destabilizes competing readings of his texts as allegories of China and the world. This in turn reveals the rhetorical, as well as historical, flux that preceded the geopolitical and economic rise of China and the intensification of globalization in the 1990s and 2000s.

Chapter 5 explores how writer and artist Dmitri Prigov appropriates and responds critically to Western conceptualism and to Russian modernist and romantic notions of strangeness and originality. Repackaging samizdat texts and the sacred figure of the Russian poet as works of contemporary art, Prigov's practice reveals continuities between Cold War oppositions and the economic liberalization and globalization of the post-Soviet period, by showing their common dependence on the binaries of East and West, local and global. Yet the singularity of the encounters that he stages between such discursive systems belies their binary oppositions, by conjoining contexts as varied as Soviet foreign policy and global dinosaur mania. Finally, chapter 6 examines how Charles Bernstein responded to the changes wrought by the post–Cold War era and the rise of multiculturalism in the United States by suggesting that poetry might transcend borders through its "commonness . . . in . . . partiality." Bernstein provides a model for comparison attuned to the rhetorical structures—the poetics—that shape cross-cultural thinking, and that all six writers highlight and explore in various ways. But his vision of "unity in diversity," with its connotations of US imperialist ideology, also helps to crystallize the persistent tension in the various appeals to textual, personal, and collective strangeness in the work of all these writers and in comparative and global theory: a tension that arises from the fact that an appeal to strangeness can easily become an assertion of commonality or global meaning, so erasing the very particularity with which it began.[40]

These six poets write in diverse languages and historical circumstances, and their work is not united by a single stylistic approach, but they all respond to the seismic shift in geopolitics, economics, and culture that took place from the 1970s through the early 1990s. In their poetic structures and personal and transnational affiliations, they reveal a shared search for alternatives to the persistent poles of commonness and strangeness found both in Cold War binaries and in the local/global dichotomies that continue to shape our understanding of literature and culture. Taken together, they highlight and unsettle the poetics of strangeness through which we conceive our new global reality. They also offer ways to imagine where a mode of writing and reading literature and history that gives up these certainties might lead.

CHAPTER ONE

Yang Lian and the Flâneur in Exile

Knowledge production would henceforth be a matter of tracking the broken lines, shapes, and patterns that may have become occluded, gone underground, or taken flight.

—REY CHOW, "The Old/New Question of Comparison in Literary Studies: A Post-European Perspective"

All an exile can do is follow a dotted line of footprints, stopping motionless on every dot.

—YANG LIAN, "Ghost Speech/Lies"

How can one acknowledge points of contact among disparate texts, times, places, languages, and cultures without eclipsing their particularity? This problem becomes especially acute in the post-1989 world when the ever-increasing connections produced by globalization result in a plurality of cultural positions whose complex entanglements undermine notions of commensurability and equivalence that derive from comparative literature's Eurocentric legacy. As a result, the discipline of comparative literature is in danger of becoming caught in a continuous movement of self-referential deconstruction, oscillating between the universal and the particular, between old Eurocentric practices and the possibility of resisting and subverting them.

I propose that the flâneur in exile addresses and offers an alternative to this endless oscillation between sameness and difference. I use the phrase "flâneur in exile" to refer to the encounter between a paradigmatic figure of European modernity, the flâneur, and Chinese poetry, especially the exilic writing of Yang Lian 杨炼, during the period of political and economic change from the 1970s to the early 1990s that gave birth to our current era. In its overlaying of places, times, languages, and cultures, this encounter embodies the bewildering complexity of the present moment. It also suggests an approach to comparative literature that would address this complexity by acknowledging the constitutive role that such moments of mutually estranging encounter play in modern literature and culture. Taken as a figure for comparability, the flâneur in exile emphasizes collision, encounter, and touch, rather than models of comparison that either claim mimetic commensurability or pit global homogeneity against local particularity. While recognizing the elision of difference that occurs through the superimposition of any text, language, culture, time, or place upon another, the figure also produces moments of particularity that emerge out of these superimpositions: moments of touch that presage the possibility of commonality in singularity, of common strangeness.

FLÂNEUR

Far from being the creation of an isolated European modernity, the figure of the flâneur was from the very beginning intertwined with Europe's others and inseparable from a global context of imperialism. The flâneur was a product of the nineteenth-century European imperial capital; while he was acutely self-conscious of his place at what he perceived to be the center of modernity, his sense of European particularity was nevertheless also born out of his relation to non-Europe. This dynamic is evident in the difference between the original popular flâneur, who assumed "that Paris, or at any rate Europe, was the center of modernity and that he could not exist anywhere else in the world," and Baudelaire's "avant-garde *flâneur*," a "man of the world and . . . a great traveler, who felt at home in all parts of the globe."[1] As a "displaced native" in a city "filled with foreigners and goods from distant lands," the latter emerges out of the experience of strangeness induced by the increasingly cosmopolitan nature of the very imperial capital (Paris) celebrated by the original flâneur.[2] Traveling beyond European boundaries and seeing the foreign within the local, the avant-garde flâneur stages the interrelationship between and superimposition of different places and times. "No one," Benjamin notes, "felt less at home in Paris than Baudelaire."[3] This "dialectic of domesticity and desire for faraway locales" is central to Baudelaire's and Benjamin's flâneur, a figure who emerges only in relation to non-Europe and so demonstrates that modernisms and modernities were and are dynamic "relational" concepts "based in global linkages," born out of and always already in cross-cultural encounter.[4]

The flâneur also epitomizes Benjamin's "peculiar fusion of the primally old within the very heart of the most fashionably up-to-date . . . as the essence . . . of modernity itself."[5] Benjamin associates this fusion with his concept of the "dialectical image," in which the superimposition of past on present shatters the illusion of progress, revealing the mythic and primal within modernity: "what has been comes together in a flash with the now to form a constellation."[6] Benjamin's dialectical image rejects "the idea that conceptual work is related to the making of generalizations" and instead offers a way to recognize each phenomenon's "singularity in details" by mapping the extreme points between each phenomenon, like stars in a constellation.[7] The constellation emerges out of the juxtaposition of texts from different places and times—texts that are not linked by causative relations or a single organizing logic; it thus marks a shift from the establishment of a "relation to reality by means of language to the plane of language itself."[8] This poetics of textual constellation is exemplified by the nonlinear arrangement and frequent cross-referencing of the quotations and commentaries that comprise Benjamin's *Das Passagen-Werk* (*The Arcades Project*). It is also allegorized by the figure of the flâneur who wanders among the many texts of the city.[9]

Benjamin associates the flâneur with the shock encounter that produces a dialectical image most clearly in his description of the failure of the visual at the conclusion of Baudelaire's "À une passante" ("To a Passerby"): "Baudelaire describes eyes that could be said to have lost the ability to look." This "crisis in perception" is marked by the shift from vision to touch that is implicit in Baudelaire's "decisive . . . experience" of being "jostled by the crowd."[10] The moment in turn figures the "immediate shock experience" through which "the sensation of modernity could be had."[11] Through Benjamin's dialectical image, the flâneur becomes not only a figure for tactile, embodied encounters that superimpose disparate places, times, and texts, but also a way of acknowledging the blindness and erasures that such encounters produce, erasures that are obscured by a view of history as progress.[12]

Because the flâneur is always already hybrid, estranged, uprooted (despite its supposed European origin) and yet also associated with European imperialism, the figure has an important connection with current debates on comparability. If, as Rey Chow puts it, the "grid of intelligibility . . . is that of literature as understood in Europe, and historical variations are often conceived of in terms of other cultures' welcome entries into or becoming synthesized with the European tradition," how can one prevent concepts of comparative or world literature from "instrumentalizing the literatures of the world as objects of neocolonial usurpation and imperial subsumption" and so from demonstrating "the arrogance of the cartographic reading of world lit"?[13] Past readings of the flâneur illustrate this problem in multiple ways. The flâneur has been read as embodying a Western imperialist and "masculine identity," who treats women and non-European others as the objects of his gaze—"as part of the representation."[14] In our present moment, the flâneur has also been said to represent the Eurocentric transnational critic who anachronistically applies Western terms to non-Western contexts in ways that elide their particularities and the economic, political, and representational power dynamics involved in cross-cultural reading.[15] To describe, for instance, "*flâneurs* with Chinese characteristics" means overlaying Paris onto Shanghai, a move that inevitably recalls the occupation of the latter by foreign powers, France among them.[16] This conception of the figure highlights critical issues in the current debate over comparability. Yet to read the flâneur only in this way creates a false dichotomy between the West and the rest, between global modernity and local tradition, between world and national literatures, or between the male subject and the female object. To trace the figure's influence on the rest of the world by enumerating similarities or differences against a predetermined European or now global norm is already to accept the "grid of intelligibility." Such a reading ignores how the flâneur is multiply intertwined with other places and times, and connected to the failure of sight and the attenuation of male power.[17]

I therefore take the flâneur as a figure for cross-cultural comparison itself—one that emphasizes the multiple figurations of encounters among places, times, peoples, and languages. Chow and others have called for new modes of comparison that similarly resist commensurability while retaining a desire to think on a world or planetary scale—modes of comparison that recognize that "the general post-European predicament . . . is by necessity inscribed in comparativism and must be grasped through comparativism."[18] Chow's archeological model of comparison would "reach for the universal" while recognizing the problem of doing so without "compromising and erasing the particularity of [the other's] alterity."[19] Emerging from the encounter between Europe and non-Europe, the flâneur exemplifies the need for an approach to comparative literature that acknowledges the already essentially comparative nature of the "post-European predicament." Moreover, the flâneur's blind, tactile wandering seems to anticipate Chow's conception of an alternative mode of comparison. Drawing on Michel Foucault's archeology, this mode would track "the broken lines, shapes, and patterns that may have become occluded, gone underground, or taken flight."[20]

By standing simultaneously for both the Eurocentric gaze and a new post-European perspective, the figure of the flâneur suggests the erasures that accompany even such attempts to oppose the grid of intelligibility. Examples of such erasures are the dependence of Benjamin's nonlinear, constellated vision on his Eurocentric reading of Paris as "the capital of the nineteenth century," or the Western imaginings of China from which Foucault derives his alternative model of knowledge.[21] But for all its acknowledgment of these negations, the comparative poetics of superimposition that I locate in the flâneur does not lead necessarily to a collapse of difference in deconstructive play, to differences that signify only through their mutual negation. The darkness of "indefinite definition by negation" produces in response a poetics of the senses and, in particular, interpersonal acts of touch that bring "intersubjective experience and meaning" into being.[22] In poetry, such sensuous moments are frequently marked by an emphasis on language's material, visual, aural, or even tactile embodiment. In the rest of this chapter, I trace the flâneur through 1970s and 1980s Chinese poetry in general and Yang Lian's later exilic writing in particular. Rethinking the flâneur in exile—outside Europe and under various forms of contradiction and negation—points to a comparative poetics at once cognizant of the erasures of transhistorical and cross-cultural comparison and attentive to moments of historical and sensuous textual encounter.

SUN

While Baudelaire has held an important place within modern Chinese literature since his work was translated by leading Chinese modernists (Lu Xun 鲁迅, Xu Zhimo 徐志摩, and Dai Wangshu 戴望舒 among them), he arguably occupies an even greater symbolic position in Chinese literature of the second half of the twentieth century, one intimately connected with the figure of the flâneur.[23] In 1972, as part of his "underground reading" during the Cultural Revolution, the poet Duoduo 多多, one of the founding and most influential figures of post-1970 experimental Chinese poetry, encountered Baudelaire's work for the first time through a selection from *Les fleurs du mal* (*The Flowers of Evil*) translated by the poet Chen Jingrong 陈敬容 and published in 1957 by the official People's Literature Press.[24]

Because Chen was a former member of the modernist Nine Leaves group, which had been attacked for not conforming to the party line, Duoduo's discovery of her translations represents an encounter not only between contemporary China and nineteenth-century France but also between 1970s Chinese poets and a suppressed Chinese literary modernism.[25] Chen's renditions of Baudelaire exemplify what Bei Dao 北岛, another major figure in experimental Chinese poetry of the 1970s, calls "translation style" (翻译文体). This style was created by talented writers who, unable to publish their own work in the 1950s, took advantage of the fact that "in the PRC's first decade the ideological criteria for foreign literature were looser than for native Chinese works."[26] Citing Chen's translations, among other works, Bei Dao argues that this style, which "exists in the strip between two languages . . . without belonging to either," represented a "quiet revolution" in Chinese literature and was crucial to the revival of modernist poetry in the 1970s.[27] Underscoring Bei Dao's point, Yang Lian emphasizes the enormous impact Chen's translation style made on his own writing when he first encountered her renditions of Baudelaire in the early 1980s.[28]

Duoduo's discovery of Baudelaire is arguably the most celebrated instance of the impact of translation style's in-between poetics of cross-cultural and cross-temporal encounter. Duoduo himself mythologizes the occasion as a crucial event in his life, which influenced his development as a poet and, more generally, his entire worldview: "the one [worldview] emanating from Baudelaire's poetry collided head-on with the glorification of Mao during the Cultural Revolution."[29] Chen's translation of Baudelaire's "Le crépuscule du matin" ("Dawn") as "Menglong de liming" 朦胧的黎明 ("Shadowy Dawn") emphasizes the obscuring of the sun's light and understanding (*ming* 明). Her translation implicitly rejects the emphasis on straightforward expression in officially prescribed literature and challenges the prevailing political ideology, since "generally in poetry and other forms of writing from the 1970s and 1980s, 'the sun' stands for Mao Zedong."[30] In this respect, Chen anticipates the resonances of the term *menglong shi* 朦胧诗 (translated variously as "obscure poetry," "misty poetry," or "poetry of shadows"), later widely used to refer to the first generation of post-Mao modernist or experimental poets (including Duoduo, Bei Dao, and Yang Lian).[31] It should come as no surprise, then, that Duoduo describes his encounter with Baudelaire through sun imagery—in particular the eclipse of one sun by another. He contrasts singing "Chairman Mao is like the sun" with Baudelaire's assertion in "Le soleil" ("The Sun") that "The sun is like a poet."[32] Duoduo's account exemplifies the "counter-discourse" of Occidentalism in China, whereby writers and intellectuals import an idea from the West by productively "misunderstanding" it. Here Duoduo produces a form of "anti-official" Chinese Occidentalism, assimilating Baudelaire into the symbolic system of Maoist China in order to counter official ideology.[33] One could thus also read the hazy light of the obscured sun (*menglong*) as standing for Duoduo's cross-cultural reading of the image of the sun as poet in Baudelaire's "Le soleil"—that is, as a figure for the act of productive misreading.

The obscured sun might equally stand for a comparative practice that emphasizes mutually estranging encounters among disparate cultures, languages, and literary works over mimetic models that claim equivalence or commensurability.[34] Indeed, another variant of *menglong*, 矇眬, literally refers to the blinding of the eyes and so to the erasure of vision associated with the flâneur. For, if "Le soleil" equates the sun with the poet, it also equates both poet and sun with the flâneur. The flâneur's blind wandering involves "Trébuchant sur les mots comme sur les pavés" (Stumbling over words as over paving stones) and so becomes synonymous with the writing of poetry and with the indiscriminate visitations of the sun. When the sun is finally said to be "ainsi qu'un poète" (like a poet), it is because "il [le soleil] descend dans les villes" (he goes down into the cities) and participates in the urban wandering undertaken by the poet who finds his rhymes on the streets in the first stanza.[35]

Just as Duoduo presents reading "Le soleil" as a collision between two suns, between China and the West, light and eclipse, so Baudelaire's poem is itself built, through the doubleness and erasures of the figure of the flâneur, on a poetics of collision and encounter. The poet collides with verse ("Heurtant parfois des vers"; Colliding at times with lines) and responds to the sun's "frappe" (blows) with his own "fantasque escrime" (fanciful fencing). We do not know whether the sun mimics the poet or vice versa, nor, if they are in conflict with one another, who wins out.[36] The poet takes on sun-like characteristics and the sun poet-like attributes, and in finding rhymes on the streets (the poet) and wandering indiscriminately (the sun) both resemble the flâneur. The ambivalent figure of the flâneur as poet and sun also relates to a battle between reality and language that is enacted most strikingly in the pun on "vers" (at once "verse," "worms," and "toward"), whose prepositional meaning allegorizes the signifying function of the sign—the movement between verse and worms. The "flickering" between language and reality that is the result of "the double allegiance of the sign to its context and something outside of that context" also enacts the ceaseless movements of the flâneur, who similarly allegorizes the signifying function in the poem, parrying with language (rhyming "la rime" itself with "escrime") the shocking blows of modernity that in Benjamin's reading cause "words to collapse."[37]

Benjamin further complicates the flickering double movements of the walker in "Le soleil" by reading him as a flâneur under erasure. The protagonist of "Le soleil" "traverse[s] the city absently." His "fanciful fencing" embodies "anything but the condition of the observer."[38] Echoing Baudelaire's description of Constantin Guys, the painter of modern life who "*stabs away* with his pencil, his pen, his brush," "parrying his own blows," the protagonist's stabbing pen implicitly marks the shift from vision to language and touch.[39] The poetics of collision in "Le soleil" figures "the subterranean shocks by which Baudelaire's poetry is shaken" and so the "shock experience" of modernity that Baudelaire places "at the very centre of his art" and that is critical to Benjamin's identification of a dialectical image in his poetry.[40]

Through the figure of the flâneur, sun and poet, reality and language, sight and touch are superimposed, merging with and erasing each other, just as Duoduo's poet as sun eclipses Maoist ideology while conforming to its symbolic structure—and even to its literal meaning. (Mao, after all, was also a poet.) Enacting the double movement of language toward and beyond its context and the shift from a poetics of generalizing vision and binary opposition to one of blind touch, the flâneur is a figure both for the specific cross-cultural encounter between Duoduo and "Le soleil" and for my act of comparison that produces a further collision out of their implicitly comparative poetics.

Also critical to the flâneur's flickering double movement is the antithesis and interconnection between town and country. This is announced in the opening stanza of "Le soleil" by the line "Sur la ville et les champs, sur les toits et les blés" (On the city and the country, on the roofs and the wheat fields) and is reinforced by the division of the remaining two stanzas into the country (stanza 2) and the city (stanza 3). Walking becomes an act of writing, and the city a text in which one finds "vers" (verse), but this city-text is intimately connected with a country-text that might at any moment bloom forth "like roses" in the "country" or "fields." ("Éveille dans les champs les vers comme les roses"; Makes verses bloom in the fields like roses.) Just as the city-text is hidden in corners ("Flairant dans tous les coins les hasards de la rime"; Scenting in every corner the chances of the rhyme), the country-text is concealed in a subterranean realm of writhing worms, through the pun on "vers" (as both "worms" and "verse"). By equating both sun and poet with the flâneur, and uniting rural and traditional symbols of death (worms) and beauty (roses) with their modern, urban counterparts—"les hôpitaux et . . . les palais" (the hospitals and . . . palaces)—the poem enacts Baudelaire's vision of the painter of modern life as an artist who combines the modern and the ancient, the "fleeting" and the "eternal." "Le soleil" typifies as well the flâneur's role in staging this connection as the interplay between, and conflation of, city and country: Benjamin describes the flâneur "botanizing on the asphalt" in a city that, in Baudelaire's words, resembles "the forest and the prairie."[41]

Duoduo's poetry similarly stages the interplay between country and city. Just as the sun signified differently to Duoduo than it did to Baudelaire, so the city-country divide reflects a very different political and historical context. Written the year Duoduo encountered Baudelaire's poetry, "Gaobie" 告别 ("Farewell"; 1972) addresses the Cultural Revolution's rustication campaign, which sent thousands of urban youths, including Duoduo himself, into the countryside. The "city lights" (万家灯火), which "stretch out in loneliness" (一片孤寂), contrast with the "dark night" (黑夜) of the countryside.[42] The "herdsman" (牧羊人) who "guards the dark night" (守卫黑夜) apparently stands for the Communist or Red power that bars the protagonist from returning to his urban home and relieving the city's loneliness.[43] Yet this exile to the countryside is treated metaphorically through the figure of a walker, who moves through streets, taking "an unfamiliar turn / in the side lane leading toward maturity" (陌生的分路 ／ 在走向成长的那条僻巷中). Negotiating a flickering path between country darkness and city lights, the walker occupies the city imaginatively, through its lonely lights and the ambiguously located "side lane," even as he is barred from it physically. His "unfamiliar turn" (becoming a poet) allows him to undercut the official opposition of country to city.

Duoduo's poems of the 1980s, such as "Wo yifu" 我姨夫 ("My Uncle"; 1988) and "Beifang de ye" 北方的夜 ("Night of the North";

1985), also address the relationship between city and country.[44] "Night of the North" blurs the two so as to uncover the primal beneath the modern: "inside our brains, shining like lamps / stretch wild forests, to this day" (在我们灯一样亮着的脑子里 / 至今仍是一片野蛮的 森林). The location of the "prehistoric" (史前) within the present and the country's wild forest among the lights of the city reflects a general trend in Chinese literature of the 1980s that parallels the "botanizing on the asphalt" in the literature of the flâneur. During this decade, many writers sought to confront modernity by staging an "imagined return to the country" in a movement known as *xungen* 寻根 (root seeking), a literary tendency that, like Baudelaire's sun, provided a counter-discourse to "urban centers of political power."[45] The *xungen* movement took place in the context of an ideological debate in the official media over both the relationship between tradition and modernity and the place of modernist literature. The more sophisticated *xungen* writers did not simply conform to the parameters of these debates by idealizing the country, myth, and tradition as counters to modernity, modernization, and the West. As in the literature of the flâneur, *xungen* writing extended beyond the boundaries of these debates "to question both tradition and modernity and dramatize the traumatic encounter between these two nemeses in figurative terms."[46]

Like most *menglong* poets, Yang Lian spent time in the countryside during the Cultural Revolution, and his 1980s work exemplifies the complex questioning of tradition and modernity characteristic of *xungen* writing. "Banpo" 半坡 (1984), for example, explores the famous archeological site through Han creation myths, and "Nuorilang" 诺日郎 ("Norlang"; 1983) stages an encounter with an eponymous waterfall in relation to various Tibetan myths and rituals.[47] These poems mark the Beijing poet's journeys to rural parts of China and Tibet in search of resources unavailable in urban centers. While neither explicitly addresses country-city relations, they implicitly conflate the conflict between tradition and modernity with the confrontation between country and city. As in "Le soleil," these works deploy the figure of the sun to dramatize the return to the countryside and the encounter between tradition and modernity.

Although Xiaomei Chen argues that Yang Lian and Jiang He 江 河 use the sun positively in their *xungen* poetry to depict a collective Chinese tradition, Yang's representation of the sun, like his treatment of the relation between modernity and tradition, in fact remains

highly ambivalent.[48] In "Banpo," for example, the sun is associated
with the superimposition of past on present and the uncertain nego-
tiation of a path between modernity and tradition. The poem depicts
the "ancestral sun" (祖先的……阳) both as a figure for rebirth (再生;
born again) and as an executioner: "the hangman's noose of the mid-
day sun's light / was long ago pulled tight" (太阳的正午之光的绞索 /早
已勒紧).[49] At the conclusion of the poem's opening section, the "set-
ting ancestral sun" (祖先的夕阳) accompanies the rebirth of the god-
dess Nüwa 女娲, a conjunction that signals both the overcoming and
renewal of tradition.[50] Through an address to a sun that figures both
the past and renewal, both oppression and possibility, modernity and
tradition are superimposed and mutually constructed in the now of
the poem.

In "Richao" 日潮 ("Suntide"), the first part of "Norlang," the sun
plays a similarly critical role in staging the interaction between tradi-
tion and modernity.[51] Because the poem's "reply to the sun" (*nuo ri
lang* 诺日郎) inheres in the literal meaning of the Chinese translitera-
tion of the Tibetan name of the waterfall, Norlang, the cross-cultural
encounter between a Tibetan word and its Chinese rendition suggests
the flickering double movement that the poem performs. Signaled in
the title "Norlang" and the subtitle "Suntide," the interplay between
sun and water embodies the poem's opposing forces.[52] Like these ti-
tles, the poem's address to the sun and Tibetan tradition is open to
multiple interpretations. It has been read as an expression of a Han,
masculine desire to dominate nature and other cultures, but also as
a counter-discourse to official ideology.[53] The poem both connects
and opposes the sun to the poet, recalling the simultaneous opposi-
tion and conflation of the two in "Le soleil" and in Duoduo's encoun-
ter with Baudelaire's poem. In addressing the sun, it also recalls and
responds to Mao and the heroic rhetoric of the Cultural Revolution.
Equally, the poem appropriates tradition for modernist ends. Like
"Banpo," then, "Norlang" overlays tradition and modernity, Maoist
and post-Maoist ideologies, the countryside and the modern urban
poet, through an appeal to the sun. As in Duoduo's reading of "Le
soleil," the poem's "reply to the sun" takes on multiple eclipsing and
reinforcing figurations.

The ambivalence and "shifting critique of tradition and moder-
nity" in *xungen* writing, including Yang's, reflected and contested the
ideological structures of post-Mao China at a time when a renewed
emphasis on tradition was accompanied by a rhetoric of progress that

led to massive modernization, industrialization, and urbanization on a globally unprecedented scale.[54] During this period of flux, writers experienced new opportunities for publication and intellectual debate, but also faced repression and political intolerance—notably the 1983 Anti–Spiritual Pollution Campaign, during which Yang's "Norlang" was harshly criticized, the 1987 Anti–Bourgeois Liberalization Campaign, and, of course, the response to the protests in the spring of 1989. Yang's *xungen* writing implicitly critiqued the combination of this renewed emphasis on tradition and rapid economic development. By superimposing the mythic on modernity and emphasizing a repetitious and entrapping intertwining of the two through the figure of the sun, he implied that the changes of the 1980s hid the continuity of political repression and located this sense of entrapment within the Chinese tradition. He thus reflected a growing sensitivity among *xungen* writers to the "paralysis that a total immersion in culture dictates."[55] He also recalled Benjamin's admonition to explore the "primal" in modernity in order to apprehend the perpetual (and hellish) recurrence of the new.[56]

EXILE

For Yang, June 4, 1989, confirmed his sense of the sameness beneath the semblance of change that forms an undercurrent in his *xungen* poetry; it also marked a shift in his life and writing. Yang was in Auckland, New Zealand, in the run up to June 4. His protests against the Chinese government at that time made returning to China seem ill-advised, and so he spent the subsequent three years based mainly in Auckland.[57] The writing he produced over this period develops the disenchantment and decentering impulses of *menglong* and *xungen* poetics into a confrontation with exile.[58]

Yang's exilic writing negotiates the temporal and physical disjunction of exile through the figure of the walker in the city. It shifts the many literary references to walking and to the figure of the solitary traveler, exile, and stranger in traditional and modern Chinese poetry and fiction (including *xungen* literature) from their largely rural landscapes to an explicitly urban and foreign environment, presenting a far more alienated subject than in the few earlier Chinese modernist representations of the flâneur.[59] In the prose, or *sanwen* 散文, cycle "Guihua" 鬼话 ("Ghost Speech/Lies") and the poetic cycle "Huanxiang zhong de chengshi" 幻象中的城市 ("City in a Day Dream"),

Yang's walker dramatizes the superimposition of two cities—Beijing and Auckland—and two times—June 4 and the aftermath of exile. He enacts the dislocation between the here and now of exile and his past in China, between the strange language that surrounds him in exile and the language in which he writes.[60]

Just as I have superimposed Baudelaire and Benjamin onto Chinese poetry of the 1970s and 1980s, so I read Yang's exiled walker in relation to the figure of the flâneur. In doing so, I redouble the superimposition of times and places found in the figure, which occurs both in Yang's texts and in Baudelaire's mythologized position at the origins of post-Mao Chinese poetry. The collisions that result, like that between Baudelaire and Duoduo, reveal as much through noncorrespondences as through points of contact, enacting the double movement of a text toward and beyond its engagement with the particularities of its own space and time, at a moment when—from Berlin to Beijing—spatial, temporal, and political boundaries and oppositions were being both contested and violently reasserted. Read through the lens provided by the flâneur, Yang's exile writing confronts this moment by suggesting the possibility of an alternative approach to comparative literature and modernity that negates commensurability in favor of superimposition, encounter, and touch.

The protagonist of Yang's Auckland writings is almost always depicted as an exile, alone and isolated, "walk[ing] the streets" (在街上走) and "walking alone in the city" (一个人在城里走).[61] This depiction combines characteristics of the flâneur with a contrasting sense of the exile's alienation from the city, its language, and people. Yang's alienated walker is a fugitive "on the run in this strange city" (在这座陌生的城市里逃), a status that recalls the association of the flâneur with the criminal and with the detective story.[62] Benjamin notes that Baudelaire frequently changed his dwelling place in order to circumvent the regulation of the city, and Yang's work repeatedly invokes this same theme.[63] In "Lao gushi" 老故事 ("Old Story"), "time and again the escaped convict changes addresses" (逃犯一再更换地址).[64] In "Yi ge ren de chengshi" 一个人的城市 ("City of One Person"), the protagonist reflects that "your whole life has changed behind your back, blurring your address so it appears to be a place you have never been before" (在你自己背后，整整一生变得地址模糊，像从未去过的地方).[65] Moreover, this constant movement is once again associated with criminality linked, as in classic detective fiction, to the capacity of the city to provide anonymity: "all you do is conscientiously record

the number of times you move house, like a criminal clearly count-
ing the number of times he has been cut on the head by the back of
a knife blade" (你只认真记下每一次搬家的数字，像一个罪犯，清清楚楚
地数着刀背砍到头上的次数).[66]

Yet if Benjamin, following Poe, locates this anonymity in the
crowd, Yang's walker is explicitly alone.[67] Like the flâneur, he oc-
cupies an urban environment both modern and decaying, containing
towers and skyscrapers, a hospital, a museum, a prison, a motorway,
streetlamps, shops and shop windows, public toilets, rumbling traf-
fic, a tumbledown house, a dilapidated graveyard, and indifferent and
impoverished inhabitants. Yang's walker, however, moves through a
city in which people are largely absent and which is in this sense anti-
thetical to the city of teeming crowds that has typically been the ter-
rain of the flâneur.[68] The title "City of One Person" not only conveys
the alienation associated with both flâneur and exile (the title is a play
on words that could equally be rendered as "Lonely City"), but also
points to the crucial difference between Yang's exile and the flâneur:
"In this city there is only you" (这城里只有你).[69] If this depiction re-
lates to Auckland's relatively sparsely populated urban environment
in comparison to China's cities, it also, and more importantly, signi-
fies the exile's sense of alienation and difference from his environ-
ment—the qualities of physical and linguistic displacement enforced
by political circumstances that define "literature in exile," narrowly
understood.[70] Yang expands this sense of alienation by referring to his
exiled protagonist in the second person. His use of a cliché of love po-
etry ("there is only you") here only serves to underscore the isolation
and self-alienation that makes it impossible to enunciate in the first
person *wo* 我 or "I."[71]

These particular and generalized conceptions of exile are super-
imposed upon one another in Yang's writing. He describes the exile's
experience as that of a "living ghost" (活的鬼魂) for whom speech
is all but impossible.[72] But he also argues that exile provides a pow-
erful—indeed the only true—basis for writing.[73] Exile in this sense
is "not just a misfortune" but "also a cultural luxury."[74] This gen-
eralized notion of exile is pervasive in modernism. In Baudelaire's
"Le cygne" ("The Swan"), for example, exile not only refers specifi-
cally to the poem's dedicatee, Hugo, but also stands more generally
for the allegorical superimposition of various places, times, and ex-
iles: Andromache, Ovid, Hugo, the swan, and the "négresse." In the
poem's words, "tout pour moi devient allégorie" (everything becomes

allegory for me). Allegory enables the rapidly shifting spatial and temporal movements of the text from "ruisseau sans eau" (dry gutter) to "boue" (mud), from Troy to Paris—what Benjamin calls the "rocking back and forth between modernity and antiquity."[75] Exilic dislocation and alienation are also products of rapid urban change (old demolished shops replaced by new monuments) and of the movements of the urban walker who registers the resulting "desolation of the big-city dweller" with the shifting gaze of Benjamin's allegorist-flâneur.[76] As a result, exile in "Le cygne" becomes both the condition of modernity ("mon esprit s'exile"; my spirit goes into exile) and the walker's means of allegorical poetic expression.[77] Yang conveys a similarly double sense of exile by producing work that is both "abstractly dislocated" and "concretely located in Auckland landscapes" and in the autobiographical details of his post–June 4 exile, during which, as he describes it, he "walked alone in Auckland city," a flâneur with "no English," able only to talk to himself.[78]

Though both exile and flâneur might seem to have become so generalized as to signify all modernist forms of alienation, estrangement, and wandering urban consciousness from *The Waste Land* to *Ulysses*, from Dos Passos to Frank O'Hara, they nevertheless embody encounters among different places and times in their singular instantiations—the passages between transnational or global modernity and local particularity to be found in what Michel de Certeau calls "spaces that cannot be seen" and paths that "elude legibility."[79] Superimposed onto each other in Yang's exilic writing just when the global-local binary was gaining currency, the exile and flâneur produce instances of singularity through encounter—moments of blind touch that also inform Benjamin's presentation of the flâneur in *Das Passagen-Werk*. Yang's protagonist recalls Benjamin's flâneur in his ability to access the city's hidden depths through the displacement of vision by touch. "City of One Person" begins with the ascent of a volcano: "You climb; you feel a stone in the thick grass with the sole of your foot; you step on it firmly and take another step. You feel the height of the mountain gradually increase through the quickened pace of your breathing. On top of the extinct volcano you are a wild animal, able to feel the fire trembling faintly in the deep layers of the earth" (你爬，用一只脚掌在草丛里摸索石头，踩稳了，再换一只。用越来越急促的呼吸，感到山的渐渐升起的高度。在死火山上，你是一只野兽，能够感到地层深处，火在微微震动).[80] The volcano, one of many that dot the Auckland isthmus, provides ancient evidence of hidden geological depths ("deep layers of the earth") that exceed the temporal and spatial boundaries of the city. The volcano stands for the primal forces that might at any minute burst forth to shatter the city's rational order and illusion of progress. The protagonist imagines how "fire once oozed from the stones on the mountains, a golden underground current gasping for breath in the silence" (山上的石头曾经渗出火来, 金色的潜流, 在寂静中喘息).[81] He at once emphasizes the volcano's ancient subterranean power and echoes Benjamin's description of the walker's descent into the city's hidden past: "The street conducts the flâneur into a vanished time. For him, every street is precipitous. It leads downward."[82] Yang's walker accesses this subterranean world by feeling "a stone," "height," "fire trembling."

Yang repeats this description of walking as an act of touch rather than vision in the cycle's title piece, "Ghost Speech/Lies," in which the subterranean depths become the old tumbledown house where the protagonist lives: "Your toes lead you. . . . Never mind that the light is broken, you can feel your way, feel it through the soles of your feet, but you cannot speak it. As soon as you speak it's just words" (脚趾带着你......灯坏了没关系, 你能摸, 用脚掌摸, 可不能说, 一说, 就是辞).[83] Benjamin describes the sensuous interaction between the city and flâneur similarly: "At the approach of his footsteps, the place has roused; speechlessly, mindlessly, its mere intimate nearness gives him hints and instructions." As the flâneur touches the place, "his soles remember."[84] The touch that provides Yang's walker and Benjamin's flâneur with access to the irrational depths of the city's past is also a point of contact between the two writers and an apt figure for cross-cultural encounter and comparison. In both cases, touch involves the unsettling of rational notions of history and temporality and the negation of speech, while walking, as a tactile and communicative act, becomes a way of negotiating—or failing to negotiate—temporal and spatial displacement. In "Ghost Speech/Lies," the protagonist attempts to—but cannot—speak his way through the dark. Instead, walking produces a painfully acute awareness and conflation of space, time, and language. "Every step" and "every moment" (每一步、每个瞬间) are felt and literalized in the laborious account of ascending the staircase, an account that is at the same time "just words" on the page or, elsewhere, "a day inside a sentence" (一个句子中的日子).[85]

Yang associates the exiled walker's difficult steps with the poet's turn to prose, or *sǎnwén* 散文, an association already implied by the character that *sanwen* shares with *sànbù* 散步 (strolling), where *san*

散 in both cases, despite divergent pronunciations, suggests leisurely, scattered indirection.[86] Just as for Baudelaire "the miracle of a poetic prose" is a dream that "is born, above all, from the experience of giant cities, from the intersecting of their myriad relations," so too for Yang exile demands a "dense and convulsive" (密集的, 抽搐的) language for which "anything that is not prose is totally insufficient" (散文之外的远远不够).[87] If the "fencing" rhyme (escrime/rime) marks the poet's embattled response to the blows of the great cities of modernity in Baudelaire's "Le soleil," Yang's shift to prose further underscores the insufficiency of a conventional poetic response to the experience of the urban walker and the shock of exile.[88]

In prose pieces such as "Weishenme yiding shi sanwen" 为什么一定是散文 ("Why There Has to Be Prose"), Yang addresses one of the nemeses with which the flâneur does battle—perpetual recurrence beneath the illusion of novelty:

> 同样的姿势、脚步, 走进这一天, 又走出这一天。岁月, 压抑在字里行间, 是不是总共只有一天? 一天中就发生了五年 (道路的日子)、五千年 (陶罐上粗陋符号的日子)? 言辞, 狂暴地展示着一个被无数街道、城市和国度折磨的经历, 高达彻底的沉寂。

> Walk into this day with the same stride and posture as you walk out of it. All in all, isn't time, shut up in lines of words, just one day? Don't five years (days on the road) or five thousand years (days in the crude symbols on an earthenware jar) all take place in just one day? Words, violently displaying an experience of being tormented by innumerable streets, cities, and nations, climax in total stillness.[89]

Here the walker uncovers the hell of repetition not only by means of Yang's earlier *xungen* themes (entrapment by tradition—"five thousand years"—and the written Chinese language—prefigured by "crude symbols on an earthenware jar"), but also through the experience of exile, which produces a similar repetition across an equally vast geographical expanse ("innumerable . . . cities and nations").[90] The comparative force of these lines equates the temporal and linguistic entrapment of tradition with the temporal, geographical, and linguistic entrapment of exile. The lines also describe a more generalized effect of modern temporality whereby the apparent escape from tradition, here through exile and travel, ironically only reinforces the experience of entrapment and repetition beneath what appears to be new. The temporality of Yang's walker is presented as a particular effect of exile and yet also as the general condition of modernity, which exile highlights; as such, it both recalls and inverts the way Baudelaire's

"Le cygne" deploys the trope of exile to figure the alienation and temporal entrapment engendered by the modernization of Paris—or what Benjamin calls the poem's "days of recurrence."[91]

Walking through a single day that is "shut up in lines of words," Yang's exile experiences the city as a text, as is often the case in literature of the flâneur, but not as "a book of consecutive pages through which one can 'browse,'" as in some representations of the figure.[92] Rather, Yang's city-text is strange, literally and metaphorically shrouded in darkness, and devoid of the crowds typically associated with the flâneur. "Ghost Speech/Lies" equates the recitation of a poem with the ghostly sound of "footsteps echo[ing] in an unoccupied room" (没有人的房间里, 脚步咚咚响), while in "Dongri huayuan" 冬日花园 ("Winter Garden"), the "empty peopleless street" (空无一人的街) walked at night "under the lamps" (灯下) becomes a "hoarse throat / reciting" (沙哑的喉咙 / 郎诵着) a muffled text, the aural concomitant of the visual occlusion of night.[93] In "Ghost Speech/Lies," the city-text is wholly illegible:

从一个路口到另一个路口, 那些同样读不懂的街名, 与你有什么关系? 从一只手到另一只手, 你读一部上千页的书, 与把仅有的一页翻动上千次, 有什么区别? 流亡者, 无非沿着一条足迹的虚线, 在每一个点上一动不动……活埋进每天重复的日子, 像你的诗, 一个关于真实的谎言。从什么时候起, 辞像陈年的漆皮一样, 酥了, 碎了, 掉下来。你不说, 才听清那个恐怖的声音——又过了一天!

From one intersection to the next, what have all those incomprehensible street names got to do with you? What's the difference between you reading a book of more than a thousand pages and turning the only page you have from one hand to the other a thousand times? All an exile can do is follow a dotted line of footprints, stopping motionless on every dot. . . . Every day you are buried alive in days that keep repeating themselves—it's like your poetry, a lie about reality. At some point, words have become brittle and cracked and have flaked off, like a timeworn coat of paint. Only when you say nothing do you hear that terrifying voice—*another day has passed!*[94]

"Incomprehensible" streets that reflect at a literal level the exile's experience of linguistic foreignness are linked once again to the temporal entrapment of modernity. The words ("dotted line of footprints") on the page mark days that are indistinguishable, while the unfolding, progressive book of the city hides a perpetual sameness revealed in the city's ancient depths and hidden decay, here represented by the peeling paint of the exile's house. (As in Benjamin's readings of "Le soleil,"

"Le crépuscule du matin," and "Le cygne," the city's "decrepitude constitutes the closest link between modernity and antiquity.")[95] By superimposing the trope of the flâneur as reader of the city-text onto both the exile and the root-seeking investigator of Chinese tradition, Yang produces a poetics of palimpsest that confronts the problem of modernity as the unresolved relationship between different times and places. In Benjamin's words, Yang's alienated walker's "perception of time is supernaturally keen." The passing days bury him, just as in Baudelaire's "Spleen" "the minutes cover a man like snowflakes."[96] Here, language is similarly materialized as flaking paint, and text, time, and city simultaneously embodied and erased through the figure of ellipsis, the "dotted line" that the exile must trace.

But Yang's walker, of course, writes as well as follows this broken line, producing a "lie about reality." This lie recalls Virginia Woolf's "complications about the claims of documentary writing and the claims or place of the documentary observer" through the transformation of walking in everyday life into words on the page and vice versa.[97] Yang documents autobiographical fact—his exile and its cause, the June 4 massacre—while highlighting the fictionality of writing. This fictionality is underscored by the title "Guihua" 鬼话: "lies," but literally "the speech of ghosts." Language's unreliability both enables the erasure of June 4 through Chinese government misinformation and suggests the possibility of different ghostlike readings within the same text. These phantasmal readings demand that the reader play an active role in order to allow literature to achieve the "precarious and temporary transfer of agency, earned through imaginative attention," that Spivak finds in Woolf's *A Room of One's Own*.[98] Because, like Woolf, Yang deploys the liar's paradox, his text transfers agency to the reader who is attentive to language—and especially to its spatial and temporal dimensions, which shift uneasily between the words on the page and the scenes they describe. The reader's tracing of the page embodies the exile's movement along a dotted line, enacting this transfer in a moment of touch. This touch in turn figures the problem and possibility of connection across the disparate spaces and times that exile, reader, and comparatist confront. In this way, language's disembodied resistance to a single position (its "lies") allows the reader to give life to the text's ghostly voices.

ECLIPSE

Among Yang's exilic prose, "Rishi" 日蚀 ("Eclipse") perhaps most clearly dramatizes the experience of the flâneur in exile that I have traced above, while simultaneously suggesting how the radically non-logical constellations of Benjamin's dialectical image might be extended into a deconstructive comparative practice of encounter, superimposition, and touch:

> 到那座桥上，站着。桥下绿阴阴的一大片，是墓地。来来往往的人看你，你什么也看不见。日子，从那时才露出真面目了。一张曝光的底片，灰蒙蒙的空白。站了多久，才回来。

> You reach that bridge and stand there. Beneath the bridge is a dark, sinister expanse of green—it is the graveyard. The people coming and going see you but you don't see anything. From that moment the days reveal their true complexion. A photographic negative exposed to light, an overcast blank space. After standing there for a time, you return.[99]

Recalling De Certeau's distinction between a rational overview of the city and the blind experience of the walker, Yang's protagonist discovers Auckland's Symonds Street Cemetery without the aid of sight ("you don't see anything"), once again displaying a flâneur-like hypersensitivity that sets him apart from "people coming and going" who "see you" but appear oblivious to what is beneath their feet. Lying, easily overlooked, beneath Symonds Street and Grafton Bridge, Auckland's first major non-Māori graveyard is a particularly apt example of the city's forgotten depths (fig. 1). Resistant to—but marked by—the rationalizing forces of progress, the graveyard's overexposed layers of history negate the "light" of its visual appearance: the graveyard contains the city's buried past (bodies) and present (the homeless people and drunks who frequent it), and some of the graves have been exhumed and moved more than once to make way first for the bridge and later for the motorway that now passes beneath the bridge and alongside what remains of the cemetery.

In the graveyard, the walker discovers the "true complexion" of "days" that bury the subject through the conflation and superimposition of text, space, and time. Walking repeatedly from his decrepit "old house" (老房子) across the bridge to the graveyard, he overlays one day illegibly upon another, producing an image akin to a "negative exposed to light."[100] Like the dotted line in "Ghost Speech/Lies," this "blank space" simultaneously marks and negates the passage of

Figure 1. Graves from Symonds Street Cemetery located directly under Grafton Bridge, Auckland, New Zealand. Photo by Joanna Forsberg.

time: "Time passes day by day," but "nothing happens. A whole year has passed" (日子一天天过去, 什么都没发生。周年也过了).[101] The tension between the passing of time and a pervasive sense of stasis is underscored through a play on words that is central to "Eclipse": *rizi* 日子 means both "time" and "day" and contains the character for "sun," *ri* 日. Because this character also appears in the title "Rishi" 日蚀 ("[Solar] Eclipse"), which is followed immediately by the line I have just quoted, the "eclipse" signifies not only the darkness resulting from the superimposition of the moon on the sun but also the erasure produced both by overloading a single sign, such as *ri*, with multiple meanings and by the spatial and temporal movements that the walker performs in his daily strolls through the city-text.

"Eclipse" likewise exploits the various meanings of the verb *guo* 过 (to pass), which, like the English *pass*, refers, among other things, to physical movement, temporal change, and the past: "The days are only needed for the past. The 'passing days' allow you inside a year to become familiar with a city step by step" (仅仅为了过去, 才需要日子。"过日子", 就是让你在一年里, 一步一步熟悉一座城).[102] Here, the context invites one to read "passing days" as "days past" (the lack of tense in Chinese makes this wordplay clearer; see, for example,

the announcement that *"another day has passed"* in "Ghost Speech/
Lies"). Time is in the "past" but is also perpetually present ("days
pass") for the exile, who enacts this stasis within change "step by
step," marking the "passing days" by repeatedly passing back and
forth across Grafton Bridge. Significant events happened only in the
"past"—"Nothing happens" anymore—and the exile can neither re-
turn to this moment of death (June 4) nor get past it. "Buried alive"
under these repeating days, he remains a "living ghost whose death
has taken him out of time" (一个死去岁月的活的鬼魂).[103] The two
times, like the two meanings of *guo*, overlay and erase each other,
threatening to leave the exile in a situation characterized by stasis,
spatial entrapment, and semantic erasure—doomed endlessly to pass
from point to point along a dotted line that marks the absence of
meaning.

Through the wordplay on *guo*, the exile's experience is also over-
laid with a reflection on what Benjamin describes as the transforma-
tion of the structure of experience in modernity. *Guo*, like the "word
perdu" in Baudelaire and Marcel Proust, "acknowledges that the ex-
perience he once shared is now collapsed into itself," that now, in
Proust's words, "only a very few days can appear."[104] The exile's sen-
sitivity to his repetitive temporal and spatial movements and to the
decrepit, ignored, development-ravaged graveyard marks not only
his alienation but also the general alienation of all those people and
things (the graveyard, the volcano, the wino, and the tumbledown
old house) in Yang's Auckland that do not conform to narratives of
progress.

The wordplay on *ri* and *guo* also links the exiled walker's appre-
hension of the temporal and spatial complexity of modernity to the
virtual and material configurations of language and writing in par-
ticular. By conflating the spaciotemporal dimensions of the city with
the page, the wordplay underscores the textual nature of the exile's
experience and so shifts attention to the plane of language, a shift
also critical to Benjamin's dialectical image. A sense of temporality
results from reading the spatial configuration of words on the page,
just as the walker's sense of temporality is created through the spatial
configuration of the old house, bridge, and graveyard, so that in the
poem "Gelafudun qiao" 格拉夫顿桥 ("Grafton Bridge") "that point
you walk to is also the point where you are aged" (你走去的还是你被
变老的那一端).[105] The "temporalized space" of the city here results
from the insertion of virtual times through the temporalized space of

the page, creating a "haunting and opening" that, although seemingly trapping Yang's protagonist, might offer "the possibility of difference rather than just repetition."[106]

The temporalized space and spatialized time of Yang's exile writing extend beyond Auckland, reminding us "that, in the course of flânerie, far-off times and places interpenetrate the landscape and the present moment."[107] "Winter Garden" repeatedly refers to "snow" (雪), practically unknown in subtropical Auckland and least of all in the Auckland Domain hothouse to which the title refers.[108] "City of One Person" superimposes Beijing on Auckland. It locates the protagonist simultaneously in a city where the sea is only a "myth" (神话)—"You still live in that ancient city buried in dust and yellow earth" (你还住在那座黄土和灰尘掩埋的古城里)—and in a city where the sea is ever present: "All you can do is live beside the sea" (你只能住在海边).[109] For "as you walk the streets, distances change. The distance from one day to another resembles the distance from shop to shop, from door to door, from bed to bed. . . . you swing each of your two hands in turn. The two days in your two hands swing you about. Which one do you belong to?" (在街上走，距离就变了。从日子到日子的距离，像从市场到市场，从门到门、床到床。……就交替地摆动两只手。两只手里两个日子，摆动你。你属于哪一个?).[110]

In "Eclipse," however, the superimposition of Beijing on Auckland does not lead even to the difficult reconciliation that in "City of One Person" is implied by the contrary directions of the walker's swinging hands and the wordplay on *rizi*, which links his visceral experience of "two days" to the repetitious modern temporality of "two times" or "two lives." The possibility of connection or touch emerges instead out of the very impossibility of such reconciliation. Temporal, spatial, and textual superimposition produces a moment of erasure that further merges the textual space of the page with the temporal and spatial movements of the walker at the point at which he witnesses the beginning of the eclipse: "You plan out a poem in the graveyard, making the poem itself embody part of the graveyard. Generations of communal burial chambers. Walking along a line of poetry is like walking along a path, words on both sides of blank space, square open graves—they exist because of blank space" (在墓地构思一首诗，就让诗本身成了一块墓地。祖祖辈辈的集体墓室。沿着诗句走[像]沿着小路走，空白两边的字，方方正正的墓穴，由于空白才存在).[111] To trace the words on the page through the physical act of touch is to parallel the path of the walker passing between the lines of graves in the darkness of the eclipse. Just as the ellipsis marks the failure of speech in "Ghost Speech/Lies," so here the words as gravestones embody the erasure of signification that accompanies the failure of vision during the eclipse. But they suggest in addition that a ghostly speech (*guihua*) of stones emerges out of the erasures produced by textual, temporal, and spatial conflation and superimposition, a speech accessible only through the sensitive walker's or reader's touch: through an embodied reading.

Like Baudelaire's play on the word "vers," these superimpositions produce the double movement of words toward and beyond their context, and between embodiment and disembodiment. Recalling Baudelaire's wordplay, the characters form lines of text while their rectangular shapes iconically represent worm-riddled graves. As the description of the sun being "bitten away" (牙咬过的) suggests, the title "Rishi" 日蚀 ("Eclipse") itself implies a sun being eaten by a worm: *shi* 食, the left-hand component of the character *shi* 蚀, means "to eat" or "food," while the right-hand component, *chong* 虫, signifies an insect or worm.[112] The title thus identifies the erasure of the sun, time, and days (*ri* 日) both with the decomposition of dead bodies in the graveyard and with the idea that each written character is a worm-riddled grave, a figure that marks simultaneously the success and failure of the attempt to make language embody meaning. On the one hand, words become the broken dotted lines of the graves they describe. On the other, the transformation of a body into language necessitates its disembodiment. The decaying "body" becomes a textual surface "covered in green dots" (身上到处是绿点子), which are simultaneously the dappling of the sun's light and "moldy spots in the flesh" (肉里……的霉斑) that suggest worms working on a decomposing body, as well as the erasure of language marked in "Ghost Speech/Lies" by the dotted line.[113] The worms consume the protagonist's decomposing body, transforming it into language: "the real you is picked out of the gaps between teeth bored by worms" (真的你，一次次从虫蛀的牙缝间被剔掉).[114] In devouring the mouth they embody the "ghost speech" (*guihua*) of the "tongueless mouths of the dead" (死者那没有舌头的嘴).[115]

"Eclipse" ends when the two cities and two times eclipse each other:

> 那里的人们，不说你，只说"去年"。谁都是"去年"。所有死亡都在"去年"。
> ……你就被甩下来。"去年"中没有你……又进不了今年。……这些阔叶树，
> 绿得发亮。不像你熟悉的松柏，本身就很黑。……日蚀那天，太阳不是太
> 阳，人不是人。……那个女孩子，才九岁，已经学会与石头谈话，让石头摸

她。老人瞎了，只能摸自己儿时的照片。黑暗平坦地落下来，黑暗中本来什么都没有。

> People there don't speak of you, they just say "last year." Everyone
> is "last year." All death was "last year." . . . So you have been left
> behind. There is no you in "last year" . . . you cannot enter this year
> either. . . . These broad-leafed trees are a luminous green. They are
> not like the pines and cypresses you are familiar with, which are the
> very embodiment of darkness. . . . The sun is not the sun and people
> are not people on the day of the eclipse. . . . The little girl, just nine
> years old, has already learned how to talk with the stone, to allow the
> stone to stroke her. When old people go blind, they can only stroke
> their own childhood photographs. Darkness descends smoothly—in
> the darkness, of course, there is nothing.[116]

Like an overexposed negative, the temporal, geographic, and sym-
bolic superimposition of "last year" on "this year," of the "luminous
green" of Auckland's subtropical trees on the darkness of Beijing's
"pines and cypresses"—in China traditional symbols of longevity of-
ten found in cemeteries—yields only "darkness." The eclipse thus su-
perimposes the generalized condition of modernity onto the exile's
experience. Just as Baudelaire's "À une passante" ends in a dramatic
collapse of vision for its flâneur protagonist, so Yang's exiled walker
"feels as though he has been dropped from the calendar." His inabil-
ity to enter "last year" or "this year" overlays the loss of the "capac-
ity for experiencing" in modernity onto the particular catastrophe
of June 4 and his exile.[117] The overloading of symbolic values on the
word "eclipse" finally threatens to plunge language into a semantic
darkness in which "the sun is not the sun . . . people are not peo-
ple," and "darkness" is layered on "nothing." If Baudelaire's defen-
sive response to the stasis and anesthesia of modernity shifts percep-
tion from vision to touch and causes "words to collapse," for Yang
the eclipse is redoubled in the language itself, marking the shift to the
linguistic plane that Benjamin associates with the dialectical image.

Here, my reading of "Eclipse" in relation to the flâneur and Benja-
min's dialectical image threatens the text with an additional seman-
tic layer that might eclipse its particularity. Yet the singular moments
of touch that emerge out of the superimposition of disparate places
and times in "Eclipse" suggest how singularity might be constituted
through the encounter between particularity and the very generaliz-
ing comparative impulse that would seem to negate it. "Eclipse" em-
phasizes the particular circumstances of a post–June 4 Chinese exile
even as it addresses the generalized problem of bringing places, times,

and languages together, just as Benjamin's general account of the catastrophic shock experience of modernity also addresses the specific historical situation that he faced in the late 1930s.[118] Yang superimposes Symonds Street Cemetery onto the graveyard on the outskirts of Beijing where he worked during the Cultural Revolution ("A great city far away; a graveyard on the edge of the city"; 远方一座大城，墓地在城市边上) and onto the ghostly nonexistent graveyard for those who died on June 4 "last year," especially the "girl" about whom Yang wrote the poem "Gei yi ge datusha zhong siqu de jiusui nühai" 给一个大屠杀中死去的九岁女孩 ("To a Nine-Year-Old Girl Killed in the Massacre").[119] The exile experiences temporal entrapment and erasure partly because he is unable to connect directly with the event that took place in Beijing "last year." But he cannot pass beyond it to be in Auckland "this year," since "any realization of being 'here' now irrepressibly mobilizes the memory of the massacre over 'there.'"[120] The impossibility of being "there" or in "last year" generates the paradox that it is both impossible to write about the event and impossible not to write about it. This particular paradox in turn produces another: that it is impossible to write history, the "speech of ghosts," without writing "lies" (guihua).

The particularity of exile produces a general sense of the impossibility of reconciling language and reality and of bridging disparate places and times without erasing differences. Yet the negation of the visual also suggests an alternative to this entrapping binary: the possibility of moments of touch among places, times, languages, and people. The grave-like characters and the darkness at the conclusion of "Eclipse" reassert the singularity of touch even as they collapse difference into a generalized breakdown of meaning. The eclipse produces a moment of blindness and touch in the graveyard: "When old people go blind, they can only stroke their own childhood photographs." Through touch, the gravestone and the dead girl communicate the speech of ghosts, a dream expressed in the epitaph Yang composed for the Auckland monument to those who died in the massacre: "you do not speak, but the stone has a cry" (你们已无言，而石头有了呼声; figs. 2 and 3). Here the unreliability of language, its capacity to tell lies (guihua), enables the wordplay on shítóu 石头 (stone) and shétóu 舌头 (tongue), which closely resemble one another visually and aurally. This play on words emphasizes language's ability both to silence and to recover the speech of ghosts (guihua). Similarly, the collapse of signification and vision in "Eclipse" is accompanied by the appearance of the girl and the stone's touch, both of which reinforce

Figure 2.   Memorial stone dedicated to the victims of the June 4, 1989, massacre, St. Andrew's First Presbyterian Church, Alten Road, Auckland, New Zealand. Photo by Joanna Forsberg.

the possibility of tracing in the path among the graves—of Auckland, Beijing, modernity—an elliptical, tactile, ghostly language of stones.

The equation of graves with characters invites the reader to stroke the page and so embody the positions of both the walker-protagonist and the ghostly nine-year-old girl. But the reader's touch also registers the impossibility of reaching across the divides of space and time that the mediation of the page viscerally marks. "Eclipse" describes and attempts to overcome this problem, deploying the word *rishi* to conflate the gaps in language with the wormholes in decomposing bodies, as in the representation of ghost speech as a tongue of worms and the depiction of words as graves on the page. The flickering double movement of signs toward and beyond their context that results enacts the superimposition of disparate places and times, just as in "Le soleil" the play on "vers" oscillates between embodiment and disembodiment through its superimposition of heaven and earth, sun and flâneur, country and city, worms and verse, reality and language. In "Eclipse," the movement also involves collision and the interplay between sun and walker, though it comes less violently than in Baudelaire's poem, taking the form of a caress. Collision or touch signals

Figure 3. Plaque on the memorial stone dedicated to the victims of the June 4, 1989, massacre, St. Andrew's First Presbyterian Church, Alten Road, Auckland, New Zealand. Photo by Joanna Forsberg.

the emergence of singularity within the very erasures effected by generalizing superimposition, whether in Benjamin's reading of Baudelaire, Duoduo's encounter with Baudelaire, Yang's exilic writing, or my reading of each through the flâneur. Touch stands as a figure for, and embodiment of, a comparative poetics that uses a flâneur-like hypersensitivity to the duality of language in order to bring places and times into contact, while acknowledging their mutually constituting and yet mutually eclipsing otherness.

Responding to a historical moment when the difference between here and there, then and now, word and meaning, history and lies was both heightened and on the verge of collapse, Yang sought alternative forms of writing and history to recognize the erasures that these oppositions produce. The ellipses and eclipses that emerge out of reading the flâneur in exile recall Benjamin's conception of the dialectical image, in that they bring disparate material together without insisting on a single overarching form. For Benjamin, the sun becomes the many stars of irreconcilably distinct positions that can nevertheless be connected in the constellation of a provisional totality. Read through the figure of the flâneur in exile, however, these positions, places, times, and languages are not isolated heavenly bodies but mutually constituted and overlaid geological layers of encounter, history, and reading. Their superimposition does not resolve into the light of a constellation but into the darkness of an eclipse: here singularity is preserved in the possibility of touch, in an imagined line traced across the night.

CHAPTER TWO

Arkadii Dragomoshchenko and Poetic Correspondences

L'homme y passe à travers des forêts de symboles
Qui l'observent avec des regards familiers.

—CHARLES BAUDELAIRE, "Correspondances"

I recall how my part of the "correspondences" began . . . I thought . . . about how a tongue is never "just a tongue"—it is always someone's tongue.

—ARKADII DRAGOMOSHCHENKO, letter to Lyn Hejinian, 26 October 1985

Arriving in Moscow on 10 June 1983, the collection of mainly San Francisco Bay Area bohemians must have made a strange sight. Comprising avant-garde musicians, writers, filmmakers, a video crew, and accompanying family, the group had come to the Soviet Union because of a letter from Alexander Kan. In 1981, Kan wrote to Rova Saxophone Quartet member Larry Ochs, inviting the quartet to the Free Music Club in Leningrad, "as a gesture rather than with any expectation of his being able to accept." Kan met the group at the airport in Moscow, where he informed Ochs's wife, the poet Lyn Hejinian, that "in Leningrad you will meet many writers. You are invited to dinner by Arkady Dragomotschenko [Arkadii Dragomoshchenko] and to a meeting of the writers' club there. The writers in Leningrad are waiting for you."[1] The cross-cultural exchange initiated by Kan's letter would lead to a much more extensive and longer-lasting friendship, collaboration, and correspondence between Hejinian and Dragomoshchenko, who met in Leningrad four days later. This history of personal encounters and correspondence began just months after Ronald Reagan had delivered his "evil empire" speech during a moment of heightened Cold War tensions, a context underscored by the title *Saxophone Diplomacy*, the name of the Rova Quartet album that followed the trip and of the documentary film about the visit, for which Hejinian wrote the narration.[2] Developing through the perestroika period and concluding in the early 1990s, Hejinian and Dragomoshchenko's most intense phase of correspondence and collaboration coincided with the period of political and cultural instability that climaxed in the collapse of the Soviet Union and the end of the Cold War. What Hejinian would later call the "geo-politics" of her "alliance" with Dragomoshchenko affects and sometimes obscures the singularity of this and other very personal cross-cultural encounters and artistic collaborations.[3] It raises a question that increasingly preoccupies scholars writing after deconstruction and cultural studies: how can we reconcile the generalized abstractions of language, culture, society, and history with a particular text and with the person who writes it?[4]

Dragomoshchenko's collaboration with Hejinian not only poses this question but also offers a way to rethink its conceptual suppositions. As the product of a cross-cultural encounter between two persons, it occupies the middle ground elided by the opposition between singular and collective that the question presupposes. Their collaboration takes the form of a bilingual correspondence that intermingles private letters with poetic texts and that addresses correspondences and noncorrespondences between Russian and English, between the Soviet Union and the United States, and between language and the world. Many of Dragomoshchenko's poems of the 1980s are dedicated to Hejinian, drafts of some poems appear in letters to her, while other poems include extracts from their letters. The poems themselves were written with a view to her translating them into English as part of their joint project The Corresponding Sky, which in its original English variant, coined by Hejinian in 1985 after her second visit to the Soviet Union, stresses the place of letter-writing in their collaboration. The Russian version, which became the title of Dragomoshchenko's book *Nebo sootvetstvii* (*Sky of Correspondences*) and which he would come to see as a mistranslation, lacks this sense, calling to mind instead "correspondence" as a key term in modernist poetics, especially that simultaneous invocation and negation of correspondence between language and the world that derives from Baudelaire's "Correspondances."[5] Baudelaire's sonnet might be read as staging either the experience of urban modernity or the endless intertextual correspondences of language. Similarly, Dragomoshchenko's poetic contribution to his collaboration with Hejinian has been taken either as a window on late-Soviet culture and its difference from the

West or as singularly resistant to representation and interpretation. Caught between linguistic universalism and ethnographic exoticism, these contrasting readings grow in part out of the historical moment of the late–Cold War and early post-Soviet periods as they were experienced on opposing sides of the Iron Curtain. Like Yang Lian, Dragomoshchenko contests these late–Cold War binaries by drawing on Baudelaire's poetics, though for him, unlike Yang, the singular encounter—the moment of touch—precedes the superimposition of places, times, cultures, and languages, and the flickering double movement between word and world. When taken as epistolary address and response to a singular other—as co-response—his correspondences provide a third term outside the binaries that have shaped readings of his work and that continue to constrain our understanding of this moment of historical change.

CORRESPONDENCES

In a letter to Hejinian written a year after their first meeting, Dragomoshchenko invokes correspondence in the mimetic sense of a relation of likeness or equation between language and the world, and between his world and hers. He writes, "the cup of Jamshid. Remember how in it one could see the whole world? I try to 'see' yours."[6] A year later, the "cup" becomes a key figure in Dragomoshchenko's conception of The Corresponding Sky, which he describes in another letter to Hejinian: "I recall how my part of the 'correspondences' began . . . every evening [Mitya and I] would take a long walk, and along the way I would discuss the 'cup' . . . I would wave my hands and come to life, because the world of objects and ideas that sprung up around the 'cup' was—and now still is—closely connected to you." But, he continues, "at the same time I thought about the *embodiment* of the tongue, about its strange sexuality in its completely simple, first sense, about how a tongue is never 'just a tongue'—it is always someone's tongue."[7] Dragomoshchenko's "cup" implies the idea of finding perfect "correspondences" between language and reality and between Russian and American worlds, while the word *iazyk* ("language" and "tongue") figures their correspondence as a linguistic, interpersonal, and even sexual encounter. The word suggests the encounter with a singular other, while also marking and bridging the collective otherness that divides the two poets between Russian and

English. It transforms the search for a correspondence between another "language" or culture and one's own into a sensual encounter with another's "tongue."[8]

In opposing the totality of the cup in which one can see the whole world to the singularity of a person's tongue, Dragomoshchenko underscores his later explicit rejection of "the hieratic model of poetry," which seeks "a universal language that can exhaust the coincidence between knowledge of the world and the real world" and which insists on "the possibility of perceiving the concealed unity and continuity . . . of Being."[9] The title of Dragomoshchenko and Hejinian's collaborative project alludes to the tradition—which has powerfully shaped Western poetics from Aristotle through romanticism to the present day—of treating the lyric as an attempt to ground the universal and transcendent in sensuous experience. The Corresponding Sky echoes Wordsworth's "correspondent breeze" and so the romantic "connection between inner experience and outer analogue" signaled by apostrophic address to the elements themselves, as in Shelley's "To the West Wind."[10] Similarly, the Russian version, *Nebo sootvetstvii*, which could be translated as *Heaven of Correspondences*, suggests the related notion of vertical correspondence between the earthly and spiritual or heavenly realms as in Swedenborg's "correspondences." *Sky of Correspondences* invokes but ultimately refuses notions of correspondence that would secure meaning and comparison: correspondence between word and world, the world and the divine; and correspondence between Russian and English, the Soviet Union and the United States. In so doing, it alludes to Baudelaire's "Correspondances," which similarly refers to but rejects Swedenborg's theories and the romantic notion of nature as a temple ("La Nature est un temple"), a notion which in turn implies a vertical correspondence between nature and the divine.[11] Instead, "Correspondances" presents "confuses paroles" (confused words), "forêts de symboles" (forests of symbols), and "de longs échos qui de loin se confondent" (prolonged echoes mingling in the distance) in which a "profonde unité" (profound unity) seems only the product of confused and uncertain relations of likeness ("comme"). These relations cannot fix meaning but rather enumerate similarities and differences in a perpetual process of response to one another. The rhyme confuses ("se confondent") echoes and responses ("se répondent"), highlighting the structure of the sonnet form and of rhyme itself, which can serve at once as a response, an echo, and a confusion of the two.[12]

Through the interplay of tongue and cup, Dragomoshchenko emphasizes that The Corresponding Sky, like Baudelaire's "Correspondances," involves a process of continuous, shifting echoes—of co-response not correspondence. "When the translation seems finished, it means one thing: translate again and again," he writes in another letter.[13] Walter Benjamin suggests that a translation, "instead of imitating the sense of the original, must lovingly and in detail incorporate the original's way of meaning, thus making both the original and the translation recognizable as fragments of a greater language, just as fragments are part of a vessel."[14] Recalling Benjamin, Dragomoshchenko describes how the "*desire* for wholeness and completion (eroticism?)"—Dragomoshchenko's "cup" or Benjamin's "vessel"—remains perpetually unfilled. Undone by the "contradictory flow toward disintegration" and "dispersal," the cup appears only in the fragments or echoes found between the embodied tongue and the longing for totality.[15] But by appealing to the "tongue," and to Hejinian, and, like Baudelaire, linking "unity to an effacement of differences," Dragomoshchenko more closely resembles Levinas, who goes further, arguing that the "whole vessel" is preceded by a relation to "the other," a relation that provides the grounds for our experiencing of the world.[16] Echoing Blanchot, whom he has translated and to whom he frequently refers, Dragomoshchenko describes poetry as a mode of "responsibility" born out of the relationship between "I" and "you."[17] Blanchot's "relation to naked presence, the presence of the other," as in Levinas, precedes and gives rise to experience and language understood as a whole vessel apprehended only in fragments—what Dragomoshchenko calls a "sourceless echo" and Blanchot terms a "plural speech" that "holds itself between" each speaker in a dialogue, but originates with neither.[18] The two poets' letters, collaborations, and translations involve neither completion nor unity but continuous co-response—an exchange of languages, of tongues. The unfilled cup results not just from the confrontation and noncorrespondence between one culture and another, nor solely from the endless possible iterations of translation, but from an encounter between two people who, even if they share the same language, have tongues that can only ever meet for an instant in erotic touch.

Dragomoshchenko's poetics of co-response engages current theories of comparative literature by addressing what happens to the idea of comparison across languages and cultures when the notion of cultural unity, totality, or vertical correspondence to a universal ceases to be tenable. Co-response does not conform to the binary structure of particular and universal, local and global, notions that continue to shape debates about comparative literature even as the idea of universal correspondence is increasingly questioned. Like Chow's Kantian vision for comparative literature, co-response involves "*reflection* on the ability to represent and evaluate [cultural difference] per se," but it differs from Chow's binary "oscillating process of judgement" between singularity and the "movement to reach the universal."[19] More than just presenting "the 'transcendental object' of the Kantian tradition" as "unknowable," Dragomoshchenko rejects Kant's notion of *Zusammensetzung*—the bringing together of fragments in a unified image.[20] He thus undermines the particular/transcendent, singular/universal, local/global dichotomies that inhere in this concept. Dragomoshchenko's poetic correspondences offer an alternative model based on encounters among particulars or fragments that respond to one another but never unify. Just as Baudelaire's poem presents the passerby's encounters with familiar but unplaceable glances ("regards familiers"), Dragomoshchenko stresses the constitutive role of encounters, which highlight the insufficiency of the fragment/whole, local/global, particular/general binary, an inadequacy felt particularly acutely during a period of historical and geopolitical transformation and intense personal, cross-cultural, and interlingual exchange.

Like Baudelaire's "Correspondances," Dragomoshchenko's letters to Hejinian emphasize how not just translations but all texts correspond to—or "echo"—other texts, a view that would seem to dismiss the individual subject and historical location but that here emerges out of his response to a singular other. Of translating Hejinian's 1984 long poem *The Guard* (which itself includes an extract from another correspondence that crossed the Cold War divide), Dragomoshchenko writes: "I called your letters poems—it's amazing, but these two parts from *The Guard* . . . naturally mixed with the letters!—they became a continuation, a foretelling . . . , and not only because they hide 'citations,' many of which now sound to me as though *I* had written them—but you too write that the letter has for you become a poem."[21] Here he echoes Barthes's view that "this 'I' which approaches the text is already itself a plurality of other texts."[22] This quotation opens Dragomoshchenko's nineteen-section long poem "Uzhin s privetlivymi bogami" ("A Supper with Affable Gods") and is reinforced at the outset of the poem by the insistence:

Что ты попросту сумма высказываний,
                                        принадлежащих другим,
Иными губами вылеплен,

That you are simply the sum of utterances
                                        belonging to others,
Shaped by other lips,[23]

Throughout, the poem presents language as an endless chain of re-
semblances without a source. By playing on the aural echoes in words
such as *rech'* (speech), *reka* (river), and *ruka* (hand), the poem empha-
sizes that language does not correspond to reality with the transpar-
ency of a windowpane but depends on a shifting series of likenesses:

Не умоляй о прозрачности,
Словно тебе не под силу и самому видеть так,
            как дан этот мир,
неуловим в переменах: «словно», «подобно», «как будто»
                        и «как» . . .

Do not beg for transparency,
As if you cannot yourself see
            how this world is given
elusive in the changes: "as if," "similar to," "as though" and
                        "like" . . . [24]

Here Dragomoshchenko presents language as a continuous series of
analogies and the subject as a nexus of other texts in lines that them-
selves echo an earlier part of the poem: "magicians in spaces bring
gifts: 'like,' 'as if,' / and 'as though'" (*volkhvy v prostranstvakh prono-
siat dary: "kak," "slovno" / i "budto"*).[25] In this, Dragomoshchenko
recalls the repetition of "comme" (like) in Baudelaire's "Corres-
pondances" and his own claim that Hejinian's letters "sound . . . as
though *I* had written them," while anticipating (or echoing, since each
"foretelling" can also be a "continuation") his later description of po-
etry as "answering the sourceless echo," as "responsibility."[26]

Yet the same section of this long poem includes extracts from let-
ters from Hejinian and from Dragomoshchenko's first English trans-
lator, the British scholar Michael Molnar. By including these let-
ters, Dragomoshchenko connects a Barthesian view of language as a
sourceless echo to encounters with specific addressees and so suggests
a poetics of co-response founded on a relation to the other. By in-
cluding the letters, Dragomoshchenko engages with and complicates
the collective framings of cultural, historical, and literary-historical

difference through which his writing has been read, illustrating how a poetics of co-response might also offer alternatives to conventional ways of thinking about literary-historical periodization, national literature, and cross-cultural comparison. The letters from Hejinian and Molnar, conspicuously headed "Berkeley" and "London," emphasize the transnational coordinates of Dragomoshchenko's poetics through a complicated triangular correspondence that does not conform to a conventional East/West formula. The letter from Hejinian reveals that both she and Molnar are translating Dragomoshchenko's writing, and both her letter and Molnar's letter consider questions of wholeness and fragmentation. Hejinian asks, "What does the line mean to you? When, for example, it is broken?" Molnar's letter suggests his discomfort with Hejinian's "fragments of sense and words," which are "oriented toward the moment when words and sounds, and commonplaces combine." In lacking unity or coherence, Hejinian's poetry risks, Molnar suggests, the "banality of common absurdity."[27] By showing Hejinian's desire to retranslate the same poems already translated by Molnar, and Molnar's uncertain reaction to reading her poetry, Dragomoshchenko emphasizes major aesthetic differences between the two and so the likelihood of their differing interpretations and translations—or echoes—of his work. Dragomoshchenko's use of fragmentation and echoes provokes a conversation about poetics. This conversation equally highlights the difficulty of placing his work within a varied and multilateral literary field that is itself exemplified by the fragmented, aesthetically contradictory positions of his translators.[28]

The poem also addresses Dragomoshchenko's Russian affiliations and the rise of interest in postmodernism that coincided with his meeting and correspondence with Hejinian.[29] It does so through its assertion of Western affiliations, the inclusion of a letter from Leningrad writer Boris Ostanin, and its venue of publication. A poem that has come to be seen as marking Dragomoshchenko's "linguistic turn," "A Supper with Affable Gods" appeared in 1985 as the opening work of the first issue of *Mitin zhurnal*, the samizdat journal that in the following few years would publish almost all his work and become the flagship for the new Russian literature associated with the term "postmodernism."[30] Writing also in 1985, the editor of *Mitin zhurnal*, Dmitry Volchek, described the journal as engaged in "a secret war" with the "realism" promoted by Boris Ivanov, a leading unofficial writer, on behalf of the "playful culture" (*igrovaia kul'tura*) of writers such as Dragomoshchenko.[31] With its appeal to transnational and Western affiliations through cross-cultural correspondence, and with its highly unconventional style and structure, "A Supper with Affable Gods" typifies the new writing's resistance to placement within the boundaries of a national literary tradition and its tendency to provoke a heated response. In December 1983, using a recording of Hejinian reading her work, Dragomoshchenko presented an irreverent multimedia recital that antagonized not only the KGB but also the more aesthetically conservative members of Leningrad's unofficial literary community.[32] Similarly, one disgusted reader of an issue of *Mitin zhurnal*, perhaps prompted by Dragomoshchenko's unconventional poetry, went so far as to burn her copy in her bath.[33] "A Supper with Affable Gods" highlights the aesthetic conflict within unofficial literary circles through a reference to the "Silver age" poetry associated with more conservative members of the unofficial community, by anticipating criticisms that those who write poetry of this kind "don't know how to write normally," and by his inclusion of a letter from Ostanin, who in 1986 would publish a highly influential essay on the rift between the conservative aesthetics dominant in unofficial culture and the new developments exemplified by Volchek's *Mitin zhurnal*.[34]

In underscoring this split within unofficial culture, Dragomoshchenko's poem illustrates more than the binary logic of late–Cold War poetics in the Soviet Union: such internal differentiations and the poem's staging of a complex series of personal interactions—including with Hejinian, Molnar, and Ostanin—belie monolithic accounts of official and unofficial late-Soviet culture and its relation to Western postmodernism. Hejinian and the Rova Quartet's visit to Russia in 1983, for example, was only possible because of the interrelationship between unofficial Soviet culture and the authorities. The Rova Quartet's concert in Leningrad took place only because of Club-81: a grouping of unofficial writers, supervised by the KGB but supposedly "independent in aesthetic matters," who were allowed to meet regularly to discuss their work at the Dostoyevsky Museum.[35] Dragomoshchenko played a role in establishing Club-81; the club itself was seen as an example of his, and some of his contemporaries', self-styled indifference to politics, an indifference that Ostanin also singled out in describing the new literature associated with *Mitin zhurnal*.[36]

Despite his multifarious personal and poetic engagements within and beyond the Soviet Union, when Dragomoshchenko's work attracted the attention of US critics in the late 1980s and early 1990s, these critics read his work for what it revealed about the differences between Russian and US culture and poetry. Responding to his connection with Hejinian and the excitement surrounding political and cultural changes in the Soviet Union, they echoed the binaries of Cold War rhetoric and the them/us structure of Cold War poetics through references to "our two poetries." Insisting that Western "postmodernism" and Dragomoshchenko's work were "incommensurate," they suggested that "Russian Postmodernism" was an "oxymoron."[37] Implicitly or explicitly opposing these socially, historically, and culturally located readings in ways that reflect their own historical, social, and political location, several Russian critics have approached his poetry outside such contexts, as an engagement with language as such.[38] Their critical approach insists on the independence of aesthetics from politics and reflects a desire to avoid easy placement within a Russian tradition. Just as US readers have seen Dragomoshchenko through dichotomized American and Russian contexts, so Russian critics have tended to privilege language as a universalized force outside history, society, and politics. In their cross-cultural and linguistic accounts, both Western and Russian scholars largely ignore how the embodied, personal encounter between Dragomoshchenko and Hejinian and the broader multilateral interconnections together unsettle the views of culture and language upon which their readings are respectively based.

The highly charged late–Cold War context prompted dichotomized readings of Dragomoshchenko's work. It also shaped our models for understanding the new, more globalized world that emerged from this period. Through its inclusion of correspondence and its poetics of co-response, however, a poem like "A Supper with Affable Gods" suggests an alternative model for thinking comparatively emerging from the moment of change that gave rise to our current era of globalization—one that would synthesize often opposed social and linguistic readings by taking seriously the singular encounter between one person and another.

MIRRORS

After the publication of "A Supper with Affable Gods" and their second meeting in May 1985, Dragomoshchenko and Hejinian augmented their conflation of poetry and correspondence by agreeing to collaborate on The Corresponding Sky, a work they decided would emerge out of their letters and poems to each other. As in his letters to Hejinian, in his contributions to The Corresponding Sky Dragomoshchenko conjoins epistolary and poetic correspondences, staging the interplay between a singular encounter and the abstractions of language and social and cultural collectivities. Just as in a June 1984 letter he writes of mistaking Hejinian's words and citations for his own, in a September 1985 letter to her he includes a poetic extract—described as coming from the eighth part of *Sky of Correspondences*—that conflates the "sourceless echo" of language with a lyric drama in which a man and a woman exchange words, literally taking each other's words for their own:

Речь пробивает в бессмертьи
первую брешь. Что кроется
в словах, которыми
обмениваются по телефону
        мужчина и женщина?
. . . и до них.

Дыхание.

Speech makes the first breach in
immortality. What is contained
in the words that
are exchanged on the telephone
        by a man and a woman?
. . . and before them.

Breath.[39]

In describing a man and woman encountering each other in "words," the poem itself mistakes the sense of language as an elemental "sourceless echo" for the lyric drama of communication between "a man and a woman." Recalling Baudelaire's "prolonged echoes mingling in the distance," the poem conflates language's infinite repetitions—its "immortality"—with the confusion of a lovers' quarrel or with the delays or echoes in a long-distance call. By mixing a universal theory of language with a lovers' conversation, the poem moves between disembodied language and embodied encounter, between the distance of "speech" heard on the telephone or written half a world away and words so close they merge with one's own and are, like a lover's, traced on the page or felt as "breath." This binary is reinforced in a later, published version, which begins with the lines quoted above and concludes by contrasting the embodiment of "speech" and "breath" with the distance of "writing":

В ожидании письма
в сентябрь превращается август.
Снег сходит утром с лица,
снились туман, апрель, поля,
в словах—дыхание.

In anticipation of a letter
August turns into September.
Snow falls from the face in the morning,
fog, April, fields are dreamed
in words—breath.[40]

These lines oppose the bodily proximity of the "face" and "speech"—
a word recalled here, in the poem's conclusion, by "breath" and the
breath-like "fog"—to the distance marked by the word *pis'mo*, which
here seems best translated as "a letter" (perhaps in the pair's long-dis-
tance, cross-cultural, and multilingual correspondence). But *pis'mo*
can also mean "writing" and so links the cultural, linguistic, and
geographic divides between them to the distancing effected by writ-
ten language as opposed to "speech." "Breath" functions as a visceral
marker of fogginess, noncorrespondence, indeterminacy, dreams,
and yet also stands for embodied closeness against the distance of
letters, telephone conversations, and written language. The poem
links proximity to distance, personal correspondence to the totality
of language and culture—the latter through the clichéd references
to Russian "snow" and San Francisco "fog" here and elsewhere in
Dragomoshchenko's contributions to The Corresponding Sky. Drago-
moshchenko locates the link "in words." "Words" mark the poem's
distance from its subject—the gap between "words" on the page and
the "snow falls" and "fog" they describe. But they are also viscerally
proximate: the poem's "words" can be touched or breathed upon by
both correspondents, by writer and reader.

Writing to Hejinian about translating her poetry, Drago-
moshchenko further merges the immediacy of face-to-face encounter
with the mediation of language. "'Becoming used' to [your] *writing*"
(*pis'mo*) again means becoming used to Hejinian's "letter" (*pis'mo*)
and even to her face: "My tongue, my eyes, my hearing, skin, sense
of smell, reactions are fully subordinate to you, to your lines, to
that which lies between them and that must arise in the Russian
language in my feelings."[41] As above, *iazyk*, as both "tongue" and
"language," figures the cross-cultural, linguistic, and interpersonal
encounter on which their correspondence is predicated. Language

is the bridge and marker of difference in the cross-cultural encounter between the two poets who speak two different languages. Language is also the conduit for the elemental force of poetry, which resists any single location and possesses an independent force, which "lies between" the lines and "must arise in the Russian language." In the same letter, Dragomoshchenko writes that his translation aims to resist "conscious interpretation . . . filling the cup of the text with content that is pure in its inexpression."[42] Yet Dragomoshchenko appeals to the abstraction of "pure . . . inexpression" through an explicitly erotic image. The image upsets the totality of the cup and of language as an abstract force. *Iazyk* as the singular, bodily "tongue" in the mouth of each poet unsettles *iazyk* as "language." As with the "breath" in the poem, Dragomoshchenko deploys the tongue to transform the abstract desire for the cross-cultural collective other—the desire to speak another tongue, to know another language, another culture—into an encounter that questions the object of cross-cultural reading.

Dragomoshchenko's poem "Obuchenie chistote v smeshannom" ("Instructing Clarity in a Confusion"), written for The Corresponding Sky, also blends text and body, language and face, but complicates his own use of the cup as a figure for perfect correspondence:

настоя терпко нетерпенье, горячечное, будто
                        муравьиный рот
кого-то,
искривленный на стакане, когда
                в лекарственном, хмельном чаду
пол с потолком меняется местами
и холодок кривой игрой у губ—
                        брат бестелесный лба,
сухого созерцанья
в семян неведеньи неслышном, точно невод,
способном ум обрушить косностью значенья
в истлевший, пресный час зари.

Но даже память здесь—не боле, чем изъян,
впивающийся центром круга . . . Не уходить.
Склонись.
И слушай гул. Бурьян. Он гол, безвиден.
Слух—это ждать, когда в ответ не ждать.

Такой удел струне завиден . . .

Нас разделяет пестрый искры миг

золою мотылька, расправленного в копоть
свободной радугой ресниц.
Нас разлучив, венчает вспышка век—
гарь десяти секунд глаз в совпаденьи,

the impatience of the brew is bitter, delirious, as if
the ant-like mouth
of someone,
distorted on the glass, when
in medicinal drunkenness
the floor changes places with the ceiling
and the crooked cold toying with the lips—
the disembodied brother of the forehead,
of dry contemplation
in the inaudible ignorance of seeds, like a net,
set to destroy the mind by the stagnation of meaning
in the dying, dull hour of dawn.

But here even memory is no more than a flaw
sucked in by the center of the circle . . . Don't leave.
Bend down.
And listen to the hum. Tall weeds. They are bare, unseen.
Sound—this is waiting, when there's nothing to wait in response to.

The string envies such a fate . . .

A spark's colorful moment separates us
with the ash of a moth spread out into soot
by the free rainbow of eyelashes.
Having separated us, the eyelids' flash crowns—
cinders of the ten seconds when the eyes meet,[43]

The poem stages the desire for "response" (*otvet*) from the other, a desire that "separates us" but allows "us" to "meet" each other face to face, eye to eye—*venchaet* can mean not only "crowns" but also "marries"—though always through a "distorted . . . glass." The reader seeking the world of the implied speaker through the "cup" of the poem finds instead the "spark" and "flash" of fragmented meaning, just as the speaker sees or hears ("listen"; "unseen") the "mouth" of the other through a glass cup: "as if / the ant-like mouth / of someone, / distorted on the glass." While the image of the cup in Dragomoshchenko's poetics promises perfect apprehension of the other's world, the distorted mouth suggests that language, translation, and cross-cultural encounter affect how one perceives and remembers, so that "the floor changes places with the ceiling" and "memory is no more than a flaw"—a pun Hejinian introduces in her translation, underscoring how language resists "the stagnation of meaning." Like the "glass" (*stakan*) the poem fragments the other's face into "mouth" (*rot*), "eyes" (*glaza*), "eyelashes" (*resnitsy*), "eyelids" (*veka*), "lips" (*guby*), and "forehead" (*lob*), transforming the concrete body into isolated, "disembodied" (*bestelesnyi*) body parts and, in the case of *gub*, *lob*, and *rot*, shared sounds. (There is also a play on *veka*—"eyelid"— and *vek*—"century" or "age.") Wordplay makes the "bare" or "naked" (*gol*) body a "hum" (*gul*). By choosing a "glass cup" (*stakan*) that distorts, intoxicates (*khmel'noi*), and turns the world upside down ("the floor changes places with the ceiling"), rather than an opaque "cup" (*chashka*) that hides its contents, Dragomoshchenko perhaps alludes to his letter to Hejinian about how to translate the word *chashka*, after she proposed her own key term "cuppings."[44] The whole "vessel" becomes a myriad of imperfect containers— *stakan*, *chashka*, "glass," "cup," and "cuppings"—that fragment into myriad meanings, like a face seen through a faceted glass.

The poem that prompted Dragomoshchenko and Hejinian's correspondence over translating the word *chashka*, "Primechaniia" ("Footnotes"), conflates not just the body and language, but also letter writing and poetry. Dragomoshchenko's "Footnotes" calls for the reader to respond to the interplay between direct address and cultural and linguistic otherness with multiple readings that would match the poem's many versions. Differing versions of the poem appear in Dragomoshchenko's first English-language collection (in Hejinian's translation), in an anthology (in Russian and in another translation by Hejinian), and in his selected poems *Opisanie* (*Description*).[45] The first of the two versions in the selected poems—really only an augmented fragment from the poem—opens *Pod podozreniem* (*Under Suspicion*) and the entire collection. The lines that overlap with the other versions read:

март ежегодно
разворачивает наст сознания,
перестраивая облака
в иное, опять в иное письмо:

вновь невнятно.

Меня больше там,
      где я о себе забываю.
Нагие,

как законы грамматики,

головы запрокинув.

March yearly
scatters the snow crust of consciousness,
transforming the clouds
into another, again another letter:

unintelligible once more.

There is more of me
      where I forget about myself.
Naked,
like the laws of grammar,

heads thrown back.[46]

The line "another, again another letter" emphasizes many versions and invites multiple readings. Dragomoshchenko again exploits the ambiguity of the Russian word for both "letter" and "writing" (*pis'mo*) to fuse particular and general readings by alluding to the letters from Hejinian, their collaborative writing project that emerges from these letters, and written language as an elemental force, like "snow" and "clouds." Letters fly like "clouds" across The Corresponding Sky that separates and unites the two, punctuating the year ("yearly"; *ezhegodno*), just as "in anticipation of a letter / August turns into September" above. The differing letters ("another, again another letter") mark time passing but also suggest that the "writing" is "other" (*inoe*), written in another language or tongue, *inoiazych-nyi*, by a foreigner, *inostranets*, and so "unintelligible" (*nevniatno*).[47]

In one interpretation, I take "unintelligible" to refer to the foreign letter and so read the lines as a personal reference to Hejinian and Dragomoshchenko's friendship. But in "another" (*inoe*) reading, the poem generalizes the personal and cross-cultural encounter, presenting "writing" as "other" (*inoe*), and the foreign language as ultimately a product of language in general, which is an "unintelligible," impersonal force, like the weather. "Footnotes" describes and enacts how language unsettles the boundaries of self and other, so that the pronouns "I" and the implied "you" and "we" (the grammatical subject of "naked" in other versions of the poem) become "naked," disembodied elements of a "grammar." This "other writing" resembles what Blanchot calls the "speech of detour, the 'poetry' in the turn of writing, . . . wherein time turns": that is, language that moves away from any fixed correspondence between word and world and between one world and another.[48] The iterating "another, again another writing" suggests Blanchot's turning of time, which turns "the world . . . upside down," an image literalized in "Instructing Clarity in a Confusion," "when the floor changes places with the ceiling."[49] Language's strange force "scatters . . . consciousness," unsettling its "snow crust" (*nast*) rigidity, pluralizing "me" ("There is more of me"), and transforming the lyric "I" into impersonal "writing." Like Baudelaire's "forests of symbols," the poem here invokes an analogy with the natural world of weather only to collapse correspondence between words and world under the force of language's relentless signification.

In transforming lyric address into linguistic play, "Footnotes" invites yet "another" (*inoe*) reading attuned to the erotic self-exposure of the "naked" (*nagoi*) lyric "I," suggesting "There is more of me / where I forget about myself," and "transforming" a generalized reading back into a particular one. The plural of the adjective "naked" (*nagie*) realizes the multiplying "I" ("more of me") and suggests a link between the "I" and the "you" who is implied by the "I" and by the letters. Their shared upward gaze mediates their face-to-face encounter through the sky, weather, and language, in The Corresponding Sky. The gaze skyward returns the reader to the "clouds" that transform into writing or letters between the "I" and the "you," setting writing and their relationship into endless motion. Because the final sentence lacks a subject, "naked" might refer to any plural noun or pronoun and so alternates between uniting the "I" and "you" and eliminating the poem's personal address. Other versions read "we are naked in bed" (*my v posteli nagie*), heightening the erotic lyric self-exposure by suggesting a sexual encounter.[50] In translating the line, Hejinian implies their location by mentioning a "bed" in the previous line, but she does not include the words "in bed," reinforcing the interplay between exposing and concealing or unsettling the lyric self.[51] Likewise, by removing the pronoun, Dragomoshchenko propels the poem away from the personal lyric and toward impersonal linguistic play, but by leaving the plural subject suggestively undefined, he equally lets the poem oscillate between revealing and concealing its own "naked" lyric self-exposure.

These rewritings comment on the "scene of writing" in the poem, which in other versions is linked, through the lines "mother stands over us at the foot of the bed, / we are naked in bed like the laws of grammar," to Freud's "primal scene" and to the "even more 'primal' . . . biblical scene of 'knowledge,'" when Adam and Eve became cognizant that they were "naked." By including this familial, primal context in one version and excluding it from another, Dragomoshchenko's self-quotation questions how a scene can be original or "primal," since the reader cannot determine which version of the poem should take precedence.[52]

Moving between self-referential, echoing language and the contrary correlation of words to nature, Dragomoshchenko presents a "naked" autobiographical encounter, while "transforming" it into writing, which the iterative power of language divorces from a single primal scene ("naked") and from the limits of the natural world ("clouds") and personal experience ("consciousness"). Rewriting the poem, from his letter to Hejinian, to her translation, to the multiple versions he "scatters" across his books, he links the vagaries of the weather to his iterating linguistic method—"another, again another writing"—and to the recursive everyday act of letter writing: "another, again another letter." He thus undermines a reading of the poem that stresses either the intertextual correspondences of language, or the search for correspondence between language and the world, over personal address and lyric self-exposure. The poem points skywards, but should we seek in that sky natural signs to be read, a rhetorical gesture toward language's infinite plurality, or a conduit through which his and Hejinian's letters and poems journey to and from Russia, as they come to us even today? Dragomoshchenko enfolds generalized deconstructive readings and readings that relate language to the world by inviting the reader to partake in his poetics of co-response, producing "another, again another" reading.

Dragomoshchenko's "Accidia" also derives from multiple readings, or misreadings, connecting letter and poetry writing, the body, reading, language, and translation to explore the relationship between generalized cross-cultural and linguistic readings and personal face-to-face encounter.[53] If "Footnotes," the immediately preceding poem in *Description*, can be read as a footnote to Dragomoshchenko and Hejinian's letters, "Accidia" presents the letters as a footnote to the poem. Dragomoshchenko frames the poem as extending his and Hejinian's letter writing by including a lengthy note to the poem taken from a letter to Hejinian. In the note, he explains how "Accidia" began with his misreading of a phrase from Hejinian, which he took to be "everything begins as an error of vision." His personal and inter-lingual reading produces the generalized ("everything") and uncon-tainable play of language and translation that, like Blanchot's "move-ment of a speech that is neither mine nor yours," replaces the subject's originary intended meaning with impersonal "error." Underscoring the personal, embodied encounter, Dragomoshchenko quotes exten-sively from the letter where he discusses his misreading.

A part of the same letter not quoted in the note describes the sen-suous pleasure of receiving a letter from Hejinian, transforming dis-embodied writing into embodied speech: "How happy I am to hear you again, to guess—perhaps mainly made up by me—at your intona-tion, your speech, reading it [the letter] again and again."[54] Inverting how his note moves from intimate encounter to generalized language, Dragomoshchenko produces an embodied encounter by misreading or mistranslating writing into speech, recalling how, in a poem dis-cussed above and sent as a letter to Hejinian, "writing" or a "letter" becomes "breath." He produces an "error of vision" in two senses, not just mistranslating Hejinian's English phrase but confusing sight and hearing, text and body, impersonal linguistic play and intimate face-to-face encounter. Dragomoshchenko's note explains that he subsequently removed his mistranslation of Hejinian's line from the beginning of the poem, presenting the poem itself as an error, an error he underscores by excluding the poem from his Russian col-lections.[55] The generalized "error" erases the singular encounter and lyric disclosure, finally eliminating the poem altogether, but the re-sultant ghost text continues to haunt his writing (Dragomoshchenko reuses the title in a 2005 work), inviting both autobiographical and generalized linguistic and cross-cultural readings.[56]

"Accidia" oscillates between the general and particular through its refrain "one should / break / the mirror / of language":

следует
разбить
зеркало
языка.   Плохая примета—разбитое зеркало. Как-то в летнее утро
я был разбужен нечеловеческим воем: кричала мать: повесился дед.
      Поднимался жаром пышущий день, мотыльков стаи в то лето мета-
лись без устали над огородами. Путался шелест в аравийских черепах
мака. Все начинается с ошибки зрения, с распыления вещи, замершей
в обреченном единстве   (учиться сквозь сон, как другое, распозна-
вать предметы и вещи,—таково обрученье).

one should
break
the mirror
of language   A broken mirror is a bad sign. One morning in sum-
mer I was awakened by an inhuman howling: my mother was crying:
my grandfather had hanged himself.

The seething day formed in its own heat, that summer swarms of
butterflies bustled ceaselessly above the vegetable gardens. In the Ara-
bian skulls of poppies their rustling was confused. Everything begins
with an error of vision, with the disintegration of the thing arrested
in its doomed unity   (learn through dream to recognize subjects and
things as other—such is an exchange of rings).[57]

Like Dragomoshchenko's "cup," his "mirror" suggests mimesis: hold-
ing a mirror up to reality. But the mirror also describes how language
reflects one's own image.[58] The poem's "mirror / of language" appears
to reflect the unspeakable real and show the lyric subject disclosing
his innermost secrets. Read in this way, the poem describes a lyric
subject haunted by the memory of the moment when his "mother"
discovered that his "grandfather," perhaps her father, "had hanged
himself." While the poem's language reflects the world and the lyric
subject's memory, "Accidia" also associates the memory with the mir-
ror's shattering and the shift from lyric poetry to prose. Beginning
the shift to prose layout, the sentence "A broken mirror is a bad sign"
immediately precedes the shocking news. The poem breaks the "mir-
ror," registering language's failure to represent the moment when a
life shatters, a moment conveyable only through "inhuman howling,"
"crying," and, in the poem's final word, a "scream" (*vizg*). The shock-
ing encounter with the real ruptures language and shifts the subject
from narcissism into an encounter with the other: "learn through
dream to recognize subjects and things as other." Breaking the mirror
not only draws language's transparency into question but also places
the self and the generalizing notion of language in doubt through
a singular encounter with the "other" (*drugoe*), implicitly here not
just "things" but also the speaker of another language, Hejinian, to
whom the poem is dedicated. "Accidia" presents a breathless, inti-
mate encounter with memory and translator, but also generalizes
the visceral embodied cry, questioning how to relate language to the
world. Errors and mirrors reveal the ghosts that haunt language and
the psyche, ghosts visible only through "the mirror / of language,"
which breaks to reveal "the disintegration of the thing arrested in
its doomed unity"—exposed in the wordplay between *obrechennyi*

(doomed) and *obruchen'e* (the "exchange of rings" in a wedding). Here two words signifying binding are also linked by their similar-sounding roots, *rech'* and *ruk*, "speech" and "hand." These semantic and phonemic resemblances at once connect the spoken word to the hand's touch and, like Baudelaire's "Correspondances," disperse language in a play of similarities that refuses the unity of mimetic correspondence. Addressing and incorporating the words of the other—be it Hejinian or the mother—the poem's broken mirror reflects the abstracting otherness of language and translation in the face of a singular encounter.

WINDOWS

Dragomoshchenko's final poem in *Sky of Correspondences*, "Nasturtsiia kak real'nost'" ("Nasturtium as Reality"), oscillates between an embodied, intimate, personal poetics and a principled resistance to location. Describing a nasturtium viewed through a rain-spotted windowpane, the twelve-part poem appeals to an immediate object and to its faraway dedicatee, Hejinian. Yet it resists reifying object and addressee, meaning and place, highlighting instead the frames, slippages, and translations through which language represents "reality" and through which the poem is read. The observer-nasturtium relationship becomes an allegory or metaphor for the reader and writer and for views from inside and outside a given context, including the differing views engendered by Hejinian and Dragomoshchenko's cross-cultural encounter and translations, which, like the rain-spotted windowpane, produce "an error of vision." By questioning the "window" through which the world is described—or, as in "Accidia," "the mirror / of language"—the poem unsettles the cross-cultural reader, who, like the reader of lyric poetry, looks, in the poem's repeated phrase, "over someone else's shoulder," seeking an intimate window on another's reality. "Nasturtium as Reality" demands a comparative poetics that negotiates between location and nonlocation—between reading literature for what it says about a particular place, time, and culture, and for its dislocated play of language.

"Nasturtium as Reality" shuttles between language and embodied, often erotic, encounter, prompting contrasting generalizing readings that emphasize either cultural and historical location or the dislocating power of language. The poem concludes Dragomoshchenko's first and only Soviet collection, *Nebo sootvetstvii* (*Sky of*

Correspondences), and his first English-language collection, *Description*, both of which were published in 1990. Due to its placement within each collection and its appearance at this historical juncture, it came to be read in the West as expressing a "post-Soviet subjectivity" that differed fundamentally from Western postmodernism: whereas Dragomoshchenko's poetry was said to be grounded in a place and time, postmodernism was placeless and globalized.[59] For Russian critics writing after the fall of the Soviet Union, however, his poetry was not "a representational practice specific to a given context, and thus . . . something . . . determined by, or reducible to, a habitual set of national attributes current at a given moment."[60] Where, for example, Marjorie Perloff argues that Dragomoshchenko's "Footnotes" presents a strange but reified poetic "vision," Mikhail Iampolski describes a poetics of "non-place" that negates vision in favor of touch and that refuses any position, frame, or location.[61]

The title "Nasturtium as Reality" invites and complicates these contrasting readings. It suggests the desire to address reality, which US poet and critic Barrett Watten takes to be "post-Soviet subjectivity," defined as "a reconciliation of collective memory and empirical truth," in which "subjectivity is constituted in its immanent horizons of lyric continuity, collective memory, and scientific objectivity."[62] But the title also represents a humorous riposte to the idea that a poem might encapsulate reality. The preposterous act of taking a nasturtium as reality parallels the act of taking a poem to provide a window on another world, such as post-Soviet subjectivity. As with the title, the poem as a whole unsettles generalizing cross-cultural, historical, located readings and dislocated, linguistic readings through intersecting relationships between observer and nasturtium, writer and reader, Russian and American poets.

The poem highlights and unsettles its own linguistic play through autobiographical, embodied, and cross-cultural encounter. Although Watten argues that "cultural and personal memory are fragmented and recombined in the form of a material text rather than the embodiment of the poet," the poem nevertheless highlights bodily encounters and invites readings that connect the poem to the literal body of the poet.[63] "Nasturtium as Reality" employs the figure of chiasmus, transforming embodied experience into language and back again, in a ceaseless movement that "continuously introduces the subtext motif of correspondence."[64] By intertwining language and body, the poem presents a phenomenological reality arising through the interactions between perceiver and perceived. Recalling Levinas, who argues that the ethical relationship or co-response precedes ontology and epistemology, "Nasturtium as Reality" insists on mutually constituting relationships with others as the precondition of "reality," on co-response before correspondence.[65]

The poem undermines the quasi-scientific objective discourse of its opening lines not only through textual play but also by appealing to embodied singular relations between self and other:

Опыт
описания изолированного предмета
определен предвосхищеньем итога—
          взглядом через плечо другого.

Настурция состоит
из дождливой прорвы окна
для себя самой «до»,

для меня—«за». Кому достоянье
рдеющей
дрожи
спрессованного обнажения
          в проеме обоюдоострых предлогов
                                        у
створчатой плоскости,
прозрачность
разящей
стекла?

An attempt
to describe an isolated object
determined by the anticipation of the resulting whole—
          by a glance over someone else's shoulder.

The nasturtium is composed
of a rain-riven mass of window
to itself it's "in front,"

to me, "behind." To whom is the property of
gleaming
tremor
of compressed disclosure
          in the opening of double-edged prepositions
                                        in
a folded plane
striking

the transparency
of the glass?[66]

The poem responds to the other, undermining any straightforward correspondence to the world—denying Benjamin's "whole vessel," or Dragomoshchenko's "cup," or here "the resulting whole," "sum," or "answer" (*itog*). Through "anticipation" (*predvoskhishchen'e*), the poem's "object" (*predmet*) becomes subjective and relational. The two words' shared, "double-edged" prefix *pred*—which also functions as a preposition signifying "in front of," "before," or "prior to"—links the words, suggesting that relation precedes object and subject. The "glance over someone else's shoulder" further implies that description depends on interpersonal relations, on "someone else," or "the other" (*drugogo*), and that the writer is glancing over his shoulder, conscious that the text addresses an audience who helps constitute the poem as "object." Just as the describer's "anticipation" undermines the attempt to describe an "isolated object" outside its relation to the describer, so the poem refuses to be "isolated" by anticipating multiple readings and diverse readers—Russian and English-speaking since the text was written to be translated by Hejinian.[67] Neither poem nor "description" produces an "answer" (*itoga*) because its half-rhyme partner, *drugogo* (pronounced *druogova*; "the other"), always undermines "the resulting whole" by suggesting someone or something else outside the object, the self, the poem, or the window.

The nasturtium becomes one figure for that other, and the poem a metaphor for embodied cross-cultural encounter. The feminine noun *nasturtsiia* confronts the implied male poet figure across the neutral—and, in Russian, neuter—space of the "window" (*okno*), suggesting a parallel between the describer and nasturtium's encounter through the windowpane, and Dragomoshchenko and Hejinian's cross-cultural correspondence across the half-transparency of cultural and linguistic difference. Dragomoshchenko reinforces this parallel by dedicating the poem to Hejinian, by positioning the poem as the concluding piece in his contribution to The Corresponding Sky, and by later naming the poem's male poet figure "A. T. D." and "Arkadii Trofimovich," Dragomoshchenko's initials and first name and patronymic, respectively. The window is a commonplace figure for the relationship between Russia and the West that derives from Pushkin's famous description of Peter the Great founding St. Petersburg, Dragomoshchenko's adopted hometown, in order to "cut a window through to Europe."[68] In *Mednyi vsadnik* (*The Bronze Horseman*), Pushkin contrasts the desire for an overnight Westernization of Russia through the creation of a new city with the less than utopian and deeply unsettled result. A number of writers, artists, and filmmakers found that Pushkin's poem articulated the uncertain relation between Russia and the West with renewed resonance during the late-Soviet and early post-Soviet periods, as, for example, in the 1993 film *Okno v Parizh* (*Window to Paris*), in which the occupants of a Petersburg apartment discover a magical window that transports them directly to Paris.[69] Written on the cusp of Russia's opening up to the West, Dragomoshchenko's poem anticipates this broader cultural moment.

Reflecting their uncertain relations, both the "I" and the "nasturtium" occupy only relative positions: they exist behind "prepositions" (*predlogi*), as well as each being positioned "behind" and "in front" of the window through the prepositions *za* and *do*. Relation undermines entity and identity in bodily, sensuous, even sensual terms. *Obnazhenie* (disclosure) derives from the word for nakedness, linking the Russian-formalist "baring of the device" (*obnazhenie priema*) to sensual, sexualized relations. The sexualized imagery centers on the flower, which guards but also displays its sexual organs, and is reinforced by the "tremor" (*drozh'*) as well as the "disclosure" and the "opening" (*proem*). Such imagery recurs in part 3, where the nasturtium is "vibrating" (*vibriruiushchaia*) as a result of the "immersion / of a bumblebee"—gendered masculine in Russian—"in the still unconsumed confusion of wings" (*pogruzhen'e / shmelia v nedopituiu otorop' kryl'ev*). In the opening section, the letter and word *u* (y in Cyrillic; translated as "in"), isolated on its own line, links this sensuality to language not only through its marking of a prepositional, relational state but also through its shape, which resembles a stem attached to the cup-like opening of a flower. Moreover, the word *u* (in) in the middle of the stanza is also the middle letter in the word *nasturtsiia* (nasturtium), literalizing in another sense the "opening" in the middle of the flower.

Dragomoshchenko's comments about the word *nasturtsiia* further link the sensuous use of language to sexualized encounter with the other:

> Из своего окна я видел настурцию на балконе, таившую в словесном своем составе, словно в слепом стручке, новые завязи, соотношения новые меры, коим в точности было предписано повторить бывшие . . . словно в сумрачном стечении согласных—в смерти—где

нарастающие, смывающие друг друга, возникающие дрожат бесчисленные связи реальности.

> From my window I saw a nasturtium on a balcony. The nasturtium was concealing in its verbal composition, as if in its blind pod, new ovaries, new measures of interrelationship, for which it was precisely prescribed to repeat former measures . . . literally in the twilight confluence of consonants—in death—where growing, washing one another away, and springing up, the innumerable links of reality tremble.[70]

The sensuous, sibilant (fifteen words in the quoted passage begin with the *s* sound) language in this description accompanies a more explicit focus on the nasturtium's sexual organs ("its new ovaries"), underscoring the interplay between linguistic and embodied encounter. Dragomoshchenko reinforces this linguistic and bodily relationship through the *so* prefix in *sootnoshenie* (interrelationship) and *soglasnye* (meaning "consonants" as in letters—but also "those who are consonant" or "in agreement," or literally those who are "covoiced"). The alliteration—the shared consonant—enacts the correspondence or interrelationship between words, even as the phenomenological description of the nasturtium is staged as an erotic heterosexual encounter—a moment of consonance—between people. The *so* prefix and sex emphasize co-response, or coming into being through mutual response.

The wordplay underscores the collaborative, co-voiced text that emerges out of the "interrelationship" not just between the lyric subject and the nasturtium but also between reader and writer, writer and translator, addresser and addressee. The window can be read as "the language of the poem, through [which] . . . occurs the possibility of description; on the surface of language, description is 'in front,' though from the point of view of subjectivity in the poem the nasturtium is 'behind' language."[71] Equally, one might take the page of the poem to be the window so that the reader becomes the viewer of the spotted, word-covered page behind which lies the writer and the nasturtium. The window as page separates not only the describer and described, nor only Russia and the West, but two persons. The window-page becomes a figure not just for linguistic and cross-cultural mediation, but for the encounters between Dragomoshchenko and Hejinian, and between the reader and the text.

"Nasturtium as Reality" further impels the reader to recognize how the encounter between describer and nasturtium and between

lovers parallels his or her own encounter with the text, by returning
to the opening glance over the shoulder in part 8:

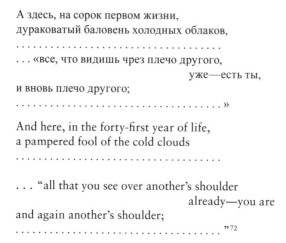

А здесь, на сорок первом жизни,
дураковатый баловень холодных облаков,
. . . .
. . . «все, что видишь чрез плечо другого,
                                          уже—есть ты,
и вновь плечо другого;
. . . . »

And here, in the forty-first year of life,
a pampered fool of the cold clouds
. . . .

. . . "all that you see over another's shoulder
                                          already—you are
and again another's shoulder;
. . . . "72

The encounter with "you"—the relation to "another" or "the other"
(*drugogo*)—impels the poet to reveal himself (Dragomoshchenko was
forty-one at the time he wrote the poem) and The Corresponding Sky
project ("cold clouds") to which he contributed the poem. This moment
of self-revelation recalls the poem's opening, which discloses ("com-
pressed disclosure") how the objective attempt to describe the nastur-
tium as "an isolated object" is "determined" by subjective "anticipa-
tion" and by the lyric subject's relation to the other—the poem's first
"glance over someone else's shoulder." The poem reveals and conceals
by playing between multiple possible readings: on the one hand, it bi-
furcates and distances the subject; on the other, its erotic and amo-
rous allusions suggest an intimate face-to-face encounter. The quota-
tion marks distance the glance over the shoulder, presenting it as the
reported speech of another. The lines could be translated as "all that
you see over the shoulder of the other / is you," further distancing the
subject by bifurcating "you" into a "you" who sees and a "you" who is
seen, so that the glance over a shoulder both recalls and hides the lov-
er's cliché "all I saw in the crowded room was you." But the line could
also be read as stating that all the "you" sees in the other is a mirror
image of the self. These multiple readings underscore how language is
prepositional: it mediates between persons, between self and other, and
between subject and object, just as the glance moves "over the shoul-
der," and the nasturtium is seen through and "in" (*u*) the windowpane.

The poem performs and invites "a glance over someone else's shoulder," but, as with the nasturtium in the window, whether one glances from "behind" or "in front" makes all the difference. From behind, the reader peers voyeuristically at the lyric subject's conventional self-exposure and at a self-consciously constructed window on Russia. From in front, the writer and lyric subject look beyond their apparent addressees to another, perhaps the reader, underscoring the lyric's "doubled 'I'" and "doubled 'you.'"[73] The poem implicates the reader, rejecting the tendency to situate reading outside the text. As Dragomoshchenko writes elsewhere, "As we read . . . , blinded by our ability to see, we are at times utterly unable to admit that we too are included in the endless weave of meanings."[74] Building on his iterative poetics of correspondence—"another, again another letter" or "writing"—Dragomoshchenko's "Nasturtium as Reality" situates the reader in the "endless weave" by offering him or her multiple views, windows, or repeating glances over "another's shoulder," and so extends the interplay between disembodied language and embodied speech to include the reader.

The desire to frame the world and language, to imagine them as a "whole vessel," cup, or glass, motivates and shapes readings across cultures that seek a world other than one's own, or a world we hold in common. In my framing, Dragomoshchenko's writing enacts and invites embodied, sensuous, singular encounter, while exploring the frames and empty spaces, absences, and transitions these encounters produce. In his poetic correspondences, the encounter with the other does not arise from reading, writing, interpretation, and comparison, but constitutes the ground of these activities, inviting an erotics rather than a hermeneutics of comparison. By emphasizing the embodied relations through which we conduct cross-cultural reading, Dragomoshchenko's writing shows that the window through which we look is distorted not just by the glass but by our own reflection, our own breath.

CHAPTER THREE

Lyn Hejinian
and Russian Estrangement

Following such a line, we would not study—to put the question into its most traditional formulation—the "encounter" *between* Orientalism and modernism, but rather work the interpenetration of those two categories prior to a generalized awareness of them as categories, understanding that each of them depends, in some way, on the apprehension of the other in advance.

—ERIC HAYOT, *The Hypothetical Mandarin: Sympathy, Modernity, and Chinese Pain*

Like a word in Russian inspiring notice of the present incorporeality of one's self

—LYN HEJINIAN, *Oxota: A Short Russian Novel*

Viktor Shklovsky's concept of estrangement (*ostranenie*) has attracted many avant-garde groups, but perhaps none more so than the Language poets, the most prominent avant-garde in English-language poetry of the last quarter of the twentieth century. Among the Language poets, this theory of poetic estrangement finds no better expression than in Hejinian. Like Shklovsky, Hejinian extends her poetics of estrangement beyond the textual, connecting the radical artifice of poetic language with the act of seeing the world anew and with the estranging effect of Russia itself: the autonomous poetics of the word as such ("form made difficult") with the renewal of perception in everyday life.

According to Hejinian, "Sensation of the world and a counter to pessimism are what Language writers, when first encountering Shklovsky in the 1970s, found in his work."[1] It was in the mid-1970s that Barrett Watten and Ron Silliman, two members of the then-nascent Language poetry group, introduced her to Viktor Erlich's *Russian Formalism*, a book she describes as making an "enormous impact" on the Language poets at that time; of the Formalists, Shklovsky exerted the greatest influence on the group's "sense of literary style and strategies."[2] Shklovsky and Russian Formalism provided Hejinian and other Language poets with a method that emphasized poetic "technique" over the "subjective aesthetic approach" based on "values from psychology or biography." They also supplied the model for, in Hejinian's words, the "utopian project" of Language poetry: to create an artistic community in which theory and practice went hand in hand.[3]

Then, in 1983, Hejinian traveled to Russia, the "home" of estrangement and, as fellow Language poet Michael Davidson puts it, the "fount" for Language poetry theory.[4] There, as we have seen, she established a friendship with Dragomoshchenko, initiating an intense personal and artistic engagement with Russia and Russian writers, which involved Hejinian learning Russian, making extensive and frequent trips to the Soviet Union, and translating the work of Dragomoshchenko and a number of other contemporary Russian poets.[5]

Hejinian's approximately eight-year period of close engagement with Russia and Russian writers exemplifies how literary practice and theory are shaped from the outset by cross-cultural encounters. Her encounter with Russia led her not only to explore the linguistic possibilities of translation but also to conflate estrangement in art and life.[6] Partly through her developing poetics of the "person," she came to link three kinds of estrangements: poetic estrangement, the estranging effect of her Russian experience, and estrangement as the basis for a community that would unite Russian and US writers. Entwining her poetics of the person with her poetic and personal engagement with Russia, Hejinian's cross-cultural encounter demonstrates that a theoretical term like "estrangement" is neither a free-floating concept of transnational modernism, nor yet localized. Its various meanings emerge out of border-transcending visions and encounters among particular places, times, and persons. So conceived, literary estrangement cannot easily be detached from everyday experiences of strangeness, nor can it be separated from the collective cross-cultural readings—such as those involved in the Cold War binaries of East and West, Russianness and Americanness—that shape those experiences.

THE PERSON

Avant-garde artists such as Hejinian were drawn to Shklovsky's theory of art by the internal contradictions within its essential term, "estrangement." These are immediately apparent in the essay "Art as Device," where Shklovsky makes the famous statement: "in order to return sensation to life, to feel things, in order to make the stone stony, there exists that which is called art. The purpose of art is to impart a sensation of a thing as vision and not as recognition; the device of art is the device of 'estrangement.'" Shklovsky immediately adds, however, that the "device of art" involves not only returning "sensation to life" but also "the device of form made difficult [*za-trudnennaia forma*], which heightens the difficulty and length of perception, for the perceptual process in art is autonomous and should be prolonged."[7] Here the conception of poetic language as autonomous language that draws attention to words as such is combined with the view that poetic language is "expected to de-automatize and 'make strange' not only language but also the objects referred to."[8] Shklovsky's emphasis on perception contrasted with that of some other Formalists, such as Roman Jakobson.[9] Indeed, Shklovsky conflates two conceptions of poetic language, apparently without noticing, let alone acknowledging it: "If the process of perception becomes an end in itself through the difficulty of form, we perceive the object less, not more; if estrangement determines the definition of art, the process of perception is imperceptible, and we see the object instead, as if for the first time."[10] Shklovsky's famous passage from "Art as Device," then, proposes the "radical artifice" of the autonomous word as the basis of poetic language, but simultaneously argues that poetic language, through the device of estrangement, can also renew our perception of the world and can thus oppose the dreaded habituation, or "automatization," of language and perception that threatens to destroy any real experience of life.[11]

Shklovsky's conflation of "form made difficult" with the device of estranging the "real" world outside automatized experience has had an enduring appeal to avant-garde artists such as Hejinian, who wish to combine radical formal experimentation with the transformation of everyday life, because it "harbors the romantic and avant-garde dream of a reverse mimesis: everyday life can be redeemed if it imitates art, not the other way around. So the device of estrangement could both define and defy the autonomy of art." Moreover, estrangement, as Shklovsky conceived of it, was a peculiarly Russian concept, because for him it was only in Russia that the estrangement of everyday life could truly be realized. Russia offered the "imagined community of fellow intellectuals" necessary for this utopian goal, just as that same community provided the model for the utopian project of the Language poets.[12]

Following Shklovsky, Hejinian links estrangement in art and life, or what she refers to as "literary praxis" and "social materiality," terms that parallel fellow Language writer Watten's key theoretical concepts "material text" and "social poetics."[13] Hejinian develops her own distinct, though related, view of this relationship over the course of the 1980s and 1990s. She elaborates Shklovsky's original emphasis on perception through her key terms "experience," the "person," and "description," even as she opposes traditional preconceptions about lyric poetry that are sometimes associated with these terms.

Hejinian's statements about her poetry express the two apparently contradictory conceptions of poetic language in Shklovsky's work, but in her poetics these conceptions are combined through her key term "experience." In defining her poetics, Hejinian consciously echoes Shklovsky's famous statement in "Art as Device": "The function of art is to restore palpability to the world which habit and familiarity otherwise obscure; its task is to restore the liveliness to life. Thus it must make the familiar remarkable, noticeable again; it must render the familiar *unfamiliar*."[14] Here, the poetic function of estrangement is to renew perception. In the same essay, Hejinian also echoingly defines estrangement as all those effects that draw attention to the language itself, through "'roughening,' dissonances, impediments, etc."[15] Elsewhere, however, she describes these literary techniques not simply as drawing attention to language but as Shklovsky's "set of devices intended to restore palpability to things."[16] Like Shklovsky, she thus conflates these two forms of estrangement, so that the literary device of form made difficult operates "to alert us to the existence of life and give us the experience of experiencing."[17] But this goes further than Shklovsky, in that the estranging poetic text (a tautology for Hejinian) imparts an experience of the process of experiencing, or what she also calls a "consciousness of consciousness," because it draws attention to its own construction.[18] Through her concept of the "experience of experiencing," Hejinian provides a rationale for Shklovsky's original and unacknowledged conflation of two conceptions of poetic language. For Hejinian, the poetic text, through its impediments (its

estranging, self-focused, "autonomous" devices), highlights the pro-
cess of experiencing (experiential structure and contingency), even as
it provides an experience that renews our perception of the world.

Hejinian thus gives "preeminence to experience," as "an exten-
sion of the poetics implied by Shklovsky's aphorism," one that she
quotes twice in her book of essays: "In order to restore to us the
perception of life, to make a stone stony, there exists that which we
call art."[19] She rejects, however, the notion that a poetics of experi-
ence must "promote immediacy and disdain critique."[20] Rather, po-
etry affirms life by saying "this is happening" in context, "which is to
say, in thought (in theory and with critique) and in history." Without
thought, critique, and history, without a self-reflexive consideration
of the basis of experience, "there is no sensation, no experience, no
consciousness of living," only automatization, the loss of experience
through the repetitions of everyday existence.[21]

Hejinian further develops her link between estrangement and ex-
perience through another central term in her poetics: the "person."
In her essay "The Person and Description," first presented as a talk
in 1988, during her period of intense involvement with Russia, she
argues, "It is on the improvised boundary between art and reality,
between construction and experience, that the person (or my person)
in writing exists."[22] In the same essay, Hejinian distinguishes the con-
cepts "self" and "person." She notes that "each person is felt to be in-
dividualizing, different, unique." However, this uniqueness remains
distinct from "essential selfhood": "Our individuality, in fact, is at
odds with the concept of some core reality at the heart of our sense
of being. The latter has tended to produce a banal description of the
work of art as an expression uttered in the artist's 'own voice.'"[23]

Hejinian's poetic practice rejects the concept of "voice" and "all
notions of the *self* as 'some core reality at the heart of our sense of
being.'"[24] Many scholars have noted this rejection in her best-known
poetic work, *My Life*, which is "a language field in which 'identity'
is less a property of a given character than a fluid state that takes
on varying shapes and that hence engages the reader to participate
in its formation and deformation." In *My Life*, there is "a studied
refusal to engage in introspection, a steady suspicion of Romantic
self-consciousness."[25] Hejinian uses the estranging device of "radi-
cal parataxis" to avoid the impression of a singular, continuous self,
taking "several complete narrative texts" and, as she puts it in *My
Life*, breaking "them up into uncounted continuous and voluminous

digressions." The effect is close "to what Gertrude Stein calls *Everybody's Autobiography*, in which the individual life is interwoven with language, perception, and social constructs in such a way that one cannot delineate where 'Lyn Hejinian' leaves off and the world begins."[26] In *My Life* "personal experiences" are transformed into "linguistic encounters" whose generalities all Americans might inhabit.[27] The self is dissolved as "my life" becomes anybody's life in language.

Yet the "I" continues to play a role in Hejinian's work, preserving a sense of individuality rather than merely linguistic play or inhabitability through a lyric mode that foregrounds the subject as a process rather than an identity, or in Hejinian's own terms, as a "person," rather than a "self," a distinction that she developed in the late 1980s, during and through her contact with Russia and Russian writers.[28] Hejinian rejects the focus on "the self of the English language, whose definition posits it as the essence of each single human being, the sole and constant point from which the human being can truthfully and originally speak."[29] She contrasts the English word "self" with the lack of an exact Russian equivalent, suggesting that notions of personhood in Russian are consequently more dynamic and less fixed than English selfhood. Although Hejinian's distinction between Russian and English may seem forced, given the strong sense of self in the Russian poetic tradition, it nevertheless allows her to develop a critical concept in her poetics.[30] Instead of the self, Hejinian envisions a dynamic entity she terms the "person": "the exercise of possibilities (including that of consciousness) amid conditions and occasions constitutes a person." This person is "a relationship rather than an essence," and "it is here that the epistemological nightmare of the solipsistic self breaks down, and the essentialist yearning after truth and origin can be discarded in favor of the experience of experience."[31] Hejinian associates a nonessentialist, dynamic personhood with the "experience of experience" and thus links the Russian language—which, in her view, lacks an exact equivalent for "self"—with Shklovsky's conception of poetic language as the language of estrangement. For Hejinian, estrangement imparts to the reader an "experience of experience," but this effect is also central to her concept of the person, which "consists of and is known by its descriptions of its own experiences."[32] Hejinian thus sees the "experience of experience" imparted through Russian estrangement as critical to her conception and poetic exploration of the person as "relationship rather than an essence."

Through her conceptions of experience and the person, Hejinian links her poetics of estrangement to the poetics of everyday life by introducing a third key term: "description." In her prefatory note to "The Person and Description," Hejinian writes of description as being "pivotal to the question of personhood and hence to everyday life": it occupies an intermediary zone between "art and reality" to create "a space through which a person might step."[33] In her essay "Strangeness," Hejinian defines "description" as a response to the world not already shaped by everyday assumptions, presented "in the terms 'there it is,' 'there it is,' 'there it is,'" citing as examples the narratives of explorers and descriptions of dreams.[34] Description thus has a "marked tendency toward effecting isolation and displacement, that is toward objectifying all that's described and making it strange," a statement that alludes to Shklovsky's concept of estrangement.[35] Description here allows Hejinian to enact her dynamic conceptions of personhood and the "experience of experience" because, so defined, it refuses preconceived notions of self and world. It also links estrangement in art and life because, as her examples show, description for her explicitly relates estranging writing to encounters with strangeness in the world. Such description is "'phenomenal' in the double sense of acknowledging the claims of both the facticity of experience and its strangeness. And this strangeness is the strangeness of some middle ground, where we are somehow caught between the generalizing, abstracting quality of language, on the one hand, and an engagement with the localized forms of a particular perceptual world, on the other."[36]

Hejinian's concept of description reflects the development of a "new sociality" in her work that seems at odds with the tendency of critics of Language writing, especially in the 1980s, "to focus almost exclusively on modes of self-reflexivity and on a subversion of conventional models of self."[37] Over the course of the 1980s and 1990s, "a decrease in fragmentation, and an increase in complete sentences and discernible narrative structures or gestures" clearly develops in the work of several Language writers, so that the "social variety of the writing is greater." This shift is evident between Hejinian's *Writing Is an Aid to Memory* (1978) and *Oxota: A Short Russian Novel* (1991), in which she most explicitly and extensively uses material from her experiences of Russia and from Russian literature and literary theory.[38] Yet this new sociality begins as early as *The Guard* (1984), in which Hejinian's first clear articulation of her poetics of the person coincides with her initial encounter with Russia.

Hejinian theorized poetic estrangement as a way to affirm personhood, sociality, and community without essentializing identity. Her contact with Russia provided another way for her to oppose the strictures of essentialist, restrictive identity, while emphasizing sociality. First, by engaging with Russia, Hejinian escaped from the realm of US poetry, in which the typecasting of the Language poets and the attacks on their poetics in the 1980s evidenced the difficulties and restrictions of community identity, even an identity based on opposition to essential identity.[39] Second, Hejinian's engagement with Russia opposed the essentialist binary models of identity central to Cold War politics, such as Russian versus American and communist versus capitalist. Instead, she can be seen partly as living out what Watten, quoting William Carlos Williams, has described as the dream of a "wedding between Russia and the United States," a utopian vision based on the model of Shklovsky's community of intellectuals, the OPOYAZ.[40] This dream is evident in *Leningrad: American Writers in the Soviet Union* (1991), an account by Hejinian and fellow Language poets Michael Davidson, Ron Silliman, and Barrett Watten of their 1989 visit to Leningrad to attend the international conference "Language—Consciousness—Society." In providing the common ground on which to unite Russian and US writers, estrangement came to stand for the idealized vision of an artistic community that would bridge the Cold War divide, just as Hejinian identified estrangement as enabling a middle ground between life and art. A US poet using utopian Russian theory could dream of reconciling both oppositions.[41]

Hejinian's Russian estrangement became a key point of contact between the material text and the social poetics of everyday life, linking art to life through the figure of the person. The encounter with Russia reinforced her sense of a relation between existential and poetic estrangement: it drew her attention to the extraordinary strangeness and contingencies of being a person and encouraged her to conflate this strangeness with the estranging qualities that she saw as essential to poetic language. Russia became a key site for poetic and existential exploration as she developed her theory of estrangement. She found that the experience of being in a radically different cultural context alerted her to the contingencies of personhood, just as the estranging effects of poetry highlighted the contingencies of description in language. Hejinian thus came to conflate poetic estrangement not only with the utopian vision of uniting Russia and the United States but also with the estrangement produced by her experience of Russia itself.

ENCOUNTERS

When Hejinian first traveled to the Soviet Union in June 1983, she had been concerned for some time about the direction taken by her circle of writers. Her letters, journals, and the texts of several talks show that, prior to her trip, she was already thinking about subjectivity and the mediation of experience as critical issues for investigation, which she felt were undervalued in the Language poetry community.[42] At this time, however, Hejinian still expressed her belief in the primacy of artistic devices and words as such in poetry.[43] Her trip to Russia seems to have encouraged her to relate poetry and poetic estrangement more directly to social and existential questions of consciousness and experience, issues that coincided or found resonance with those current in Russia's unofficial writing community.

Hejinian's first trip to Russia was very brief, but her correspondence with poets and translators after that trip may have made her look at her own work in a new way, because it forced her to explain her poetics to Russian writers who were not necessarily familiar with her approach to writing or its underlying assumptions. In Leningrad, she left behind several books of poetry, one of which included her poem "The Altitudes." The poet Vladimir Kucheriavkin began translating "The Altitudes" immediately after Hejinian left. He sent her questions about the poem, which he clearly found somewhat bewildering.[44] In response, Hejinian explained the estranging impediments of her poetic language by linking these techniques with existential estrangement, describing her poem as "an autobiography . . . whose subject is the life of the mind."[45]

The influence of Hejinian's experience of Russia on the link she developed between poetic and existential estrangement becomes more evident in her long poem *The Guard*, begun before her first trip to Russia and completed in 1984. The poem represented a new stage in her attempt to combine linguistic materiality with a socially located poetics of the person.[46] Hejinian herself draws a connection between her experience of existential estrangement in Russia and her use of poetic estrangement in *The Guard*: the poem resulted not only from the "disorientation and longing" that she experienced through her encounter with Russia and the Russian language, but from a "similar disorientation and longing" that informed much of her writing.[47]

Her increasing interest in the phenomenology of experience, already evident in her comment to Kucheriavkin, and a new interest in the strangeness of Russia are both evident in the poem. One clear Russian influence in *The Guard* is the use of Russian animal noises:

> But I tell you that cats "say" *mya-ew, mya-ew*
> dogs *gav-gav*, trains *sheex-sheex-sheekh*
> (while whistling *ta-tooo*), roosters cry
> *coo-caw-reh-coo*, frogs croak *kva-kva*, birds
> in a flock sing *fyou-eet*, except ravens
>
> which prefer *karr-karr*, and the ducks quack *kra*
> bells ring *bom-bomm*, and pigs grunt *hryou-hryou*[48]

The use of foreign animal noises highlights the arbitrary nature of onomatopoeic words. This conventionality is only revealed in the quoted passage when translation is compared to transliteration. Hejinian writes about this effect in section 44 of *My Life*, which corresponds to the forty-fourth year of her life (1984–85), the time just after she had written *The Guard*: "But any translator will complain, woof is translation and gav transliteration."[49] The plain everyday English "woof, woof" also becomes strange when compared to the bark of a dog, because it is shown to be not a transliteration of the dog's bark, but a translation from animal sound into language, which is conventionalized and uses a limited number of phonemes. Through a Shklovskian device of poetic estrangement, the passage draws attention to its linguistic materiality and also makes the reader attend to the phenomenal reality of that which it describes—or, as Shklovsky might have said, it renews the barkness of the dog's bark. This passage from *The Guard* thus establishes a direct link between Hejinian's experience of Russia and Russian and her poetics of estrangement.

Hejinian's second trip to Russia in May through June 1985 had an even greater impact on her developing linkage between estrangement in art and life. On 28 May 1985 in Leningrad, Hejinian gave a talk on contemporary US poetry, in which she discussed Language writing and talked about her own work, focusing on *The Guard*. Her talk emphasized her interest in writing lyric poetry that was a site for consciousness and that addressed the lyric problems of self-expression and mediation. In relation to *The Guard*, she noted that "the question of mediation, of poetic language as mediation, is an old problem with lyric poetry—the lament in lyric poetry of the poet unable to say, unable to capture in words, his or her desire to say whatever it is he or she wants to say."[50] Here one sees Hejinian seeking to relate the resistance or impediments of poetic estrangement, which emphasize the mediating role of language, to questions of experience and its expression in language.

During her 1985 trip, Hejinian began to recognize that Russia played a crucial role in her exploration of such relationships. Soon after leaving Russia, she wrote in her journal: "In Russia I felt the inadequacy of my description . . . of my writing—the subject and the metaphysics of my project. In our circle, discussion is more technical than metaphysical, and I suspect us of being embarrassed by our potential metaphysics. . . . One element of my attachment to Arkadii—my need for him, or at least, my *use* for him (he too uses me, and this reciprocal necessity is part of the amorous dynamic that is characteristic of our imagination of each other)—involves a displacement—or replacement, rather, of the emotional center of my work, *away* from the Language School condition." Hejinian then attempted to list the contents of her work in her journal. First on that list was "a phenomenology of consciousness: perception, psychology, reality," which addressed "the position of a person in the real world." This phenomenology was to be "located within the context of *poetic* language," and language was to become "the site of a *poetry of consciousness.*"[51] Hejinian thus interrelates the poetics of estrangement with a poetics of phenomenology and consciousness, insisting that mediation and the strangeness to which it gives rise are necessary parts of the experience of being a person in the world, or what she would later call her experience of being a person as a "relationship rather than an essence."[52]

Her heightened interest in this interpolation arose in two ways from her experience of Russia. The first was simply the estranging effect that Russia itself had on Hejinian. Her list of the contents of her work ends with the following comment: "For days at a time in Russia I was not conscious of being conscious."[53] The foreignness of everyday Russia unsettled both her assumptions as a person and her experience of the world, thus heightening her awareness of the contingencies involved.

Second, the discussion of what Hejinian referred to as "meaning"—and what she had missed within her own group of poets in the United States—was central to her literary conversations in Russia and also had an impact on her work. In a letter to the Russian poet Ilya Kutik, she describes the importance of a particular conversation:

> By the way, did you know that you yourself had a certain influence
> on my writing, beginning in 1985? In our circle here we often talked
> about writing, and sometimes about what we were working on at the
> time, but usually our discussions were technical, about devices rather
> than "meanings." . . . Then in Moscow, in 1985, when we were sit-
> ting at a table . . . we began talking about poetry, but at the level of
> "meaning"—which I found strangely exhilarating and liberating—
> while it was clear that we all assumed that poetic language is, as you
> say, the object-subject of thinking, of inquiring, of such "meaning."
> In any case, that conversation gave me the courage and context for
> clarifying my writing and my intentions. Or, to put it another way, I
> began to insist on acknowledging not just *how* there is writing, but
> also *why* there is writing.[54]

This letter refers specifically to Kutik's statement that "in his poetry
he was asking the question, 'Do objects die?'"[55] Kutik thus began with
the existential status of objects in the world, rather than with a ques-
tion of poetic technique, in contrast to the emphasis on technique and
its priority to meaning that Hejinian noted within her own circle. By
paying greater attention to objects in the phenomenal world, Hejin-
ian came, like Shklovsky, to articulate the relationship between the
techniques of estrangement and the very things observed and expe-
rienced. By allowing meaning, experience, or abstract ideas to come
before their formal realization, she could develop further her phe-
nomenology of description and strangeness. Moreover, Kutik's par-
ticular question resonated with the link that Hejinian was developing
between poetic estrangement and the disorienting loss of objects that
characterized her experience of Russia.

Hejinian immediately started building on what she had gained
from her trip to Russia. In June 1985, the same month she returned
to the United States, she attended the New Poetics Colloquium at the
Kootenay School of Writing in Vancouver. There she presented a talk
on *The Guard*, titled "Language and 'Paradise.'"[56] In a letter, she de-
scribed her talk as "broaching various metaphysical concerns à la dis-
cussions in Moscow and Leningrad."[57]

At the colloquium, Hejinian also read from her unfinished poem
"The Person," the very title of which emphasizes Hejinian's increas-
ing interest in writing about the lyric problem of personhood. "The
Person" would later provide the inspiration and materials for Hejin-
ian's essay "The Person and Description," which, as seen above, iden-
tifies the "person" as a key middle term between everyday life and the
estranging effects of art. In September 1985, after her second trip to

Russia, she worked on the final three sections of "The Person." These sections are strikingly lyrical and show her interest in direct confrontation with metaphysical and epistemological issues related to her concept of personhood: the last section begins with the line "Realism is an unimaginable ballad" and includes the word NATURE twice in capital letters. In this section, Hejinian investigates the phenomenological relationship of a person to the world and the way a person is simultaneously a part of that world:

> Described, the corresponding sky
> in circumstantial detail goes up
> as if having yielded—blue
> seems to yield to our gaze—
> having as its object something unknown but
>   conscious
> Below the brain are overt gates[58]

Hejinian here cites the collaborative poetic project The Corresponding Sky that she and Dragomoshchenko had recently embarked upon. As I noted in the previous chapter, the name most obviously referred to the extensive correspondence between the two poets that formed such an important part of their relationship. It was, however, also suggestive of the relationship between words and things, which was at the heart of the project. Both poets set out to write works that explored the phenomenology of perception and description.[59] Hejinian's part of the project was "The Person," while Dragomoshchenko produced a large number of poems that he published under the title *Nebo sootvetstvii* (*Sky of Correspondences*). Both poets focused on description in these poems. In the quoted passage, Hejinian undermines the common association of "circumstantial" with something anecdotal, and not generally valid, by suggesting that, far from being imprecise, the description of "the corresponding sky" is detailed. Further, "circumstantial" implies being located in time, which human consciousness always is.

The "corresponding sky" also sets up a link between things: not only between the person and nature but also between one person and another. Hejinian describes the processes of perception and description as sensuous. Object and subject are animated: "blue / seems to yield to our gaze." The object of the gaze is "unknown but / conscious," not only because what is out there in the world is perceived only through the conscious mind of the observer but, less obviously, because being conscious entails the registration of what is unknown, or strange. The world yields to the gaze, but the gaze must also yield to the strangeness and estranging effects of the world. Hejinian thus presents phenomenal experience as an interactive process among mind, eye, and world in which existential estrangement plays a central role. The final line also suggests interaction. The "overt gates" imply that the interaction is sexual, although the phrase could also stand for oral communication through the gate of the mouth, or, perhaps most clearly, of the eyes. The line makes the normal strange by describing eyes, mouth, or sexual organs as "overt gates." Strange in itself, "gates" is made stranger by the use of "overt" instead of "open." "Overt" in turn opens up a connection with the idea of making something visible implied by "yields to our gaze." This estranging use of "gates" draws attention to the bodily nature of consciousness, the brain, and the bodily organs implied by the word. But significantly, this bodily aspect of the person (in the poem's title) is a portal, not an essence. That person consists in a dynamic process of interaction between subject and object: the "gates" of perception and the mediation of language highlighted by the poem's estranging devices.

Notwithstanding her continued avoidance of direct, unmediated self-expression, Hejinian confronts the phenomenal nature of being a person in *The Guard* and "The Person" more directly than in her earlier writing. Even her apparently more personal work *My Life*, first published in 1980, focuses more on the language that makes up a life, than it does on the phenomenology of being a person. Hejinian's increasing tendency to link estrangement to her notion of the person can be attributed at least partly to her contact with Russia.

Russia became, however, more than just an aesthetic pivot for Hejinian. Her intensive involvement with Russia was motivated by her deep personal attraction based in part on a certain aesthetic quality of estrangement that she found in everyday life there. After a visit in 1987, she wrote to Michael Molnar about her "romance" with Russia: "I was thinking that surely Russia isn't magical. That is, I was forgetting. It is—I'm mystified, but it is. I had moments when I felt completely isolated, and thought maybe I was losing personality and would become no one. . . . [But then] I began speaking Russian. . . . It is amazing how direct the link between personality (or person) and language is."[60] Hejinian here locates her romance with Russia in her experience of the loss and then transformation of self: the estranging effect of being unable to speak the local language and, as her fluency increased, of being translated into a Russian person. She was attracted by the similarities between this loss of self in Russia and the loss of essential selfhood that she sought to enact in her poetry.

RUSSIAN LOSS

In her contribution to the collaborative book *Leningrad*, Hejinian further develops the distinction between Russian and American notions of personhood that she had implied in her 1987 letter to Molnar and explicitly articulates in her 1988 talk "The Person and Description": "Subjectivity is not the basis for being a Russian person. 'Our independent separate singularity can hardly be spoken of, but,' Arkadii said, 'many people wish it.' 'You know,' I said, 'many of *us* wish to overcome it. We think that if we can surpass or supersede the individual self we can achieve a community.'"[61]

In *Leningrad*, Hejinian repeatedly associates the difference between American and Russian experiences of being a person and of the world with different kinds of light. Whereas she finds in the United States that each individual and each object is sharply separated from others by American light, in Russia she encounters what she sees as a communal mingling caused by Leningrad's strange light. Russia provides her with an escape from the self through strangeness, just as her poetry dismantles divisions between objects through linguistic estrangement. She quotes Dragomoshchenko as saying: "You are afraid of your finitude, and we are afraid of our infinitude."[62] "Finitude" implies a selfhood that is not dynamic, that is delimited and contained. For Hejinian, this essential selfhood is resistant to community and therefore dangerous. "Infinitude" implies the lack of sharply defined selfhood or objects and accordingly an emphasis on community over the individual. Russia thus offers Hejinian an escape from the finitude of the Western individual through the diffusion of objects and the self: a diffusion that she sees as naturally occurring in Russia and that is central to her own poetics of the person as a dynamic rather than an essence.

In *Leningrad*, as in her letter to Molnar, Hejinian describes Russian strangeness as not only liberating but also passionate. Her "love affair with Russia," she writes, "is stirred by an insatiable identity. Being there is to be in a state of incommensurability, and hence of inseparability, as if that were the status or 'human' nature of Not-me."[63] Hejinian escapes the finitude of "me" in the "Not-me" of Russia, and clearly finds this loss of self suggestive, even erotic:

> An array of images without corresponding objects, without correla-
> tives, wasn't alienating, although I was sad, as if grieving. The images
> were saturated. And my own ego was disintegrating. . . . The title of
> one of Ostap's paintings . . . is *This Time We Are Both*. Sveta gave me
> a small pin on which she had intertwined the words St. Petersburg
> and San Francisco in Cyrillic. And I can't say I felt split but rather, so
> to speak, doubled—and this was erotic.[64]

This statement employs disjunction, the estrangement device that
Shklovsky called "semantic shift" (*semanticheskoe izmenenie*), be-
tween sentences.[65] Three seemingly unrelated things appear in quick
succession: a disintegrating ego, Ostap's painting, and Sveta's pin.
This semantic disjunction is linked with the feeling of being doubled
in Russia. The semantic shifts between the sentences enact the multi-
plying of self, even as the content of the sentences gives examples of
doubling: being "both," a pin with the names of Hejinian's native city
and the Russian city she is visiting intertwined on it. The estrange-
ment of semantic shifts here combines with a doubling of self, which
implies a loss of essential selfhood. These in turn are associated with
a connection between Russia and the United States implied by the pin
and the title *This Time We Are Both*.[66] Estrangement and union thus,
paradoxically, come together in a moment of doubling.

This doubling gets associated with Russia once again in the fol-
lowing passage from *Leningrad*: "There is something indetermi-
nate about a Russian's place in history, caused by the separation be-
tween his or her simple being and his or her life. We often assume
that we construct ourselves and our lives simultaneously, in the same
gestures, within a continuum of options. Soviet friends enjoy point-
ing out the surreal effect of such constructing in their world."[67] The
effect of simultaneous construction is surreal in the Soviet context,
because people maintain a distinction between their "simple" exis-
tential being and everyday grind, which are referred to by the terms
bytie and *byt* respectively.[68] Hejinian, therefore, implicitly identifies
the doubling of the self in Russia with the distinction between *byt*
and *bytie*: in Russia, there is no essential selfhood, but a dynamic
personhood, resulting in a "surreal effect" and the "indeterminate"
place of the Russian in history. The doubling of self in Russia also re-
lates to the objectlessness that Hejinian finds in Leningrad. "Without
objects to organize," she writes, "one doesn't develop a strong sense
of organization, nor a method which stretches events taut over the
framework of time."[69] Russia dislocates objects, including "essential

selfhood," and so allows an escape from the finitude of the self. He-
jinian's experience of Russia thus corresponds to the experience of the
person as a dynamic, which she aims to convey through her poetics
of estrangement.

Hejinian's long poem *Oxota*, written between 1989 and 1991, fur-
ther develops the connection between poetic estrangement and the
estranging effect of Russia. Indeed, while writing the work, she ex-
plicitly described it as an attempt "to accomplish something on those
grounds and within the terms of that disorientation" that she had ex-
perienced in Russia.[70] *Oxota* is loosely modeled on Pushkin's *Eugene
Onegin* and consists of 270 "chapters," each fourteen sentences in
length, and an eleven-sentence coda. Hejinian's use of the sentence-
line in *Oxota* recalls Shklovsky's distinctive one-sentence paragraphs
in works such as *Third Factory*. In broader terms, Hejinian conceived
of the work partly as Shklovsky had described *Eugene Onegin*—as a
"game with [the] story," in which the artistic structuring of narrative
is more important than the ostensible story of Onegin and Tatiana.[71]

Oxota is "packed with narrative, but 'minor' narrative."[72] Em-
ploying "weak narrativity," it both "triggers our narrative sensing
apparatus" and frustrates our search for narrative "by the dispersal
of narrative fragments."[73] Narrative materials are disrupted to slow
down perception, a key feature of estrangement as Watten, following
Shklovsky, outlined it.[74] A number of estranging devices act on narra-
tive materials in *Oxota* including "fragmentation, interruption, dis-
persal, and juxtaposition," and the device of rhyme, which is used
to add additional "noise."[75] The use of these estranging devices in
Oxota asserts Hejinian's vision of dynamic personhood, rather than
the essential selfhood implied by a single overarching narrative.

This resistance to essentialism is associated with the estranging ef-
fect of Russia itself. As in *Leningrad*, the Western narrator in *Oxota*
becomes, in Hejinian's words, "estranged from the markers of self
and incapable of self-location" through her experience of Russia.[76]
Chapter 251, for example, plays with and half accepts the idea that
the ego or individual disappears in Russia, and this disappearance
once again involves erotic interplay and doubling:

> A situation is erotic at many points
> There is sex at intersections and at vanishing points
> A person will always submit to a time and place for this
> A novel of non-being, a moan of ink
> A Russian loss

The eros of no individual, the sex that is impersonally free
It might be pornography, stripping and gears
But only if I speak
I could say I like music but I don't like rhythm when it's too much in
     the air
It's water that's the light of the sky
There's no *a* and no *the* there
Not much is
Heat's weight and cold's weight bouncing
Hot and cold heights[77]

Hejinian begins by stating that points are erotic. What could be points in time in the first line (the usage here is ambiguous about time and space) are defined in the second as points in a geometric field: at the intersections of lines and at vanishing points in pictures. Therefore, combining line 1 with line 2, points of intersection are erotic. In line 2, Hejinian's substitution of "sex" for "erotic" is gently undermining, because it strangely associates sex in public spaces, possibly prostitution, with the rules of perspective in painting. Another meaning here, however, seems to be that when a person accepts that he or she is always located at an intersection of time and space (or place), at a point, the person is in an erotic state. Erotic and sexual connection appears positive—it can be "impersonally free" because it is not about a single individual, but about two individuals, like two lines meeting at some point. Points represent a meeting in space-time and are therefore free and unbound by the lines that describe them. Points stand for the doubling that resists essentialist selfhood. Points thus free us from the self; they are encounters and experiences, as opposed to generalizations. In Hejinian's poetics, to reject the self as a fixed identity is to acknowledge being as becoming through encounter. The erotic, sexualized encounter of lines at an intersection or point therefore creates the "eros of no individual." Hence *Oxota* is a "novel of non-being," a novel not of the individual essential self, but of an erotic encounter on paper—"a moan of ink." (The title *Oxota* could itself be translated as "desire.") This is at one level Hejinian's encounter with Russia. The erotic point of "non-being" becomes the "Russian loss" of self.

In this chapter, Hejinian also refers to the nebulousness caused by what she sees as the lack of definite identity in Russian, where "There's no *a* and no *the*." The following line can also be related to the grammatical strangeness of Russian, in which the copula is omitted. Just as in her essay "The Person and Description," here the grammatical peculiarities of the Russian language mirror those of existence in Russia. The line "Not much is" could equally refer to the uncertainty about the reality of things in Russia. Things have no essential qualities but exist only as dynamics. The thermodynamic movements between "Hot and cold" at the end of the chapter are like the uncertain oscillations between things that constitute this Russian state of being for Hejinian.

In many chapters in *Oxota*, Hejinian alludes to the loss of self and of objects that she explicitly associates with Russia in *Leningrad* and that she sees as a central quality of her estranging poetics of the person. As in *Leningrad*, she also frequently connects this loss of self and objects to the city's strange light. Observe how chapter 157 explores Leningrad's light, the "Russian loss" of objects and self, everyday life, and the relationship of life to art:

> We can take no time, we can take no light, but they appear and we
>   have accounts
> New pictures and defects
> No objects
> The poetic—this means loaned
> Daily life presents matters for practical reason (free will)
> Or it isn't so
> There are parts of the light—agency, green, pink, and grime
> No subject to light, and no discontent with life
> Zina shrugged when I wanted to speculate
> No innate love of forms
> Then dispersal and reform
> And Misha?—we laughed
> It is impossible to study it all equally
> Our curiosity cannot be practically applied[78]

Many of the typical features of Hejinian's descriptions of Leningrad as a landscape of estrangement appear here: light, a lack of objects, and the strangeness of time. The relationship between "objectlessness" and light is also worked out in this chapter. Neither time nor light can be possessed like objects. All one can do with them is notice appearances and give accounts, from which come "New pictures and defects" (perhaps photographs, which are created through the exposure of light-sensitive material to light for an instant of time), but "No objects." The essences of things themselves cannot be possessed: all we can own is the mark things leave in our memory and their representations, like the mark of light on photographic paper. Poetry as the language of estrangement provides new pictures and thus renews perception, but is not about possessing objects by giving them identity. Instead, it presents a dynamic affirmation that "this is happening" in context and through encounters. Poetry, therefore, is not about owning things, but "means loaned." "The poetic" is always already a product of exchange, such as loaning, and thus concerns not objects but relationships. Hejinian associates this objectless poetics of exchange and estrangement not only with daily life but also with free will, so that the light becomes the catalyst for creating "agency" in life. Hejinian even uses paronomasia to connect "light" with "life." Light acts to eliminate both objects and subjects ("No subject to light"), producing a utopian effect—"no discontent with life."

Hejinian also gently challenges her own further speculation ("Zina shrugged") that there are no objects and subjects, that there is "No innate love of forms," the anathema of Hejinian's poetics of estrangement. Following Shklovsky, Hejinian aims to overcome predetermined structures for experience, such as the essential self, to restore perception of words and the world. The next line demonstrates both linguistic estrangement and the effect supposedly achieved. It suggests the "dispersal" of essential objects and selfhood through the "reform" of "form." The rhyme with "form" draws attention to the form of the words and thus suggests that the reworking of form is a necessary part of the way estrangement reforms language to renew perception and disperse essentialist, or "innate," notions about the self and about objects.

The romantic view put forward here that poetic estrangement is embodied in Leningrad's light and Russian life is then debunked through a semantic shift involving a category error. The abstract nouns "dispersal and reform" are combined with a proper noun, the unidentified "Misha," in a question probably used facetiously by Zina, Arkadii Dragomoshchenko's wife: "And Misha?" Zina's skepticism helps to point out the incompleteness of Hejinian's dream of the sublimation of art and the everyday in Leningrad's light, but the recording of Zina's attitude in the poem also expands the realm of the everyday. It shows how a piece of everyday conversation can provide the material for a semantic shift, a key estrangement device.

The final two lines articulate the difficulty that Hejinian confronts in including the everyday, while maintaining her poetics of estrangement. On the one hand, not everything in the everyday can be attended to "equally" and so, by implication, brought into the poem. On the other hand, the view that the light possesses the values of

Hejinian's poetics of estrangement—it disperses objects and provides a utopian space in which there is "no discontent with life"—is impractical in the real world: "Our curiosity cannot be practically applied." While Hejinian here appears to conflate poetic estrangement with her everyday experience of Leningrad, she also acknowledges the tension between them.

Light plays a similarly key role in chapter 249 of *Oxota*:

> Leningrad was made of light and my eyes were moths
> They were both
> Floating even rudely—no way to brush them off
> They reverberated whole
> They returned to the skull
> A compassion
> The twilight glowed from within its own plum blindness
> I climbed a little slope pressed to its birches
> But Leningrad was stayed in light
> A crow rose
> Puppet night
> A flutter of knees
> Nerves of an oily shadow, a protraction
> There above I didn't remember how I'd been below[79]

In the opening line, the image of flying moth-eyes in a city made of light links the experience of seeing Leningrad with disembodiment: if "my eyes were moths," they would be unattached to my body and would be able to dart anywhere. Besides granting freedom from an essential, singular selfhood, Leningrad with its light is also attractive to moth-eyes. This attraction is implied in line 2, "They were both," which recalls the opening line of *Oxota*, "This time we are both," and so the title of a painting by Ostap Dragomoshchenko from which it derives and which Hejinian mentions in *Leningrad*.[80] "Moth" and "both" thus rhyme semantically because each stands for the loss of self that is achieved, according to Hejinian, through estrangement. They also create a visual rhyme, and the third line ends in "off," half-rhyming with "moth." Essential entities break down in Russia, where things can be "both," and, at the same time, slippage at the boundaries between things is reinforced through the estrangement device of paronomasia. Hejinian conflates the estranging effect of Russia, in which objects merge into one another, with poetic estrangement, which analogously blurs the boundary between words by highlighting their common qualities and placing them in unexpected combinations.

STRANGENESS

In her poetry, letters, and other writing about Russia, Hejinian came to link various estrangements across the usual art-life divide. In this, she followed Shklovsky, whose internationalist modernist outlook was, ironically, based in part on his belief that only in Russia could everyday life yield to the artistic device. Shklovsky believed there was simply inescapable everyday existence in the West, because it lacked the opposition between everyday grind (*byt*) and existential being (*bytie*). The uniquely Russian opposition opened up the possibility of taking life out of the daily grind through artistic devices of estrangement that would make it perceptible again as *bytie*.[81] Similarly, Hejinian came to link poetic estrangement, which for her opposed essential selfhood, with uniquely Russian experiences of estrangement in everyday life. These experiences, like poetic estrangement, dissolved subjects and objects, including essential selfhood. For Hejinian, the "theme of dislocation and disorientation" of the self in *Oxota* reflected not only the experience of being a foreigner but was also a particularly "Russian theme."[82]

In associating Russia with the dispersal of essential selfhood in favor of dynamic personhood, Hejinian drew on the image of the Russian soul as communal rather than individual. Boym points out that this image has been common in Russian and Western discourse since at least the nineteenth century: the "Russian soul" is "the product of Russian fiction and Western interpretations and of a peculiar two-way love-hate relationship between Russia and the West."[83] Whether this image is fictional or has its origins in a real cultural difference, Hejinian continues the tradition of contrasting the communal Russian soul with Western conceptions of private life and selfhood.

Shklovsky saw estrangement as a means to experience the world outside the automatized daily grind, the dreaded *byt*, which proved so perilous for Vladimir Mayakovsky's "boat of love."[84] Hejinian likewise sought poetic devices that would "alert us to the existence of life and give us the experience of experiencing."[85] Like Shklovsky, she and her fellow Language poets used Formalist estrangement to emphasize their affinity with modernist internationalism against Romantic nationalism and so to oppose the Cold War divide between Russia and the United States. Through her use of Russian estrangement, Hejinian was not only, like her fellow Language writers, reviving a modernist method of combating ever-mounting levels of automatization in the West's experience of everyday life.[86] She also sought to exploit the "radical difference between the American dream of the private pursuit of happiness in the family home, and the Russian dream" of "transcendental homelessness" discernible in Shklovsky's association of estrangement with Russia.[87]

In this respect, Hejinian was undertaking a utopian project akin to US critical theorist Susan Buck-Morss's collaboration with a group at the Institute of Philosophy in Moscow. From 1988 to 1993, Buck-Morss visited Russia frequently and dreamed of creating "a new, shared cultural era" that would avoid the pitfalls she saw in capitalism and communism, by examining the "mass dreamworlds" of both systems.[88] For her, "the cultural forms that existed in 'East' and 'West'" were "uncannily similar," and these similarities between the two systems were the source of potential liberation. For Hejinian, however, the differences between Russia and the West were just as important.

Shklovsky perceived "the safe haven of West European everyday existence . . . as a major threat to his survival as an intellectual and as a Russian theorist and practitioner of estrangement."[89] Unwittingly, Shklovsky repeated the romantic cliché of the Russian writer loathing European *byt* and searching for Russian poetic *bytie*. Like him, the Language poets worried about the everydayness of everyday life in the West. Indeed, Watten judged the level of automatization in the United States in the 1980s as far worse than in Russia in the 1910s and 1920s.[90] For Shklovsky, in the West "everyday life would remain everyday life, no more and no less. It would not yield to the Russian artistic device."[91] Hejinian experienced things in Russia somewhat similarly. She found that "Russian loss"—of objects and singular, essential selfhood—corresponded to the dynamic conception of personhood that she sought to enact through her poetics of estrangement. Hejinian also found in Russia the possibility of opposing the discrete identities of Russian and American by creating a community of writers like the "imagined community of fellow intellectuals and artists" that Russia meant to Shklovsky.[92] Hejinian thus discovered in Russia a place where estrangement could merge art and life, Russian and American poetry.

CHAPTER FOUR

Bei Dao and World Literature

to the world
I is always a stranger
—BEI DAO, "Duiyu shijie" 对于世界

The world actually writes itself with the many-leveled, unfixable intricacy and openness of a work of literature.
—GAYATRI CHAKRAVORTY SPIVAK, *In Other Worlds*

How could lines of poetry written secretly by a poet in his early twenties become rallying cries for a generation, and a decade later, in 1989, appear on protest banners that sought to change the course of a nation? How could some of these poems be read the following year as representative of a new placeless, transnational world literature without a history or identity?

These shifting readings of Bei Dao 北岛 could be seen as an allegory of the transition from a national to a postnational world. But to read them in this way would be to ignore how the stories we commonly tell about this historical moment are still largely shaped by the preceding era. The accounts of fragmented transnational subjects caught between global homogenization and local difference emerge from the late–Cold War binaries of East and West, of collective subject and fragmented individual, that they were meant to supersede. Bei Dao's poetry and its reception reveal a more historically and rhetorically complex story about poetics and politics, cross-cultural encounter and translation, economics and ideology, personal and international relations. It is a story that has lessons for how our recent past and present might be written and read.

Bei Dao's experience during the Cultural Revolution gave him an acute sense of how any form of individual expression can easily come to be read as the product and allegory of a collective. Even after Mao's death in 1976, individual expression was frequently interpreted in relation to the people or nation. There is evidence for this in the shared sense of post–Cultural Revolution disaffection that many readers found in Bei Dao's poetry and in the quotations used in the spring 1989 protests in Tiananmen Square.[1] These circumstances, along with what was initially—"despite the translations and other textual evidence that there was a world outside China"—a stiflingly closed Chinese world, encouraged Bei Dao to appeal to another, larger world beyond the bounds of the nation and outside national allegorical readings.[2] His writing highlights how the allegorical mode of reading subsumes singularity within a larger collectivity, or world. Yet it also shows how allegory and the multiple worlds it invokes—experiential, national, global—might unfix limiting one-to-one correspondences between world and text. It does so by emphasizing the unstable and ceaseless process through which we translate literature into worlds, and worlds into words.

Bei Dao has provoked one of the most extensive critical debates about translation, globalization, and national and world literature. Yet what has gone unnoticed is how his appeal to the world and use of allegory address the allegorical readings and translations that produce and repeatedly transform conceptions of the national, the world, and the global. Like the multiple meanings of the terms "world" and "world literature," these readings and translations are inflected by history, ideology, and unequal cultural and economic power relations. Thus a poem describing the isolation and erasure of tradition in the Cultural Revolution comes to be read as an allegory of an international literature without connection to a place, time, people, or language. As the contrasting readings of his work illustrate, allegory not only establishes a correspondence between text and world; it also reveals the gap between the world and our words for it. Instead of fixing literature and history within a single story—a single world or world literature—or set of binaries (local/global or individual/collective), Bei Dao's use of allegory emphasizes the historical flux and contested readings that gave birth to our current era. Although this emphasis recalls the work of Yang, Dragomoshchenko, and Hejinian, Bei Dao's writing does not lead to the closeness of touch, in which text and world seem, if only momentarily, to merge. Instead it produces forms of alienation that stress a continuous process of re-presentation and rereading. His work undoes the apparent fixity of its own allegorical relations between text and world.

WORLD POETRY

Bei Dao became central to Anglophone debates over world literature in 1990, when Stephen Owen used a review of Bei Dao's collection *The August Sleepwalker* to describe the emergent phenomenon of a "world poetry" in which nothing is lost in translation.[3] Appearing just a year after the fall of the Berlin Wall and the massacre of June 4, 1989, which forced Bei Dao into exile, Owen's review and the response it provoked are entwined with a critical moment in recent Chinese and world history. The debate surrounding Bei Dao's work illustrates how the end of the Cold War and the rise of globalization led scholars to address literature on a planetary scale.[4] More than just recognizing the limitations of a national paradigm, this transnational turn took literary texts as allegories of our global condition.

Owen described Bei Dao's poetry as a product and allegory of the global economic system: the unequal international distribution of cultural capital and economic power that means writers working in many countries and languages look to an international marketplace where literary value is dominated by European languages, especially English. Highlighting "the *structural inequalities* that underlie the creation and consumption of world literature," Owen's review described a world literary system framed by normative European values presented as universal and underpinned by cross-cultural exchanges "mired in unidirectionality."[5] This system is reflected in the Western domination of institutions of symbolic value and cultural capital, such as the Nobel Prize, which relies on translation into Western languages. So understood, world literature would seem to condemn Chinese literature to unequal cross-cultural exchanges in which it adapts to the West and not vice versa, and where it is trapped by paternalistic Western critics' desires for it to be different and yet universal.[6]

Acute as such analyses are, however, they ignore "the varieties of the world's world literatures," when world literature is taken to encompass not just a unitary global literary system but the many lives that literary texts lead beyond their place of origin, and the diverse literary canons and values that, depending on the place and time, the term names.[7] Like the "complex flows of cultural and financial capital within the Chinese-speaking world," the diverse conceptions of the term operating within Chinese literature complicate Owen's notion of a hegemonic, unidirectional system of world literature.[8] Equally, those who have responded to Owen pay little or no attention to how the concept of world literature motivates diverse readings of literary texts as allegories of the world and global modernity, readings that are in turn inflected by the various meanings of the term "world" itself.

Owen himself not only describes Bei Dao's work as a representative product of the transnational literary system—a new international poetry devoid of historical, national, and linguistic tradition—but reads several poems as presenting metaphors or allegories of the global condition reflected in this new homogeneous, dislocated "world poetry." Owen alludes here to Jameson's then recently propounded concept of "third-world allegory," which contrasts the "psychologized and subjectivized" nature of the political in Western modernism with the national, social, and political allegorical structure of modern non-Western literature, of which Chinese modernism is exemplary.[9] Both Jameson and Owen cite and embody the renewed interest in the concept of world literature during this period. But Owen replaces national allegory with the international allegory of the dislocated modernist poem, implicitly rejecting Jameson's treatment of China as the privileged counterexample to the fragmented Western subject. Instead, Owen's global vision echoes Francis Fukuyama, who the previous year had taken China's "peasants' markets" and "color television sets" as his first example of "the end of history" in the global "triumph of the West, of the Western *idea.*" In Owen's hands, however, Fukuyama's utopian anticipation of a globally recognized "universal right to freedom" becomes the "frightening vision" of a world devoid of history and place.[10]

In Owen's review, the "world" stands for global homogeneity and so for the loss of connection to the world in another sense—the world of singular experience, which lyric poetry in its former incarnation conveys in all its linguistic and historical particularity. The shift to "world poetry" that Owen describes involves the relinquishing of certainty about the relationship of language to the world of experience, as in Walter Benjamin's conception of allegory.

Giving up any "attempt to elucidate things through research into their properties and relations," the allegorist "dislodges things from their context" so that "the world ceases to be purely physical and becomes an aggregation of signs."[11] For Benjamin, Baudelaire's allegorical, flâneur-like gaze was a response to the overwhelming complexity of modernity. Similarly, Owen suggests that Bei Dao's poetry succumbs to placeless fragmentation as part of the cultural logic of a new era of globalization. This post–Cold War diagnosis of the condition of global modernity depends, however, on a clear distinction between the global and the local or national, just as Jameson's late–Cold War description of the fragmented Western subject depends on the contrast between China and the West. Yet allegory, to which both appeal, is precisely what undermines such clear distinctions in properties and relations, as Jameson's stress on the "heterogeneities" of Lu Xun's national allegory itself suggests.[12] Owen's use of the semantically slippery term "world" enacts the slippage of meaning that this modernist sense of allegory describes, suggesting, among other things, the global, the national, the social world, and an individual's world of experience. Likewise, the binaries of East and West, global and local through which Owen and Jameson attempt to delimit and gain some purchase on an emerging global modernity fail to do justice to the complex encounters that characterized this historical moment.

Owen's appeal to the world had powerful resonance, not least because of this unacknowledged allegorical mutability. The multiple and contested meanings of the "world" are evident in the responses to Owen's review. Some of his critics appealed to a more positively framed notion of the world—including China—as a hybridized, heterogeneous space, opposing the assumptions about Chineseness that underpinned Owen's distinction between Chinese and world poetry.[13] Others affirmed the Chineseness of Bei Dao's poetry, disassociating it from the negatively framed, homogenized notion of the world deployed in Owen's review. They denied that Bei Dao's was a poetry without a history and without connection to its language of composition, highlighting the historical and political context and untranslatable qualities of the Chinese originals.[14] In both cases, however, critics of Owen presented a version of precisely the "ethnographically essentialized image" that they criticized because they largely ignored Bei Dao's writing and instead based their opposing interpretations on the heterogeneity of modern China. Their focus on context rather than language, reinforced through translation, perpetuated the socially and politically determined approach to literature from which Bei Dao sought to break free. An alternative to these approaches might be to argue that Bei Dao's aesthetic form transcends the borders of nations and literary traditions, if not always the Chinese language.[15] But this merely replaces ethnographic essentialism with the aesthetic-essentialist claim that Bei

Dao's language and poetic form evince the literary values of a uni-
versal world literature.

The responses to Owen's review depend on what Paul de Man
terms the "metaphorical model of literature as a kind of box that
separates an inside from an outside."[16] Yet they ignore how Bei Dao's
allegorical writing unhinges this model by continuously redrawing
the line that separates inside from outside. Most respondents to Owen
reproduce this binary mode of literary analysis in cultural terms, so
that the "world" designates that which is either extrinsic or intrinsic:
Bei Dao's poetry is either inside a heterogeneous world literature sepa-
rated from homogenous national and global literatures by its hybrid
multiplicity, or it is inside a heterogeneous Chinese literature sepa-
rated from a homogenous global literature by its Chineseness. In this
box metaphor, inside and outside tend to bolster one another so that,
as in the readings applied to Bei Dao, nationalism and cosmopolitan-
ism, "universalism and particularism reinforce and supplement each
other."[17] They may even become one another, through what De Man
calls "chiasmic reversals." Even concepts such as "hybridity" and "di-
aspora," which have been developed to resist this binary thinking,
risk producing new forms of homogenization and essentialism by cre-
ating new boxes for separating what is inside—hybrid, diasporic, dia-
logic—from what is outside—essentialist, monologic, binary. When
a concept like hybridity is treated as "in itself a radical gesture," the
"claim to effortless resistance" short-circuits "efforts to translate,"
including the allegorical translations of individual expression into na-
tional and international allegory in Bei Dao's work and its reception.[18]
It is easy to argue in response to Owen that we need to investigate
"the question of borders" in a way that would find a path between
Orientalism and nativism.[19] But it remains difficult to know how to
do this without falling back into one position within these binaries.

Bei Dao's poems and their reception suggest an alternative ap-
proach that would attend to how the box or world of a text and
of its interpretation is formed, reformed, deformed. This approach
would explore the translations and readings that continuously open
up new figural and allegorical interpretations, while considering how
Bei Dao's writing itself anticipates and allegorizes these readings. It
would also reveal the historical context and geographical location of
these diverse readings, even those that are imagined to be somehow
timeless or universal, such as Owen's reading of Bei Dao as world
literature.

Bei Dao's poetry can be read, simultaneously, as an allegory of his own political situation and as an allegory of world literature. These interpretations depend on the historical and political position of the reader and frequently intermingle with and infect each other. This is clear in his appeals to the world and world literature from the Cultural Revolution to June 4, and in the national and international allegorical readings that his poems have prompted. His poetry engages with allegory in the sense De Man describes it: his poems not only comment on the impossibility of a single denotative interpretation, they reflect on the process of interpretation itself—they are "allegories of the impossibility of reading."[20] In abjuring any single context or box, Bei Dao's poetry emphasizes the impossibility of a single national or world literature and produces an allegory of that impossibility.

ANSWERING THE WORLD

Owen's review and the ensuing debate are anticipated in the many complex and contradictory engagements with notions of the world, translation, and world literature in Bei Dao's literary career up to the publication of *The August Sleepwalker*. From the beginning of that career in the 1970s, Bei Dao's appeals to world literature functioned dialectically. On the one hand they resisted official ideology, censorship, and nationalism, but on the other they strategically collaborated with these forces. This dialectical appeal to world literature derives from particular historical circumstances and political pressures but also complicates the national/international binary through which his poetry was subsequently read.

Bei Dao's conception of world literature was shaped by state selection and censorship of, and restricted public access to, foreign literature published in Chinese translation; by resistance to official restrictions on these texts through illegal underground reading; and by his focus on the construction of a new national literature. For Bei Dao and other young underground Chinese writers of the early 1970s, world literature was specifically Chinese translations of Western modernists including Lorca, Beckett, Camus, Sartre, and Baudelaire. Published officially in the 1950s and 1960s, these translations were either banned or distributed only to a restricted group of high-level party officials during the Cultural Revolution.[21] Bei Dao claims that he began to write poetry in a modernist style after illegally reading these foreign examples, which furnished Chinese literature with a new "translation style."[22] Officially selected and translated texts of world literature illicitly became Bei Dao's model for a new, alternative national literature.

Bei Dao's dialectical appeal to world literature continued after the Cultural Revolution when a national and even international audience suddenly came within reach. On 23 and 24 December 1978, Bei Dao and Mang Ke produced the initial issue of the literary journal *Jintian* 今天 (*Today*). This was perhaps the first openly published and certainly the most important independent literary magazine in the history of the People's Republic of China.[23] It appeared at a moment during Deng Xiaoping's consolidation of power when statements of political dissent were briefly tolerated, especially those pasted on Xidan Wall, which thus became known as the Democracy Wall. Pasted on walls around Beijing—including the Democracy Wall—the opening issue of *Today* invokes world literature through its editorial and selection. Perhaps conscious of the international attention that the Democracy Wall was attracting, the editors included an English version of the journal's title on the front page and used their editorial, "Zhi duzhe" 致读者 ("To the Reader"), to assert the right of a new generation of writers to create a national literature defined by its ability to take its place in world literature.[24] Echoing Deng Xiaoping's call earlier that month to "open up to the outside world" (*kaifang* 开放), the editors hail the "beginning of a new era . . . for our ancient motherland" that will "affirm the status of the Chinese peoples among the peoples of the world."[25] Here the claim to status within world literature functions to affirm the value of the new generation of writers against the classical tradition of "several thousand years." It directs the reader's attention away from this tradition and toward the "surrounding horizon" of other nations. About a third of the editorial is devoted to a quotation from Marx's "Comments on Prussian Censorship," a text that also implicitly appeals to the concept of world literature, anticipating his later, better known use of Goethe's term.[26] The editors cite Marx's assertion that "there are no black flowers" and that likewise human culture should not be devoid of color and variety. The Chinese refers to the absence of black flowers in the "natural world" (*ziran jie* 自然界), clearly implying a link between the diversity of nature cited by Marx and "the peoples of the world" (*shijie minzu* 世界民族) mentioned later in the editorial. The editors' claim to a place in world literature is also implied by the first issue's inclusion of translated works by two recent Nobel Prize winners, Vincente Alexandre (1977) and Heinrich Böll (1972), and by Graham Greene, who was then "a celebrated candidate" for the award.[27]

The editorial provides competing allegories through which to read its contents and the journal as a whole in relation to the world. Just as with his notion of "translation style," Bei Dao's figuring of world literature in *Today* both appeals to and opposes Chinese nationalism. By asserting the place of the Chinese people among the peoples of the world, Bei Dao deploys the notion of world literature—and one of its key Western institutions, the Nobel Prize—to align the journal with officially sanctioned nationalism: the drive to modernize China and to reassert its rightful place as a leading nation in the world.[28] The citation of Marx also functions to align the writers with the orthodoxy. Yet in each case, world literature equally offers a border-crossing cosmopolitan model that works against this nationalist and Communist Party agenda.

The editorial and translations in issue 1 of *Today* also point to Bei Dao's engagement with the concepts of the world and world literature in his poetic work. This engagement is especially evident in "Huida" 回答 ("The Answer"), the poem that opens the selection of his own poetry included in the first issue:

回答

卑鄙是卑鄙者的通行证，
高尚是高尚者的墓志铭。
看吧，在那镀金的天空中，
飘满了死者弯曲的倒影。

冰川纪过去了，
为什么到处都是冰凌？
好望角发现了，
为什么死海里千帆相竞？

我来到这个世界上，
只带着纸、绳索和身影，
为了在审判之前，
宣读那被判决了的声音：

告诉你吧，世界，
我——不——相——信！
纵使你脚下有一千名挑战者，
那就把我算做第一千零一名。

我不相信天是蓝的；

我不相信雷的回声；
我不相信梦是假的；
我不相信死无报应。

如果海洋注定要决堤，
就让所有的苦水都注入我心中；
如果陆地注定要上升，
就让人类重新选择生存的峰顶。

新的转机和闪闪的星斗，
正在缀满没有遮拦的天空，
那是五千年的象形文字，
那是未来人们凝视的眼睛。

THE ANSWER

Debasement is the password of the base,
Nobility the epitaph of the noble.
See how the gilded sky is covered
With the drifting twisted shadows of the dead.

The Ice Age is over now,
Why is there ice everywhere?
The Cape of Good Hope has been discovered,
Why do a thousand sails contest the Dead Sea?

I came into this world
Bringing only paper, rope, a shadow,
To proclaim before the judgment
The voice that has been judged:

Let me tell you, world,
I—do—not—believe!
If a thousand challengers lie beneath your feet,
Count me as number one thousand and one.

I don't believe the sky is blue;
I don't believe in thunder's echoes;
I don't believe that dreams are false;
I don't believe that death has no revenge.

If the sea is destined to breach the dikes
Let all the brackish water pour into my heart;
If the land is destined to rise
Let humanity choose a peak for existence again.

A new conjunction and glimmering stars
Adorn the unobstructed sky now:

> They are the pictographs from five thousand years.
> They are the watchful eyes of future generations.[29]

Probably Bei Dao's best-known poem inside and outside China, "The Answer" was interpreted primarily as a political allegory about the Cultural Revolution until Owen's review brought it into Anglophone debates about world literature.[30] Yet as Bei Dao's lead poem in the first issue of *Today*, its engagement with the idea of world literature is evident from its original publication and not just its subsequent life in translation.

Read in this light, "The Answer" oscillates between national allegory and an appeal beyond China's borders. By inviting two readings that would subordinate its individual voice to a national or translational whole, the poem stages the reciprocal but antithetical and hostile relations between individual lyric subject and the collective social "world" (*shijie*) of which he is part ("I came into this world"). While he addresses this social realm ("Let me tell you, world"), he also seeks to free himself from it by disbelieving. The conventional approach has been to read "world" here as referring to contemporary Chinese reality and thus to take the poem as allegorically depicting the Cultural Revolution and expressing a lone voice of dissent against it.[31] Yet in "The Answer," a sense of global reach functions as a counterpoint to a reading of the poem as national allegory. The "Dead Sea" and "Ice Age" not only refer to the Cultural Revolution, but, together with the "Cape of Good Hope," mark the lyric subject's refusal to be limited by contemporary Chinese reality and so by the very allegorical reading that they seem to suggest. By reaching beyond the spatial and historical boundaries of China, these lines enact the movement beyond the Chinese tradition for which the *Today* editorial calls. They establish the poem's theme of response and inversion as a relationship not only between the individual and the social collective, but also between historical and geographical location and a generalized appeal to the wider world. The poem claims a planetary geographical and geological perspective that estranges it from its ostensible political and social preoccupations, gaining a degree of individuality at the expense of an appeal to two generalized worlds. This double movement toward and beyond the individual and toward and beyond China itself enacts the poem's disbelief by undercutting its allegorical stability.

Underscoring how its appeal to the "world" points toward and beyond China, "The Answer" has attracted a variety of allegorical

interpretations inside and outside China. Read as an allegorical poem
about the Cultural Revolution, the "thunder" in the fifth stanza signi-
fies the violence and power of the era and the way it shook many like
"thunder out of a blue sky."[32] This reading is encouraged by the open-
ing lines of the editorial, which assert that "History has finally pre-
sented us with an opportunity, enabling our generation to sing aloud
songs that have been deeply buried in our hearts for ten years, for
which we will no longer suffer from the punishment of the thunder."[33]

In the first issue of *Today*, Bei Dao further encouraged this reading
by erroneously dating "The Answer" to connect it with the Tianan-
men incident of April 5, 1976, when the authorities suppressed a mass
memorial in Tiananmen Square to the former prime minister Zhou
Enlai: a memorial that had served as a demonstration against the Cul-
tural Revolution and the Maoists.[34] Bei Dao no doubt sought politi-
cal protection for his poem by associating it with the recent reversal
of the official verdict on the incident. The reversal opened the way
for the Democracy Wall (on which *Today* was initially posted), and it
helped Deng Xiaoping, who had been ejected from Mao's inner circle
after the incident, consolidate his power. As a result, "The Answer"
appeared in its first published form and has subsequently been widely
read as a retrospective and public comment on the Cultural Revolu-
tion. In fact, it was written for a coterie audience in the early 1970s
and so might be read as the statement of a private dissenter rather than
either a public speaker addressing a collective, or an individual meant
to stand allegorically for the collective response of the Chinese people
to the suffering and disillusion of the Cultural Revolution. Like Bei
Dao's appeals to the nation in *Today*, his redating of the poem invited
it to be read as a national allegory and aligned it with official culture,
an effect realized when the poem was published in the March 1979 is-
sue of China's premier official poetry journal, *Shi kan* 诗刊 (*Poetry*).

Yet another allegorical interpretation became popular in the late
1970s and 1980s, when the poem was adopted by "a generation of
young Chinese readers desperately in need of alternative heroes" and
so came to stand more generally for resistance to conformity.[35] Out-
side China, the reference to thunder also allows the poem to be lo-
cated in world literature conceived from an Anglo-American perspec-
tive, through its implicit response to Western modernism. Donald
Finkel's translation of the line as "I don't believe what the thunder
says" alludes to Eliot's *The Waste Land* with its appeal to the "East
for timeless wisdom to refresh his dried-up Western roots."[36]

Finkel's translation omits, however, the crucial word *huisheng* 回 声, or "echo." The echo not only underscores the allusion to—or echo of—Eliot, but is critical to the poem's thematic and formal emphasis on response, mirroring, reflection, inversion, shadow, and translation, through which it questions any single meaning or allegorical reading. The opening stanza underscores this structure through the repetitions and inversions of *beibi* 卑鄙 (debasement) and *beibizhe* 卑鄙者 (the base) and *gaoshang* 高尚 (nobility) and *gaoshangzhe* 高 尚者 (the noble). It also does so through the repetition and transformation implied by "shadows," or *daoying* 倒影, which are more precisely the inverted images or reflections produced by a body of water. The poem heightens this sense of inversion by turning these images upside down (*dao* 倒) so that they appear in the sky, establishing the interplay between sky and water that continues throughout the poem. The poem's rhyme scheme also contributes to its poetics of echoes, opposites, and inversions: the final lines of each stanza rhyme with one another so that the sound that ends the word *daoying* or "reflection" is refracted from quatrain to quatrain, concluding in *yanjing* 眼睛 (eyes). In echoing the opening stanza, the poem's final sound returns us to the beginning; so too its final image, the "eyes of future generations," suggests a retrospective glance, which itself emerges from the intergenerational echo that links an ancient civilization to the future.

This poetics of echo, repetition, and inversion also manifests itself at the level of the entire poem, which is presented as a response, or an "answer." The answer poses the paradox whereby any allegorical reading of individual expression as a collective assertion of difference eliminates the very individuality that made it stand for this collective resistance in the first place. The Chinese word for "answer," *huida* 回答, shares the character *hui* 回 (return) with the word for "echo," *huisheng* 回声, so that the lyric subject's "answer" itself contains an echo of the "thunder's echoes" that it disbelieves. This complex structure of echoes and inversions also appears in the liar's paradox that the poem invokes through its statements of disbelief, which "deliberately disavow the communicative obviousness of language."[37] The apparently heroic subject insists, in the poem's central and best known lines, that "I—do—not—believe": this implies that the reader should disbelieve his or her own statement of disbelief. Although this seems to indicate an escape from official reality, this escape is incomplete because the lyric subject assumes the position of answerer, not initiator, in the dialogue. Reinforcing this reciprocal relationship, the statement of disbelief mirrors, in its rhetorical form, the bold, simple slogans of the official propaganda it seems to oppose, just as its retrospective dating in relation to the Tiananmen incident conformed to the new official government policy on the event.[38]

Equally, the lines elaborating this disbelief are built on the inversion of normal reality. The lyric subject implies that the sky is not blue and dreams are not false. Maghiel van Crevel and Bonnie McDougall suggest that this inversion and other such appeals to "lies" represent straightforward resistance to the lies of officially proclaimed truth.[39] Yet instead of directly addressing and opposing the "world" of false official reality, the poem's rhetorical structure is anything but straightforward. The poem names its objects through inversions, negations, shadows, echoes, and allegories. Even apparent assertions of truth appear only in the form of a double negative, of double falseness: "I don't believe that dreams are false." If "the speaker's solidarity with dreams shows an instinctive resistance to Evil," it expresses that resistance not through "easily paraphraseable, often historically-referential subject matter," as Van Crevel suggests, but through circuitous poetic constructions and dreamlike imagery.[40] To do otherwise, the poem seems to say, would be to fall into the propaganda-like directness of statements such as "the sky is blue." In this sense, the message of the poem might be the opposite of Zhang Longxi's call to resist allegorical readings as politically pernicious: literalness, it suggests, can be equally dangerous.[41]

Through stylistic complexity that belies its declarative directness, "The Answer" demands a mode of reading attentive not just to the poet who composes but also to the audience who listens. The poem's "answer" is directed toward the "world," but what this world signifies is open to question: the poem flaunts its potential for multiple interpretations and so demands a further response. Through its structural openness, the poem draws attention to the answers we find in texts: the heroes and reflections of ourselves we identify. The final lines produce the same precarious transfer of agency as Yang Lian's deployment of the liar's paradox. Not knowing who to believe, the reader must judge for him or herself. Meaning is found in the "watchful eyes of future generations": both the eye of the individual beholder and the collective social text or literary source that lies behind each individual expression. One person's reference to the rootedness of the text in Chinese history, the "pictographs from five thousand years," becomes another's refraction of that history through Western modernism, through Pound's conception of the Chinese ideograph. This effects a further reverberation of the "thunder's echoes" that underscores the mutual engendering of the individual "I" and collective "world" throughout the poem.

Through this process of mutual engendering, national allegory and world literature readings become inseparable in "The Answer," just as the *Today* editors turned to Western models, such as the Nobel Prize, and nationalist ideology about China's greatness, in their appeal to world literature. Through these competing interpretations, the poem unsettles the allegorical readings that it seems to invite. It addresses the search for significance in the absence of certainty about how to read its signs and so is allegorical in Benjamin's sense: "Transforming things into signs is both what allegory does—its technique—and what it is about—its content."[42] Employing the same image of constellation through which Benjamin described nonlogical, allegorical connections, the poem transforms concrete historical reality into a set of signs—a "conjunction and glimmering stars." It does so while addressing this transformation and the collapse of belief in what these signs, not least the "world," might mean. True to De Man's description of allegory, the poem both comments on the impossibility of reading without believing in the relationship of signification to reality, word to world, and produces an allegory about that impossibility. "The Answer" questions its own rhetorical structure of originary voice and response through a poetics of echoes and mirrors. Situated inside and outside its immediate social and political context, it highlights the process of allegorical translation that constitutes national and world literatures.

GREETING THE WORLD

In July 1981, Bei Dao was appointed to an editorial position at *El Popola Cinio*, China's official Esperanto magazine, published by the Foreign Languages Press in Beijing.[43] As in his poetry and editorship of *Today*, in this new role Bei Dao occupied an uncertain position between official and unofficial culture within China and between China and the wider world. Just as *Today* had implicitly appealed to a universalist notion of world literature, the Esperanto journal embodied the dream of a universal literature and culture, even if the officially prescribed content and artificial language were not to Bei Dao's liking. At *El Popola Cinio*, Bei Dao presented China to an international audience at a time when the country was opening up to the outside world after the insularity of the Cultural Revolution period. Bei Dao's job at *El Popola Cinio* contrasted with his avowedly unofficial representation of China and Chinese literature in *Today*, with his uncertain position as a poet vis-à-vis official literary culture, and with the position he was about to assume as a representative of unofficial Chinese literature and culture to the wider world.[44]

The situation in which Bei Dao found himself in the early 1980s augured his entanglement in debates over the use, value, and place of literature nationally and internationally. Over the course of the subsequent decade, Bei Dao's poetry was repeatedly read negatively and positively through national allegory: either it expressed the recent history and aspirations of the Chinese people, or conversely it exemplified the infiltration of decadent Western bourgeois values into Chinese culture. At the same time, competing readings sought to situate his work outside these national allegories by representing it as pure, border-transcending world poetry, a representation as politically motivated, partial, and, in its own way, allegorical as the former. The reception of Bei Dao's poetry in the original and in translation reveals how both inside and outside China allegorical readings shaped debates over shifting relationships between literature and politics and between China and the world. By inviting and destabilizing these readings and their binary oppositions, his poetry also suggests how allegory's ceaselessly shifting mode of signification might model a more complex set of relations.

These dichotomous approaches to reading were also experienced by Bonnie McDougall, when in the early 1980s she met Bei Dao and began to translate his work. At the time she was working as a translator at the Foreign Languages Press. There her official literary translations had the utilitarian political goal of engendering "a favourable impression of China in the non-Chinese world." Unofficially, she translated Bei Dao's work "free-lance without a specific contract with a client," aiming to produce "pleasure" in what she describes as "disinterested" English-language readers "with universalistic expectations of literary values."[45] Correspondingly, in her introduction to *The August Sleepwalker* and elsewhere, she insists on the "universal nature" and "universal meaning" of Bei Dao's poetry, its easily translatable images, and its "grasp of human dilemmas present . . . in all modern societies."[46]

McDougall's translations and her reading of Bei Dao's work as universal world literature were part of an attempt made by several

Western scholars at this time to free the study of modern Chinese literature from the reductive political approaches prevalent both inside and outside China. While Western literary studies as a whole were preoccupied with undoing traditional and New Critical universalist assumptions about literary value, McDougall asserted the universal value of Bei Dao's poetry in response to both the pressures of the Chinese political climate and the place of modern Chinese literary studies in the Western academy. The neo-Marxist hermeneutics of suspicion popular in the West were uncomfortably close to the official Chinese Marxist interpretations clearly in evidence in 1982 when McDougall first began to translate Bei Dao's poetry. Their force was heightened during the Anti–Spiritual Pollution Campaign of 1983, when Bei Dao and his colleagues came under attack for writing ideologically incorrect poetry informed by decadent Western modernism.[47] Partly reflecting this politicization of literature within China, in the West the study of modern Chinese literature tended to focus on strategic geopolitical information: it adopted the "world target" model of area studies, or what McDougall referred to at the time as the "usual line of literature as pulp for the historian/social scient[ist]'s mill."[48] Opposing this tendency, McDougall's essays on Bei Dao in the first issues of the US journal *Modern Chinese Literature* contributed to the institutional consolidation of the study of modern Chinese literature in the West, as did her translations of his work for a groundbreaking special issue of *Renditions* focused on contemporary Chinese poetry.[49] McDougall hailed the issue as "At last something imaginative and thoughtful about Chinese literature & art, not just another dreary repetition of a t = problems + bureaucratese."[50] Reissued as the book *Trees on the Mountain*, the issue helped establish contemporary Chinese writing's presence in the English-speaking literary world, so that by 1988 Bei Dao's work was being reviewed in publications such as the *TLS*.[51]

In these respects, the apparently apolitical, universalistic reading of Bei Dao's poetry was itself highly political: McDougall and others appealed to world literature as a counter to the national allegories through which Bei Dao and his contemporaries were being read and even persecuted. McDougall's attempts to publish Bei Dao's translations were motivated directly by a desire to win recognition and so protection for him during the 1983 Anti–Spiritual Pollution Campaign and the 1987 Anti–Bourgeois Liberalization Campaign. In 1983, responding to the political pressure and the need to legitimize

contemporary Chinese literature in the West, McDougall first sought
international recognition for Bei Dao, enlisting the aid of the Scan-
dinavian embassies through her Swedish husband Anders Hansson,
then also resident in Beijing. Though McDougall claims she never
explicitly promoted Bei Dao as a candidate for the Nobel Prize in Lit-
erature, these links certainly encouraged an association between Bei
Dao and the foremost legitimizing institution of world literature.[52]
Likewise, in 1987, her efforts resulted in the publication of *The Au-
gust Sleepwalker*, which would become a key text in Western debates
over world literature.[53]

The appeal to Western institutions of world literature and notions
of universal literary value also situated Bei Dao's poetics in relation to
the work of Western poets. Artistic approaches as wide-ranging as the
modernism of Ezra Pound, the deep image of Robert Bly, and the eth-
nopoetics of Jerome Rothenberg called for a universalistic world po-
etry. Bei Dao directly engaged with this conception of world poetry
when in 1985 he was allowed abroad for the first time to attend the
Rotterdam Poetry International Festival. The festival had been a sym-
bol of a border-transcending, universal world literature since its incep-
tion in 1970 in emulation of the London Poetry International Festival,
which Ted Hughes founded in 1967 with the vision of poetry becom-
ing a "Universal language of understanding, coherent behind the many
languages, in which we can all hope to meet."[54] Shortly after attending
the festival, Bei Dao was invited to contribute to another Western in-
stitution of world literature, the journal *Poetry World*, a revival of the
influential *Modern Poetry in Translation*, which Hughes and Daniel
Weissbort founded just prior to the first London festival. The publisher
of *Poetry World* was Anvil Poetry Press, which would in turn publish
The August Sleepwalker.[55] Such festivals and publications helped pres-
ent Bei Dao's poetry within the Western modernist discourse of univer-
sality to which he himself had appealed as an editor introducing West-
ern literature to China, and Chinese literature to the world. Yet the
renaming of *Poetry World* and its inclusion of a Chinese poet presaged
the new emphasis on global poetics and local difference—rather than
European-oriented international poetry—that accompanied the transi-
tion from the Cold War era to our post–Cold War age of globalization.

A decade after the inaugural issue of *Today*, Bei Dao's first major
book of poetry in English translation was published in the United
Kingdom. Appearing two years later, in 1990, Owen's review of
the subsequent US edition of *The August Sleepwalker* reflects the

dramatic events of the previous year in both China and Eastern Europe. The review articulates yet another conception of world literature and another allegory through which to read Bei Dao's work. Owen picks up on McDougall's insistence that Bei Dao's poetry is translatable by translating her claim into the new historical situation. In the Cold War context, McDougall emphasized the translatability and universal images of Bei Dao's poetry. By appealing to the notion of a world literature based on universal literary values, she sought greater scholarly recognition for contemporary Chinese literature in the West, and so to gain political protection for Bei Dao. In the post–Cold War world, Owen connected translatability to globalization and the end of history. In this new era of globalization, Owen read Bei Dao's work not as national but as global allegory, marking the shift to a postnational condition that he wished to suggest.

In the review, Owen cites the final stanza of Bei Dao's poem "Nihao, Baihua shan" 你好, 百花山 ("Hello, Baihua Mountain") as an example of how "When Bei Dao's poetry succeeds—and sometimes it succeeds wonderfully—it does so not by words, which are always trapped within the nationality of language and its borders, but by the envisagements of images possible only with words."[56] Carefully chosen by Bei Dao to open his major Chinese and English collections of the 1980s, this early poem in fact positions itself much more ambiguously in relation to the various national and international allegories through which his work has been read.[57] It provides a greeting not only to the reader first encountering his work, but also to the world in relation to which Owen seeks to position him. Like "The Answer," the poem's structure of call and response anticipates and questions the collective identities and allegorical frames through which its assertion of individual voice might be read:

你好, 百花山

琴声飘忽不定,
捧在手中的雪花微微震颤。
当阵阵迷雾退去,
显出旋律般起伏的峰峦。

我收集过四季的遗产,
山谷里, 没有人烟。
采摘下的野花继续生长
开放, 那是死亡的时间。

沿着原始森林的小路,

绿色的阳光在缝隙里流窜。
一只红褐色的苍鹰，
用鸟语翻译这山中恐怖的谣传。

我猛地喊了一声：
"你好，百——花——山——"
"你好，孩——子——"
回音来自遥远的瀑涧。

那是风中之风，
使万物应和，骚动不安。
我喃喃低语，
手中的雪花飘进深渊。

HELLO, BAIHUA MOUNTAIN

The sound of a guitar drifts through the air,
Cupped in my hand, a snowflake quivers lightly,
Thick patches of fog draw back to reveal
A mountain range, rolling like a melody.

I have gathered the inheritance of the four seasons,
There is no sign of man in the valley.
Picked wild flowers continue to grow,
Their flowering is their time of death.

Along the path in the primordial wood
Green sunlight flows through the slits.
A russet hawk interprets into bird cries
The mountain's tale of terror.

Abruptly I cry out,
"Hello, Bai—hua—Mountain."
"Hello, my—child," comes the echo
From a distant waterfall.

It was a wind within a wind, drawing
A restless response from the land,
I whispered, and the snowflake
Drifted from my hand down the abyss.[58]

For Owen, "Hello, Baihua Mountain" is not only an example of a poem in which nothing is lost in translation; it is an allegory for the entire homogenizing process of globalization. The image of a "snowflake in the hand, caught and carried by the wind of a poet's whisper and blown into an abyss, where there are no margins and no frontiers" is a "frightening vision of the truly international poem."[59] The snowflake drifting into the abyss is at once a perfectly translatable, international poetic image and an allegory of the dislocated "international poem," which "is an intricate shape on a blank background without frontiers, a shape that undergoes metamorphoses." Unlike "national poetry," which has "a history and a landscape," this international poetry, Owen writes, "does not have a history, nor is it capable of leaving a trace that might constitute a history." Presumably, like the snowflake it remains in one's hand momentarily, only to vanish into the abyss without a trace.

Inverting Owen's interpretation, however, one could read the poem as allegorizing literature deeply rooted, even trapped, within a place, history, tradition, and language. Though written much earlier, by inviting multiple allegorical readings, it anticipates and complicates not only the negotiation between official and unofficial, nationalist and internationalist perspectives in China in the 1980s but also the local/global binary of post–Cold War world literature through which Owen reads Bei Dao's work. Snowflakes often leave a faint trace of moisture, a sign of life. Likewise, inasmuch as the poem implicitly compares itself to a snowflake (its momentary capture frames the poem), it also points to the contrast between the two. When composed by Bei Dao in the early 1970s, the poem was under constant threat of confiscation and destruction—and in this sense was like a snowflake. Yet even then, the poem's permanence as a literary artifact, its reproducibility through memorization or hand-copying, would have stood in marked contrast to the fleeting, singular, unrepeatable moment that it recounts.[60] Later this contrast was heightened by the poem's appearance in a collection that by 1988 had run to 35,000 copies in its second Chinese edition.[61] And in the poem itself, although the snowflake is lost, the abyss does not swallow everything, but reciprocates with a verbal response to the lyric subject's greeting. The landscape of a specifically designated mountain is an essential voice in the poem. The mountain's echo not only confirms a living connection between the lyric subject, the poem, and a specific landscape (a site near Beijing) but also emphasizes historicity through intergenerational exchange: "my—child."

Equally, the poem depends crucially on the linguistic materiality of the Chinese word for snowflake—the very word through which Owen discerns an example and allegory of the dislocated "international poem," of a perfectly "translatable" poetry that relies not on words but purely on images.[62] In fact, the Chinese word used here, *xuehua* 雪花, literally "snow flower," makes for a completely different image to that connoted by the English "snowflake" and contributes to the full resonances of the reference to "wild flowers" (*yehua* 野花) in the second stanza. (The two words are further connected by the rhyme of *xuě* and *yě*.) Far from connoting a brittle, detached, undefined piece of the world, the "snow flower" suggests a thing of beauty that is, significantly, rooted in the earth, in the landscape, and so connected with a particular land and nation. The flowers' impermanence ("Their flowering is their time of death") is part of a cycle that will also bring renewal—a sense of reciprocity affirmed by the "echo."

The "flower" in "snowflake" also links it with the name of the mountain. "Baihua" 百花 uses the same "flower" character, *hua* 花, and means "one hundred flowers." While names in Chinese, as in English, become conventionalized so that one is not immediately conscious of their original meanings, the individual characters of the name of the mountain are clearly emphasized in the echo in the penultimate stanza: *bai—hua* 百——花, or "one hundred—flowers." The connection between the name of the mountain and the snowflake further reinforces the rooting of the word for snowflake in a particular Chinese landscape, a connection between land and poetic image that takes place in and through the Chinese language.

If, as Owen argues, the snowflake in part stands for the poem, then the poem is also a flower. The image of poetry, and of art generally, as flowers that bloom coupled with the "one hundred flowers" of the title cannot help but recall Mao Zedong's famous directive "let a hundred flowers bloom, let a hundred schools contend," which gave the 1956–57 One Hundred Flowers Campaign its name. Later, in 1978, Bei Dao and the other *Today* editors would connect their own moment of liberalization to this earlier thaw by insisting with Marx that "there are no black flowers." Here, however, the allusion to cultural liberalization contrasts with the Cultural Revolution era of the early 1970s, when the poem was written and when the poet had no hope of publishing his work and only dared share it with a group of close friends. As in this poem, in the 1950s the flowers died even as they bloomed, cut down by the Anti-Rightist Campaign that followed. The poem that survives in the inclement weather of the early 1970s must be hardy; it is a "snow flower," frozen, waiting for another moment of thaw so that an audience of readers, and not just the empty valley, will hear and respond to its voice.

Read from the historical perspective of the poet at the time of composition, the lost snowflake falling into the abyss becomes a symbol of the Cultural Revolution and so the impossibility of a world poetry. Read in the Chinese, the word *xuehua* (snowflake) is marked by its historical and linguistic specificities. Translated by Owen into a symbol of world poetry, the snowflake is "essentially translatable": it is a universal figure that both exemplifies and stands for detachment from historical events that, in the other reading, might have seemed to trap the poem, freeze its flower, and cut it off from the possibility of translation and an international audience.[63] The dislocation, isolation, and erasure of history that Owen identifies emerges out of the historical and political context of early 1970s China. It is expressed in the untranslatable linguistic materiality of Bei Dao's Chinese words.

Yet the two interpretations are not as exclusive as they may seem. Each appeals to a historical moment—the Cultural Revolution or the end of the Cold War—that is imagined as marking the end of history and the erasure of tradition. Together these interpretations produce a third allegory of poetry as both frozen within a particular place and time and, like allegory itself—which Benjamin envisages as profoundly alienated, the "opposite of all poetry of the soil"—able to bloom forth anywhere, to float on the wind, knowing "no nationality."[64] Reflecting the competing pressures of his poetry's position as national allegory and world literature in the 1980s, Bei Dao chose to open his major English and Chinese collections with a poem that both invites and unsettles each allegorical reading. As in "The Answer" and in Bei Dao's appeal to a new national literature based on "translation style," the poet's act of finding his voice is staged through an echo, suggesting a poetics focused on translation among languages, voices, and interpretations, including allegories of national and world literature. The poem greets Baihua Mountain, the reader, and the world at large: thus it addresses and enacts the moment of encounter between the emptying out of historical and linguistic specificity and the particularity of the text's Chinese linguistic materiality and of its historical and political location. In so doing, the poem calls into question the opposition itself, the rhetorical structure of originary voice and echo upon which it is predicated.

ESTRANGING THE WORLD

In his 1990 review, Owen singled out for particular criticism a four-
teen-line untitled poem written in the early 1980s. The poem's open-
ing lines explicitly position the lyric subject in relation to the world:

对于世界
我永远是个陌生人
我不懂它的语言
它不懂我的沉默
我们交换的
只是一点轻蔑
如同相逢在镜子中

对于自己
我永远是个陌生人
我畏惧黑暗
却用身体挡住了
那盏唯一的灯
我的影子是我的情人
心是仇敌

a perpetual stranger
am I to the world
I don't understand its language
my silence it can't comprehend
all we have to exchange
is a touch of contempt
as if we meet in a mirror

a perpetual stranger
am I to myself
I fear the dark
but block with my body
the only lamp
my shadow is my beloved
heart the enemy[65]

Of the opening two lines, Owen writes: "I thought I destroyed the
only copy of that poem when I was 14, a year after I wrote it. I
thought we all did. We destroyed it the moment we discovered the im-
mense difference between writing and reading what we have written.
Such sentimentality (or, perhaps, self-conscious posing) is, however,
the disease of modern Chinese poetry, and a deception far deeper
than all the stifling weight of the past in classical poetry."[66] This senti-
mentality itself derives, however, from McDougall's English rendition

combined with Owen's reading. McDougall and Owen thereby illustrate the difference between a text and its translation or interpretation, the very difference they downplay in order to locate Bei Dao in a generalized world literature.

A retranslation of the lines actually highlights Bei Dao's engagement in an international poetic dialogue. When more neutrally translated, they read "to the world / I am always a stranger," echoing Rimbaud's "*je* est un autre." Indeed, given the lack of verbal conjugation in Chinese, the opening lines could be translated more radically as "to the world / I is always a stranger." The latter translation is suggested by the parallelism between "I" and "it," reinforced by the lack of a distinction between the first- and third-person verbal forms in Chinese. The repeated phrase *bu dong* 不懂 (do/does not understand) stresses the parallelism between "I" and "world," but McDougall downplays this parallelism by translating the phrase as "don't understand" in reference to the "I" and as "can't comprehend" in reference to "the world." The work's poetic and syntactic structure, combined with the uniformity of the Chinese verbs, undermines the distinction between human subject and thing. The shift of agency from subject to things is underscored through their common description through the verb "to be," *shi* 是, which in the Chinese is the same for both "I am" and "my shadow is." By the end of the poem, the active subject, the "I," appears only through synecdoche, "my shadow" and "my heart," objects that in their third-person descriptions are distanced from the "I" as "beloved" and "enemy."

The poem's theme of alienation is reinforced through the same transformation of the singular individual into a commoditized type that Benjamin sees as the condition of modernity and of Baudelaire's allegorical gaze.[67] McDougall's translation and Owen's interpretation underscore the very problem of alienation that the poem addresses: how to relate the individual to the collective, and language to the world. As the poem's mirrors, shadows, and reflections suggest, reading across cultures and languages puts a mirror up to oneself, even as it seems to offer a window on the lives of others. Owen's reading produces a moment of self-recognition in the mirror—here his looking back on the time when his fourteen-year-old self recoiled from his own earlier expression of teenage angst. From this moment he derives not a reflection of the self at all but of the world, a collective "we all did."

Building on the rhetorical strategies of "The Answer" and "Hello, Baihua Mountain," Bei Dao's poem suggests a vision of world poetry

with as many facets and reflections as readers. Written just as Bei Dao
was entering the Western literary marketplace via McDougall's trans-
lations, the poem allegorizes the ceaseless linguistic and allegorical
translations involved in interpretation and in conceptions of national
and world literatures. It stages these translations between text and
world, individual and collective, through its emphasis on "exchange,"
communion (the relationship between the "I" and his "lover," or "be-
loved" in McDougall's rendition), and indirect image (reflections, a
"mirror," a "shadow") rather than essence: the "heart/mind" (*xin* 心)
is the "enemy."

   It equally reads as an allegory of the poet's political isolation within
China and of his self-distancing—coinciding with his first publica-
tions abroad in translation—from his earlier, apparently more public
poetic persona. Reinforcing but also complicating this reading, Bei
Dao originally dedicated the poem to a foreign friend, emphasizing
both a personal context and the alienation of cross-cultural commu-
nication. The dedication further stressed the theme of alienation by
associating the poem's "I" with its dedicatee rather than himself. He
removed the dedication before the poem was published most likely for
reasons of privacy and because publicly dedicating a poem to a for-
eigner might have had negative political repercussions, or otherwise
alienated his Chinese readership.[68] In removing the dedication, Bei
Dao opened the poem's generalized and abstract language to multiple
interpretations, while obscuring the specific cross-cultural encoun-
ter and so the appeal to a world beyond the Chinese one in which it
originated. As with his other works, this poem seems to play on the
potential for multiple translations, reimaginings, and echoes, framed
around the poem's relationship to the world and world literature. Un-
like Bei Dao's poetry from the early 1970s, which referred to the Cul-
tural Revolution as a frozen landscape or "Ice Age," however, this
poem written more than a decade later is much less easily locatable
within a national political allegory. It seems a better fit for the poetry
bereft of history and location that Owen describes as "world poetry."
Yet the poem's abstraction and indeterminacy of location also em-
phasize the multiple literal and allegorical translations involved in ad-
dressing the "world" and in imagining a world poetry.

   McDougall's English and Owen's reading together show how
translation may estrange a writer from the "world" beyond his or
her own language, exacerbating the already "immense difference
between writing and reading what we have written." In seeking to

convey the formal tone of Bei Dao's original in English, McDougall contributes to what Owen sees as the contrived "poeticalness" and angst of these lines. First, McDougall deploys syntactic inversion so that in several key lines the verb precedes the subject, giving these lines an old-fashioned, poetic feel. (Compare "my silence it can't comprehend" to the flatter-sounding corresponding line in Chinese: 它不懂我的沉默, which might be translated as "it doesn't understand my silence").[69] Similarly, "perpetual," which transforms the Chinese adverb *yongyuan* ("always," or "forever") into an adjective, has a formal and poetical flavor that is even more apparent in McDougall's decision later in the poem to translate *qingren* as "beloved" instead of "lover." While the former avoids the perhaps now overly sexualized connotations and informality of the latter, "beloved" situates the poem in an older English poetic—exemplified by works such as Elizabeth Barrett Browning's "Beloved, my Beloved, when I think" and Yeats's "A Poet to His Beloved"—giving the poem a somewhat old-fashioned and poetical tone in the context of late twentieth-century English-language poetry.[70]

Through declarative statement and abstraction, the poem accentuates the difficulty of reading, of translating acts of language into the world—and from one language or world into another. In so doing, it also highlights the problem of an individual speaking to or for a collective. For Van Crevel, the poem's abstraction means "The text bears little commentary, inasmuch as it arguably is commentary itself—poetical or otherwise—and employs words such as *world, stranger, language* and *disdain* that remain unwieldy for want of imaginative usage."[71] The poem's abstraction and declarative tone also lead Owen to describe the poem as a sentimental "pose," an instance of simplicity and directness that has not been "earned."[72] But the problem of language's connection to the "world" and the possibility of speaking to and for that world are what the poem is about. Equally, then, the poem could be read as enacting the alienation it describes, precisely through its use of abstraction and direct statement seemingly disconnected from reality—neither "earned," nor provided with "imaginative usage." Read in this way, the apparently unsettling, cringe-worthy abstraction and generality of the opening illustrate how "Bei Dao's thematic of alienation manifests itself not only in more or less paraphraseable content but also in his style."[73] Thus the apparent stylistic infelicities function in Shklovskian terms to renew perception of the world precisely by pointing to the alienation of language and the individual from it.[74] The poem shatters the idea that art puts a mirror up to the world through its own apparent directness of statement, while by implying an equation between "I" and the collective social "world" it signals their mutual estrangement.

The poem stresses the complex nonmimetic translations that follow from this alienation through its emphasis on mirrors, shadows, replications, doubles, and echoes at both formal and thematic levels. The mirror becomes the point of contact and exchange between the "world" and the "I" in the first stanza, underscoring the poem's structural devices of repetition and inversion. Because the world becomes a mirror image of the "I," or the "I" a mirror image of the world, "self" replaces "world" in the opening lines of the second stanza, which otherwise repeat the poem's first lines. This mirroring and inversion is matched by thematic inversions in the poem. The "I" is taciturn and the world has a language. This inverts normal expectations and suggests the erasure involved in taking an individual or an individual poem as speaking to or for a larger group, be it a generation, a nation, or a new era of globalization.

The second stanza highlights the replications and inversions that separate the "I" from the world and from itself. Self-alienation is emphasized by the division of the person into parts: a "body" and a "heart" or "mind" (*xin*); the reflection in the "mirror" implied by the address "to myself" or "to itself" (对于自己); the silhouette or "shadow" created by the blocked "lamp"; and the antithesis of "beloved" (or "lover") and "enemy." In addition to all the other repetitions, mirror images, inversions, and replications, the poem itself comprises two seven-line stanzas that closely parallel one another. The fourteen-line structure also alludes to the sonnet, another form that relies on thesis and antithesis and so inversion, echo, and translation.

The poem's various shadows and reflections highlight how the individual "I" and collective "world" are mutually constituted by and estranged from one another. The poem's opening, "to the world / I am always a stranger," marks both their interrelationship and inability to communicate, to read each other, so that, instead of strangeness, one merely finds a mirror image of oneself. While Dian Li detects in the poem a theme in Bei Dao's poetry whereby "the world is the enemy and so is the self," the poem names neither the self nor the world as the enemy.[75] Rather it is *xin*, "heart/mind," that is the enemy. This "enemy" contrasts with the "lover," a figure for the nonessentialist exchange, communication, and translation signified by shadows and mirrors and by the replacement of "world" with "self" and their estrangement from one another. Just as Owen recontextualizes the poem outside its history as a product of teenage angst, Dian Li reads the poem in relation to the disillusionment and doubt Bei Dao experienced as a result of the Cultural Revolution and the political crackdowns of the late 1970s and early 1980s. But the poem seems limited neither to a dehistoricized world poetry context nor to a historical and autobiographical reading, nor even to the poem's veiled reference to a close but troubled friend. Instead, the poem plays on the potential for multiple translations, reimaginings, reflections, and shadows, illustrating that Bei Dao "may have a more thoughtful, ironic stance toward home tradition and foreign audiences alike than Owen allows."[76] Bei Dao explicitly situates this poem in relation "to the world," but both "I" and "world" are multiple and "strange," and the translations involved in their relation are open to potentially endless reflection, just as the window on another world provided by a work of "world literature" is "multiply refracted in the process of transculturation" and so serves as a window "on two worlds at once: the world beyond us, and our own world as well."[77] If the "I" in the poem seems imprisoned by his or her alienation from the world, the poem—through its many possible allegories, reflections, translations, and refractions—suggests the possibility of living in this uncertainty and multiplicity rather than being trapped by it.

Reading Bei Dao's poetry within and beyond its immediate historical situation highlights how a text is translated into different contexts, including the national and the world, or global. The tension between historically located and dislocated world-poetry readings of Bei Dao is a structurally critical part of the work. Like the individual "I" and the collective "world" in his poetry, each reading both reinforces and negates the other. Bei Dao's poems anticipate and address the multiple refractions through which his work has been interpreted, as seen in the shifting place of the "world" in multiple senses in China in the 1970s and 1980s, and in the debate over his "world poetry" in the 1990s and 2000s. The responses to his work are enmeshed in the moment of historical flux from which our current era of globalization has emerged; they reveal the historical and rhetorical binary structures through which we have come to conceive of our own era. They also expose the complexities that have been elided in the process. The qualities later identified with a dislocated world literature or world poetry are, ironically, precisely locatable in the political situation of

Bei Dao in China in the 1970s and early 1980s, in a personal, cross-cultural relationship, and, through his English translator, in the tensions between literary and politically oriented approaches to China studies in the 1980s. The specific location of these apparently dislocated qualities of world poetry underscores how notions of world literature both depend on local features and erase their specificities, just as the Cultural Revolution and the dawn of our era of globalization were each imagined in their time as the end of history.

This conflation of historical moments in readings of Bei Dao as "world poetry" reflects an allegorical sense of the contingent and uncertain relation between word and world, past and present: one that characterizes modernity at large but which was felt most strongly during a period of national and global change. Bei Dao's in-between position is evident in his poetics of translation, reflection, and echo, and in the tension between historically contextualized readings of his poetry and those that claim a universalist view. His poetry and the allegories through which it is interpreted reveal how national and world literature are mutually constituted and contested by acts of translation. These acts relate language to the world, but reach no dialectical resolution in the end of history, nor in a truly global literature. Instead, they underscore the estrangement of language from the world that makes possible the endless allegories and translations that constitute national and world literatures in their common strangeness.

CHAPTER FIVE

Dmitri Prigov and Cross-Cultural Conceptualism

The card reads "Dmitrii Prigov, Poet, Artist," and his address is written in roman characters, as though for Western export.

—MICHAEL DAVIDSON, *Leningrad: American Writers in the Soviet Union*

No single language can encompass a person entirely.

—DMITRI PRIGOV, "The Art of Penultimate Truths:
A Conversation with Dmitri Prigov"

The late 1980s and early 1990s witnessed the rise of an international market for contemporary Chinese and Russian artworks. Indicative examples are Zhang Hongtu's portrait of Mao Zedong on a Quaker Oats container (*Long Live Chairman Mao Series #29*; 1989) or Aleksandr Kosolapov's combination of an image of Lenin and a Coca-Cola advertisement (*Lenin Coca-Cola*; 1980, but widely exhibited and reproduced a decade later). Such works and the Western pop and conceptual art practices on which they draw illustrate the subordination of local and national traditions to the global economic and artistic system. They belie the view that conceptual art constituted a "decisive break" with "Western hegemony" and "a radical shift . . . in the pattern of art's development and diffusion worldwide."[1] Marking the enthusiastic entry of their countries into global capitalism, they cash in on the appeal of dated communist iconography to a Western audience. They capture the mood of Owen's view that Bei Dao's work foretold a world literature without history or nationality.

Yet the case of writer and artist Dmitri Prigov tells a different story about the fate of national literary and artistic traditions in the transition to our era of globalization, a story that involves a complex interplay between his native Russia and the West, and between his local milieu and the international world of contemporary art. His work has largely been read in the context of Russian literary and artistic culture, everyday Soviet and post-Soviet life, and Soviet ideology and post-Soviet Russian nationalism. His most famous poetic persona is a Soviet policeman, and he relentlessly recycled the mythologized figures and texts of Russian culture, most prominently Alexander Pushkin and his masterpiece *Eugene Onegin*. But like Bei Dao, from the beginning Prigov's address to this national context was intimately related to an appeal to a wider world. If conceptualism "sought to enable a critical engagement with art, media, mass culture, and technology," then in Prigov's practice part of this engagement had to do with its relation to the institution of Western art and to notions of Russianness and Westernness.[2] Prigov came to be seen as a conceptualist in the early 1980s. The term was adopted by critics, writers, and artists of his milieu in a strategic appropriation from Western art. The appropriation built on Vitaly Komar and Aleksandr Melamid's coinage in 1972 of *sots-art*—a linguistic and cultural adaptation of the term "pop art" that implied that Americans replaced "things" or "objects" whereas Russians replaced "concepts and ideologies."[3] During the 1980s, when an international audience became increasingly within reach, Prigov likewise defined himself in relation to Western conceptualism. Exhibiting and performing in various countries around the world for the last two decades before his death in 2007, he responded to the "end of history" that some identified in the collapse of the Soviet Union and saw anticipated in his work.[4] He staged the death and resurrection of national literary and cultural traditions and mythologies, and did so in the face of the disappearance of his earlier targets within Soviet culture. He continued this practice even while his strategies of iteration, copying, and appropriation were transformed into commonplaces of global capitalism and contemporary art.

Rather than simply contrasting local iconography with a global language of contemporary art, as in the works of artists such as Zhang Hongtu and Kosolapov, however, Prigov brings together various local and transnational languages and cultural systems. His method reveals how none alone can encompass the complex intersections between these languages that characterize our contemporary condition. Prigov's extensive use of a practice as specific to Soviet bloc conditions as samizdat publishing, for example, connects the Russian intelligentsia's fetishization of the universal value contained in these fragile, laboriously reproduced texts to the pervasiveness of repetition and copying in conceptual and postconceptual art. Through such intersections, his work illustrates how the global is not one thing but many, founded in diverse discursive systems including the Russian literary and cultural tradition, Soviet ideology, post-Soviet Russian nationalism, the discourse of the global economy, and the transnational world of contemporary art. Each of these discursive systems appeals to a relationship between the particular and the general: the lyric subject and universal moral and literary value; the Soviet hero and the people; or the consumer and the world economy. By reproducing them together in unexpected and complex intersections, Prigov reveals their parallel systems of binary opposition—the local and global; the particular and the universal; East and West; Russia and the world—while presenting alternatives that emerge from their very moments of encounter.

POLICEMAN

Prigov's vast literary and artistic output constitutes a "global project" that combines genres, media, discourses, languages, and frequent references to countries and cultural material from around the world.[5] His diverse practice is unified by a common iterative strategy. He uses iteration in a variety of ways, including the recurring forms of serial structures; the re-presentation of existing texts and cultural material in a new context, or with a new inflection; the repetition of existing works or forms across diverse media; the thematizing of iterative processes, including technologies of reproduction; and iterations across multiple languages and cultural contexts.[6] Iterative techniques allow for infinite extension across media, source material, and repetitions of texts. Together with the sheer volume of his output (his poems and drawings alone number in the tens of thousands), these techniques emphasize how the cultural, ideological, and economic systems with which he engages claim a similarly global or universal position—be it the idea of Russian literary culture's universal value, the Russian imperial dream of Moscow as the third Rome, the related Soviet ambition to leadership of the communist world, or the notion of a seamless global market.[7]

In reproducing existing texts, discourses, and images, Prigov adopts estranging regimes of organization, or "intervals," which "regulate one regime in a way that distorts others. With one variable held—perversely . . . —constant, others are allowed to be set radically, reeling, free."[8] Found among twentieth-century artists from Duchamp to Cage, systems of interval appear frequently in Prigov's

Figure 4.   Dmitri Prigov, *Banka podpisei* [Can of signatures], n.d. Tin can, plaster, wood, cardboard, paper with typed text, 8 x 7.5 x 7.5 cm. Photo courtesy of the Moscow Museum of Modern Art. Reproduced with the permission of the Estate of Dmitri Prigov.

work. We can see examples in his diverse, alphabetically arranged *Az-buki* (*Alphabets*) series, or in his exploitation of the regular spacing of the typewritten—as opposed to typeset—samizdat page, or perhaps most strikingly of all, in his extensive 1970s *Banki* (*Tin Cans*) series (see, for example, figs. 4 and 5). Here a vast range of materials is all presented on or within the regular structure of a standard tin can—the cans become, in Prigov's words, an "entire language" or "single form of life."[9] Like the containerization of freight that was transforming the global economy at this time, or the equally global adaptability suggested by works such as Warhol's *Campbell's Soup Cans* (1962), Prigov's *Tin Cans* emphasize that "value . . . lies not in what it is, but in how it is used."[10]

By bringing these diverse systems of regulation together, Prigov refuses to allow any single language to encompass him entirely. Instead, he produces singular points of encounter that belie the binary oppositions—East/West, local/global, particular/universal, male/female—upon which systems from Cold War discourse to gender conventions are built.[11] Each instance of iteration—whether a performance, a text,

Figure 5.   Dmitri Prigov, *Banka stikhov* [Can of poems], n.d. Tin can, plaster, wood, cardboard, paper with typed text, 8 x 7.5 x 7.5 cm. Photo courtesy of the Moscow Museum of Modern Art. Reproduced with the permission of the Estate of Dmitri Prigov.

or a physical object—remains an embodied intersection of sources, media, and forms, and of spatial and temporal vectors. Each one is intertwined but in tension with the regularity of its intervals and the reproducibility of the texts, genres, and discourses on which it draws.[12] Prigov's practice can be understood as one of "re-accentuation," a term Mikhail Bakhtin uses to describe the re-presentation or mixing of genres in ways that are "parodic-ironic" (or that otherwise alter their conventional meanings) and the similar effects produced by the re-presentation of speech.[13] Prigov's re-accentuations are neither simply sincere nor ironic.[14] Instead, they involve the complex relation of sincere imitation to stylization and parody that shifts across historical periods, including in the rereading of literary texts over time and—we might add—across places, cultures, and languages.[15] By linking diverse discourses, genres, and media, he allows them to articulate in new ways—a process he repeatedly describes as *peresechenie*, or "intersection."[16] Prigov's work extends this process of re-accentuation along further vectors of reiteration and recombination, including citation, serial form, translation, medium, and mode of reproduction.

Many theoretical and avant-garde visions of our global condition stress that "the belief in a *total system*" inflects "any attempt to think beyond local and particular circumstances currently."[17] By contrast, Prigov refuses to be limited by any one system, language, or mode of discourse. He undermines each system's claim to totality by staging its encounter with another such system. Extending Bakhtin's view that the command and manipulation of genres is a form of agency, Prigov's iterative poetics emphasizes both the unfreedom of endless repetition and the freedom of each gesture among the infinite possibilities of intersecting systems, iterations, languages.[18]

Prigov's much-loved policeman persona illustrates his technique of iteration and intersection. This persona exemplifies how even in the 1970s, when he was working exclusively for an unofficial, samizdat audience using forms and figures particular to Russian culture— "Soviet mythology, local mentalities, artistic styles and traditions"— his work was concerned with a global perspective and deployed methods deriving from the "international language of art (from Pop Art to Conceptual Art and Performance)."[19] In these policeman poems, Prigov adopts a figure of state power as his hero, combining Soviet ideology with a doggerel version of the Russian romantic lyric. His policeman emerges out of his reproduction and intersection of Soviet ideology, popular or folk discourse, and the Russian intelligentsia's commitment to the universal and eternal values of literature and art. A heroic figure of state authority committed to the Russian poetic tradition, he is also associated with a semiliterate folk tradition signaled by the nonstandard spelling of *militsaner* (pliceman) and by the stylistic ineptitude of his verse. Through this figure, Prigov juxtaposes the clichés of socialist realism to the mythologies of the Russian intelligentsia. Although his policeman persona is intimately tied to national tradition and Soviet ideology and mythology, he equally allows Prigov to explore the global ambitions of these local discursive systems, focusing on their appeal to transcendent, all-powerful, universal perspectives. One of his best known and most frequently performed policeman poems, originally circulated in samizdat in 1976, highlights this global reach:

Когда здесь на посту стоит Милицанер
Ему до Внуково простор весь открывается
На Запад и на Восток глядит Милицанер
И пустота за ними открывается
И центр, где стоит Милицанер—

Взгляд на него отвсюду открывается
Отвсюду виден Милиционер
С Востока виден Милиционер
И с Юга виден Милиционер
И с моря виден Милиционер
И с неба виден Милиционер
И с-под земли . . .
        Да он и не скрывается

When here on duty stands a Pliceman
For him an expanse opens up as far as Vnukovo
To the West and to the East looks the Pliceman
And emptiness opens up behind them
And the center, where the Pliceman stands
From evrywhere a sight of him opens up
From evrywhere can be seen the Policeman
From the East can be seen the Policeman
And from the South can be seen the Policeman
And from the sea can be seen the Policeman
And from the sky can be seen the Policeman
And from under the earth . . .
        And he isn't trying to hide[20]

Here the "Pliceman" becomes an archetypal figure of authority and power who spans the entire globe: "To the West and to the East," "from the sky" and "from the sea." If we note that Vnukovo lies on the outskirts of Moscow and is also the location of one of the city's international airports, we can see how the poem reinforces the interplay between Russian locality and global reach. The poem also plays on Soviet ideological discourse and the Russian cultural imaginary, which envisages the country and especially Moscow—seen as the third Rome—as a "center" that mediates between East and West, Europe and Asia. The sense of operating within traditions that replicate themselves is reinforced by the repetition of the word "Policeman," which through its capitalization and all-encompassing position becomes an archetypal idea that transcends the policeman character's mundane physical existence. Yet the variation in spelling within the poem also suggests the possibility of iterations that allow for differences. When in 1978 Prigov wrote an introduction to his policeman poems, he claimed that the figure was not ironic but a mythic hero who functions as a mediator: a "dynamic" "uniting heaven and earth."[21] The poem, through its hyperbolic repetitions, which seem at the end to disconcert even the poem's own implied speaker, attempts to encompass the whole world: West and East, sky and sea, above and

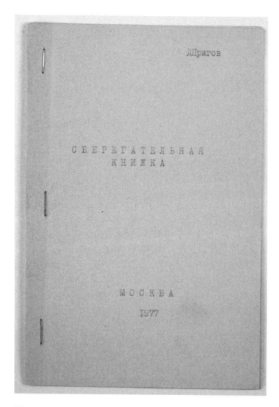

Figure 6. Dmitri Prigov, *Sberegatel'naia kni-zhka* [Savings book], 1977. Paper, typescript text, 19 x 13 cm. Photo courtesy of the Moscow Museum of Modern Art. Reproduced with the permission of the Estate of Dmitri Prigov.

below ground. In this respect, it invokes the hyperbolic pretensions of the Russian poetic tradition. (Prigov later explained that in his main artistic project he sought to create an "ideal poet" who "covers all the world with his words.")[22] Prigov has these pretensions intersect with the Soviet ideological system's claim to universal values. The divine mission of the poet meets the divine mission of the Soviet policeman, while the awesome power of each is emphasized and deflated by the poem's naïve, child-like tone, ridiculous hyperbole, and folk-like incantation.[23]

Prigov's policeman seems a world away from what we might expect from conceptual art, but its relation to Western conceptual

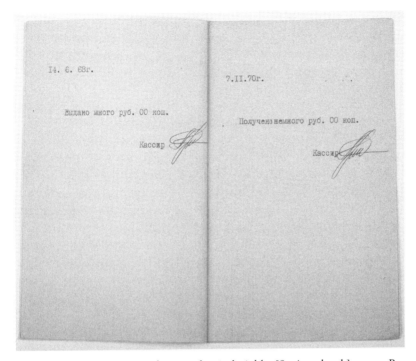

Figure 7. Dmitri Prigov, *Sberegatel'naia knizhka* [Savings book], 1977. Paper, typescript text, 19 x 13 cm. Photo courtesy of the Moscow Museum of Modern Art. Reproduced with the permission of the Estate of Dmitri Prigov.

art becomes clearer when it is read alongside other works from this period, such as Prigov's *Kniga dekretov* (*Book of Decrees*), which appeared the following year (1977). This work likewise conjoins Soviet ideological practices to the mythologizing of the artist, writer, and particularly the poet in Russian culture, and to the extension of this mythologizing in the development of samizdat literary culture. The entire book comprises labeled decrees, one on each page and each accompanied by Prigov's signature, so linking Western conceptual art's preoccupations with authorship to the Soviet ideological system.[24] Another similar work from this period, *Sberegatel'naia knizhka* (*Savings Book*; 1977), comprises a record of deposits and withdrawals signed by Prigov (figs. 6 and 7). Like the policeman poems, the *Book of Decrees* and the *Savings Book* relate the authority of the artist or poet to the authority of the state. Moreover, by presenting a figure of state power—a policeman, an issuer of decrees, or a cashier in a state bank—in a form associated with resistance to state authority (the samizdat book), Prigov not only comments ironically on both samizdat's sacral myths and Soviet ideology but highlights their common commitment to the world-making power of their authoritative word.

At this time Prigov was also questioning the mythologies of the Russian literary tradition through verbatim reproduction. As early as his 1974 *Kul'turnye pesni* (*Cultural Songs*), Prigov had rewritten lines of classic Russian poems by writers such as Pushkin and Lermontov, and in his 1978 *Prodolgovatyi sbornik* (*The Elongated Collection*), he went further, including the wholesale reproduction of the opening line of Pushkin's *Eugene Onegin* in what would become a signature iterative procedure recurring across hundreds if not thousands of his works in various media for the rest of his life. Prigov's appropriative approach coincided with the publication of the influential essay "Ekzistentsial'nye predposylki kontseptual'nogo iskusstva" ("The Existentialist Preconditions of Conceptual Art"; 1977) by Boris Groys in the samizdat journal *37*. Groys's essay introduced Western conceptualist art by way of Borges's Pierre Menard, who sought to reproduce *Don Quixote* "word for word and line for line." Apparently unwittingly, Groys described Prigov's approach and anticipated his later, more radical verbatim reproductions.[25]

Groys's follow-up essay, "Moskovskii romanticheskii kontseptualizm" ("Moscow Romantic Conceptualism"), led to the application of the term "conceptualist" to the writers and artists of Prigov's milieu. In this essay, Groys emphasizes national characteristics (as in his reference to the "French manner" or "spirit": *frantsuzskii dukh*), in order to distinguish between the hermeneutic transparency of Western conceptual art practices—such as copying and algorithmic text generation—described in his previous essay, and the similar procedures now being employed by artists and writers in Moscow. While noting that conceptualism originated in the West, Groys identifies distinctive elements in Russian conceptualism such as the "continued unity of the 'Russian soul'" (*sokhraniaiushchee edinstvo 'russkoi dushi'*) and "mystical experience" (*misticheskii opyt*). For Groys, these distinctively Russian elements allow Moscow conceptualism to address the Hegelian collective human "Spirit" or *Dukh*. (The word *dukh* is etymologically related to *dusha*, the Russian word for "soul.") The essay does not, however, refer to Prigov, whose conceptual policeman interrogates the very clichés about Russianness and the Russian poet and

artist to which Groys appeals.[26] For both Groys and Prigov, what af-
ter this essay comes to be known as Moscow conceptualism depends
on Soviet and Russian cultural mythologies and texts seen in rela-
tion to the West. For Prigov, however, that wider world stands within
as well as outside these local discourses, which become correspond-
ingly both all-encompassing and drawn into question. He thereby re-
fuses to be limited by the cultural assumptions in Groys's analysis.
Where Groys seems to want to police the boundaries between Rus-
sian and Western conceptualism, Prigov seems more concerned with
rearticulating clichés about the power of Russian literature and the
Soviet state alongside that other trope of national consciousness: the
dynamic figure of the mediator who stands between East and West at
the crossroads of many languages, cultures, and traditions.

A ТО Я

In the 1980s, partly in response to Groys's essay and its influence, and
partly as a result of growing contact with the West as the decade wore
on, Prigov came increasingly to define himself as a conceptualist and
to address Cold War oppositions and clichés about Russian cultural
difference. *Azbuka 1* (*Alphabet 1*; 1980) reflects his concern at this
time with addressing an international context and the dichotomy be-
tween East and West:[27]

> Американец—это враг
> Англичанин—тоже враг
> Бедуин—уже не враг
> Болгарин—друг и младший брат
>
> An American is an enemy
> An Englishman is also an enemy
> A Bedouin is no longer an enemy
> A Bulgarian is a friend and younger brother[28]

As in his policeman poems, Prigov iterates Soviet ideology—giving
the party line on international relations circa 1980—and lets it inter-
sect with the appeal to the power of the poet:

> Пушкин—это чистый гений
> Пригов—это тоже гений
>
> Pushkin is a pure genius
> Prigov is also a genius[29]

The poem combines the preference for the collective over the individual in Soviet ideology with a romantic emphasis on the individual poet's universal genius. Pushkin here functions as the point of intersection, allowing Prigov to connect nationalistic collective discourse to the individual writer through the figure of Russia's national poet, whose mythologized status has revolved in part around "the dispute over 'my' vs. 'our' Pushkin," between an "intimate" and a "public figure."[30]

The interplay between international relations and self-presentation is emphasized by the poem's serial form. *Azbuka 1* is the first poem in Prigov's extensive series of works that deploy an interval structure of alphabetically arranged units from the first letter of the Cyrillic alphabet to the last, from *a* to *ia* (*a* to *я*). Each work produces a unique intersection between the serial form and its content and medium of presentation, so marking the point of contact between each individual gesture and the cultural system—signified by the alphabet—in which that gesture operates. Prigov uses the final letter of the Russian alphabet, which is also the first-person singular pronoun *ia* (the equivalent of the English "I"), to emphasize the conjunction of collective system and individual act:

> Я—такого слова нет
> Я на все здесь дал ответ
>
> I—there is no such word
> I've provided answers for everything here[31]

The lines play on the "obvious paradox of stating the absence of a word one has just used, presumably to declare that in the collective there are (or should be) no egocentric individuals, and then using it emphatically again to underline one's own dictatorial declarations which allow for no individual opinion or disagreement."[32] The paradox serves as a site of intersecting discourses, revealing the interplay, as in the policeman poems, between assertions of the Soviet Union's world leadership and the universalist pretensions of its literary tradition. Just a year after "Moscow Romantic Conceptualism" had first appeared in samizdat, Prigov here critiques the collective forms of identity invoked by Groys and the Russian avant-garde's paradoxical combination of individualism and collectivism.[33] By combining official propaganda and allusions to the literary tradition in the childlike simplicity of an alphabet book, he questions generalized notions of Russia, whether conveyed through the official line on other countries, the popular mythology surrounding Russia's national poet, Pushkin, or Groys's summation of Russian conceptualism. In negating the "I" through Soviet ideological clichés and the propagandistic insistence that "I" comes last—as in Samuil Marshak's use of this play on words in *Veseloe puteshestvie ot A do Ia* (*A Happy Journey from A to Z*; 1952)—Prigov questions the relationship of the individual to his or her Russianness and the cultural assumption that the poet should give voice to collective identity and memory.[34]

The poem stands at the intersection of multiple iterative systems. On the one hand, the serial form of the alphabet emphasizes an appeal to totality, a claim to encompass everything with the comprehensiveness of a dictionary. Likewise, the poem invokes the system of Soviet foreign policy with its divisions of the entire world into enemies and friends. The claim to encompass the entire world is reinforced in the poem's final line: "I've provided answers for everything here." A similar claim to totality is highlighted within the Russian literary tradition through the invocation of Pushkin, which in the context of the alphabetical form recalls Belinsky's famous characterization of *Eugene Onegin* as an "encyclopedia of Russian life."[35] The poem highlights the similarly world-encompassing pretensions of the Russian cultural tradition and Soviet Cold War ideology. Yet by staging the encounter between these systems and the serial alphabet form, it also suggests that no one frame can provide "answers for everything," can encompass the person, Russia, or the world.

Prigov's 1982 painting *Nebo i more* (*Sky and Sea*; fig. 8) seems an even more direct response to Groys's attempt to encompass Moscow conceptualism within a single theory and define its difference from the West. Prigov had first made use of the term "conceptualism" in 1982, when he responded to the criticism that his work lacked international reach—that it was "timid, inadequate, and home-grown." He replied to this criticism by insisting that "conceptualism . . . takes readymade stylistic constructions and uses them as signs of language," so that "if earlier an artist was a 'Style,' was wholly within confines created by him according to rules of depictive or textual reality, now the artist is read on a meta-level as a kind of space in which languages converge."[36] Reflecting this understanding of conceptualism, *Sky and Sea* unites a specifically Russian context with an appeal to a wider, expressly Western, world through its combination of Russian and English. Just as Prigov's policeman occupies the center of a world defined by both the East/West Cold War axis and the limits of the natural

Figure 8.   Dmitri Prigov, *Nebo i more* [Sky and sea], 1982. Ink and acrylic on paper, 102 x 138 cm. Traisman collection. Photo courtesy of Yuri Traisman. Reproduced with the permission of the Estate of Dmitri Prigov.

world ("and from the sea can be seen the Policeman / and from the sky"), the world of the visual work is defined by the natural limits of its title and repeated words, *Sky and Sea*, inflected by the East/West axis of the juxtaposed English and Russian in their contrasting Roman and Cyrillic scripts. The central red Russian *dukh* (in Cyrillic, дух) or "spirit" transcends the clearly demarcated lines of the canvas and its binary divisions between East and West, sky and sea, black and white. It thus parodies the idea that the Russian national spirit, unlike the individualistic West, is also a border-transcending collective human spirit, as in the familiar notion of the "Russian soul" or *russkaia dusha*: the very idea to which Groys had appealed three years earlier in contrasting Western and Russian conceptualisms.

Although it first appeared in the samizdat journal *37* in 1979, Groys's essay was published the same year as the lead article in the opening issue of the bilingual Paris-based Russian-English émigré art magazine *A-Ya*, establishing the essay as a key cultural mediator between Russian and Western contemporary art. The first issue of *A-Ya* also includes a page of work by Prigov that fuses poetic and artistic practices through Russian samizdat culture (figs. 9 and 10).[37] Like *Sky and Sea*, these visual poems, which Prigov termed *Stikhogrammy,* or *Poemographs*, oscillate between text and image and negotiate between Russia and the West. They complicate Groys's clear distinction between Russian and Western conceptualism by staging the intersection between multiple discursive systems and iterations through the interplay between visual and verbal languages. Just as the term "conceptual poetry"—which thanks to Groys would come to be applied to Prigov's work—suggests, the *Poemographs* demonstrate how the peculiarly Russian cultural status of the poet creates the possibility for a particular kind of conceptual art. In the context of the bilingual art magazine, Prigov's work stands out because it requires translation and cultural contextualization, even as its visual elements suggest that reading the text might be unnecessary. Prigov's work emphasizes the international languages of appropriative conceptual art and of concrete poetry, viewed, in Max Bense's 1965 statement, as a form that "does not separate languages; it unites them."[38] Prigov builds image-based poems out of repeated lines of appropriated texts, mainly commonplaces of Russian literature, everyday life, and Soviet ideology, allowing the discursive systems of Russian literature and Soviet culture to intersect with the international languages and transnational appeal of conceptual art and concrete poetry. Playing on the irony that meant fellow Russian conceptualist Ilya Kabakov's notion of "'seeing words instead of objects' was ironically fulfilled in a refractive form when the Western viewer was subjected to 'seeing' rather than 'reading' the language-saturated works of Soviet conceptualism," Prigov stages the junction between reading and seeing through a series of encounters that reveal and undermine the all-encompassing pretensions of each discursive, ideological, and artistic system—Russian and Western—that he invokes.[39]

The first of Prigov's two visual poems published in *A-Ya*, entitled *Nas vyrastil ~~Stalin~~ partiia na radost' narodu* (*We Are Grown by ~~Stalin~~ the Party for the Joy of the People*; fig. 9), deploys the universal claims of Soviet nationalism and Russian poetic authority. Its crude, ungrammatical replacement of the word "Stalin" with "the party" (*partiia*) refers to the official introduction in 1977 of new words for the Soviet National Anthem that removed any mention of Stalin (the national anthem had been played without words for the previous two decades). In this way, Prigov makes a cultural reference that is obvious to a Soviet reader, but that might be lost on a Western audience.

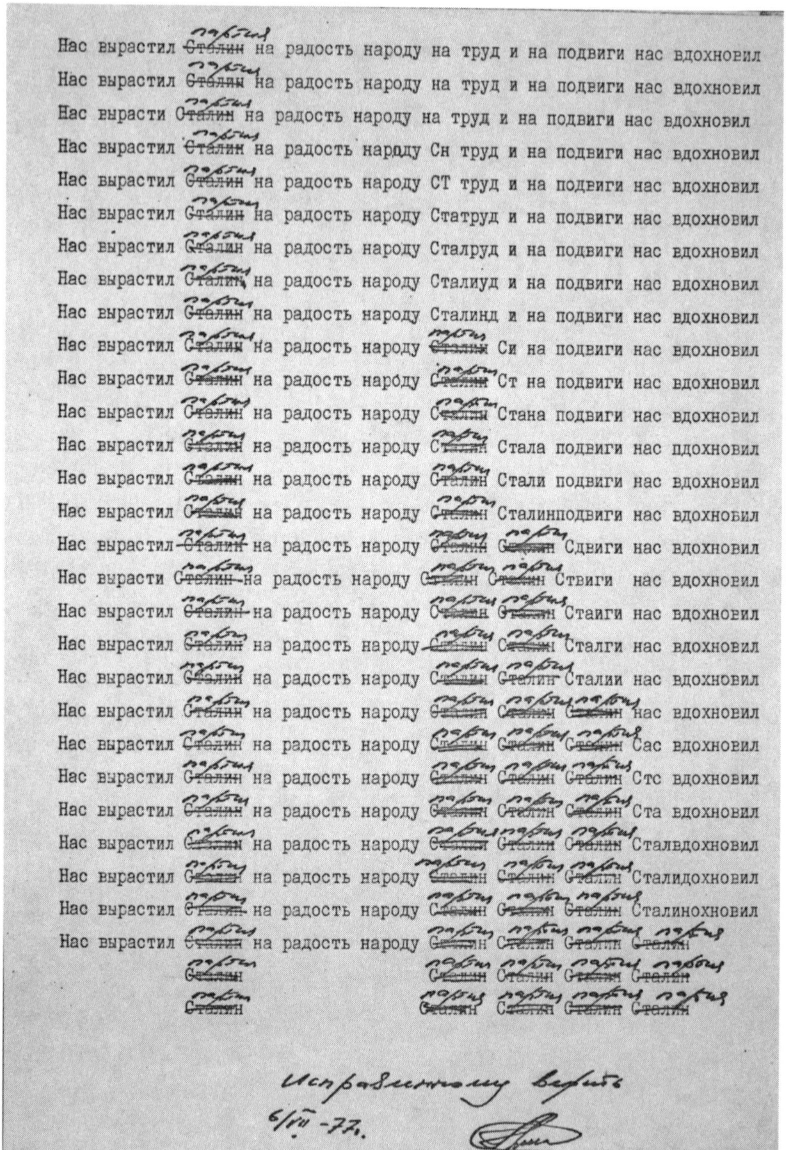

Figure 9. Dmitri Prigov, *Nas vyrastil* ~~Stalin~~ *partiia na radost' narodu / We Are Grown by* ~~Stalin~~ *the Party for the Joy of the People*, n.d. Typewritten text and ballpoint pen on paper, 30 x 21 cm. From the *Stikhogrammy* [Poemographs] series. Published in *A-Ya* 1 (1979): 52. *A-Ya* Archive, Norton and Nancy Dodge Collection of Nonconformist Art from the Soviet Union, Zimmerli Art Museum at Rutgers University, O-071.001.027.01. Photo by Peter Jacobs. Reproduced with the permission of the Estate of Dmitri Prigov.

At the same time, however, by using the national anthem, Prigov acknowledges how a foreign audience might read his work as representing the nation. His handwritten changes and signature approving the corrections (*ispravlennomu verit'*; correction approved) underscore how he playfully assumes the position of national representative. As in the *Book of Decrees* and the *Savings Book*, here Soviet ideology and authority intersect with the questioning of authority and originality in appropriative conceptual art. This is underscored by the way the words "Stalin" and, in the handwritten text, "the party" gradually and ridiculously come to subsume the high-minded words of the other line quoted from the anthem, a line that remained unchanged in the 1977 version: "inspired us to labor and to acts of heroism" (*na trud i na podvigi nas vdokhnovil*). All that remains at the bottom of the page is the repeated "Stalin" replaced by "the party," the words "We are grown," or "raised" (*Nas vyrastil*; cut from the 1977 version of the Soviet anthem), and a phrase that never appeared in the national anthem, "for the joy of the people" (*na radost' narodu*), which ironically substitutes for the official 1944 version's "for loyalty to the people" (*na vernost' narodu*). Through the omitted word *vernost'*, which can mean both "loyalty" and "truthfulness," and the use of his signature, Prigov explores the relationship between Soviet authority and the notion of the Russian poet as the true voice of the nation.

While such details might be lost on a Western reader, Prigov's humorous enactment of de-Stalinization and his satirizing of national representation are clear enough to a non-Russian-speaking audience from the translated title or caption to the piece given in *A-Ya*: "We are grown by ~~Stalin~~ the Party for the joy of the people." Prigov stresses the double function of the national anthem as both representing the nation to others (in which music dominates over words) and reinforcing a sense of national identity (for which words and so the act of collective singing are important). Analogously, the visual elements of the piece are accessible to a non-Russian-speaking reader of *A-Ya*, while aside from the translated title the words resist interpretation. Prigov underscores the breakdown of this dual role for the national anthem by alluding to the absence of any agreed words for the anthem during the period between Stalin's death and the introduction of the new words in 1977. By restaging the 1977 word substitution, he also links Soviet and Russian nationalist propaganda to conceptual art by showing how the same serial forms he uses to create works enable official culture to perpetuate and transform itself. Just as the work operates at the intersection of verbal, visual, and musical media, it conjoins international conceptual art and concrete poetry to the similarly global pretensions of the Soviet Union and the Russian literary tradition.

Similarly, in his second work in the first issue of *A-Ya*, Prigov combines cultural and national representation with a border-crossing appeal through his use of the Latin cliché "in vino veritas" (fig. 10). Prigov here engages in a European literary and philosophical tradition dating back to Plato's *Symposium*, but, against convention, he transliterates the cliché into Cyrillic, rather than preserving the Latin script. In playing on the relation of Russian to a Latin and European text, Prigov also alludes to the Russian literary tradition, specifically to Alexander Blok's poem "Neznakomka" ("Unknown Woman"), in which Blok uses the phrase "in vino veritas" first in Latin and then, to conclude the poem, in Russian translation. Prigov's equivalent translation is the question: "BUT WHAT'S IN BEER?" (*A V PIVE CHTO?*) The question is distinguished from the transliterated Latin by the use of block capitals, which form a shape that might be an upturned wine glass or the stylized outline of a woman—like the "stranger" or "unknown woman" of Blok's poem, who appears to the drunken lyric subject after he sees himself "reflected in my glass" (*V moem stakane otrazhen*).[40] Like Blok's poem, Prigov's poem-image both translates a foreign phrase into a Russian one and assimilates a vision of foreignness (the "stranger") into a recognizable form (the reflection in, or image of, the wine glass). In contrast, however, Prigov's work bathetically transforms the "key" (*kliuch*) and "truth" (*istina*) discovered through the strange woman and wine in Blok's poem into a crude joke. It thus contributes to Prigov's ongoing deflation of what he elsewhere terms the "enchanting fairytale" (*charuiushchaia skazka*) of classic Russian literature.[41] Prigov juxtaposes Russian to Latin, beer to wine, text to image, the transcendent otherness of the Russian romantic tradition and the pan-European symbolist movement to the apparently universal languages of concrete poetry and conceptual art. In doing so, he emphasizes moments of singular intersection that conform to not one of these supposedly all-encompassing languages or traditions.

In the context of *A-Ya*, Prigov's use of the typewriter itself constitutes an implicit cross-cultural commentary. His *Poemographs* emphasize the typewriter as a site of production and publication, even as they are ironically transformed into printed images of artworks,

Ин вино веритас Ин вино веритас Ин вино веритас Ин вино веритас Ин вино верита
с Ин вино веритас Ин вино веритас Ин вино веритас Ин вино веритас Ин вино вери
тас Ин вино веритас Ин вино веритас Ин вино веритас Ин вино веритас Ин вино ве
ритас Ин вино веритас Ин вино веритас Ин вино веритас Ин вино веритас Ин вино
веритас Ин вино веритас Ин вино веритас Ин вино веритас Ин вино веритас Ин вин
о веритас Ин вино веритас Ин вино веритас Ин вино веритас Ин вино веритас Ин в
ино веритас Ин вино веритас Ин А но веритас Ин вино веритас Ин вино веритас Ин
вино веритас Ин вино веритас И А ино веритас Ин вино веритас Ин вино веритас
вино веритас Ин вино веритас И А В вино веритас Ин вино веритас Ин вино верита
с Ин вино веритас Ин вино вери А В   вино веритас Ин вино веритас Ин вино вери
тас Ин вино веритас Ин вино ве А В П н вино веритас Ин вино веритас Ин вино ве
ритас Ин вино веритас Ин вино А В ПИ Ин вино веритас Ин вино веритас Ин вино
веритас Ин вино веритас Ин вин А В ПИВ Ин вино веритас Ин вино веритас Ин вин
о веритас Ин вино веритас Ин в А В ПИВЕ с Ин вино веритас Ин вино веритас Ин в
ино веритас Ин вино веритас Ин А В ПИВЕ ас Ин вино веритас Ин вино веритас Ин
вино веритас Ин вино веритас И А В ПИВЕ Ч тас Ин вино веритас Ин вино веритас
Ин вино веритас Ин вино верита А В ПИВЕ ЧТ итас Ин вино веритас Ин вино верита
с Ин вино веритас Ин вино вери А В ПИВЕ ЧТО ритас Ин вино веритас Ин вино вери
тас Ин вино веритас Ин вино ве А В ПИВЕ ЧТО? еритас Ин вино веритас Ин вино ве
ритас Ин вино веритас Ин вино А В ПИВЕ ЧТО? веритас Ин вино веритас Ин вино
веритас Ин вино веритас Ин вин А В ПИВЕ ЧТО? но веритас Ин вино веритас Ин вин
о веритас Ин вино веритас Ин в А В ПИВЕ ЧТО? вино веритас Ин вино веритас Ин в
ино веритас Ин вино веритас Ин А В ПИВЕ ЧТО? н вино веритас Ин вино веритас Ин
вино веритас Ин вино веритас А В ПИВЕ ЧТО? Ин вино веритас Ин вино веритас
Ин вино веритас Ин вино верита А В ПИВЕ ЧТО? ас Ин вино веритас Ин вино верита
с Ин вино веритас Ин вино вери А В ПИВЕ ЧТО? итас Ин вино веритас Ин вино вери
тас Ин вино веритас Ин вино ве А В ПИВЕ ЧТО? еритас Ин вино веритас Ин вино ве
ритас Ин вино веритас Ин вино А В ПИВЕ н ЧТО? веритас Ин вино веритас Ин вино
веритас Ин вино веритас Ин А В ПИВЕ ас ЧТО? веритас Ин вино веритас Ин вин
о веритас Ин вино веритас И А В ПИВЕ ритас ЧТО? о веритас Ин вино веритас Ин в
ино веритас Ин вино верита А В ПИВЕ верита ЧТО? но веритас Ин вино веритас Ин
вино веритас Ин вино вери А В ПИВЕ яно верит ЧТО? вино веритас Ин вино веритас
Ин вино веритас ин вино А В ПИВЕ н вино вери ЧТО? вино веритас Ин вино верит
ас Ин вино веритас Ин в А В ПИВЕ ас Ин вино ве ЧТО? н вино веритас Ин вино вер
итас Ин вино веритас И А В ПИВЕ аеритас Ин вино ЧТО? Ин вино веритас Ин вино в
еритас Ин вино верита А В ПИВЕ о веритас Ин вино ЧТО? Ин вино веритас Ин вино
 веритас Ин вино вер А В ПИВЕ ино веритас Ин вино ЧТО? с Ин вино веритас Ин ви
но веритас Ин вино А В ПИВЕ н вино веритас Ин вин ЧТО? ае Ин вино веритас Ин
вино веритас Ин ви А Б ПИВЕ с Ин вино веритас Ин ви ЧТО? тас Ин вино веритас И
н вино веритас Ин А В ПИВЕ тас Ин вино веритас Ин в ЧТО? итас Ин вино веритас
 Ин вино веритас А В ПИВЕ аеритас Ин вино веритас Ин ЧТО? ритас Ин вино верит
ас Ин вино вери А В ПИВЕ о веритас Ин вино веритас Ин ЧТО? еритас Ин вино вер
итас Ин вино в А В ПИВЕ вино веритас Ин вино веритас ЧТО? веритас Ин вино в
еритас Ин вин А В ПИВЕ Ин вино веритас Ин вино веритас ЧТО? о веритас Ин вино

Figure 10.   Dmitri Prigov, *In vino veritas*, n.d. Typewritten text on paper, 30 x 21 cm. From the *Stikhogrammy* [Poemographs] series. Published in *A-Ya* 1 (1979): 52. *A-Ya* Archive, Norton and Nancy Dodge Collection of Nonconformist Art from the Soviet Union, Zimmerli Art Museum at Rutgers University, O-071.001.027.01. Photo by Peter Jacobs. Reproduced with the permission of the Estate of Dmitri Prigov.

where their hand-produced, self-published quality and linguistic func-
tion are reduced when approached by a non-Russian audience view-
ing them in a glossy magazine. As Prigov emphasized this problem in
the commentary accompanying the works he sent to *A-Ya*: "Ideally,
they should be reproduced only in a way that copies all the specifics of
a typed text."[42] The boundary between samizdat and Western print-
ing that Prigov emphasizes here intersects with the boundary between
the visual arts and poetry. As a samizdat writer, Prigov typed and si-
multaneously published texts whose physical manifestation thereby
became an auratic original work of art and a nonauratic product of a
laborious form of mechanical reproduction. These typescripts empha-
size their status as both reproductions and as unique artistic works
by comprising short repeated phrases of copied text that produce sin-
gular images, which are themselves part of an endlessly expandable
series. Reproducing these works in an émigré-run art journal adds
another layer of auraless reproduction while establishing their trans-
national status as works of art. Each of the *Poemographs* constitutes
a singular intersection of multiple forms of repetition along the vec-
tors of Russian linguistic commonplace, serial form, and mode of re-
production, and between the poles of the verbal and visual, Russian
cultural tradition and international art.

Prigov chose an image of himself at the typewriter and amongst his
artworks to represent himself in the inaugural and only issue of the
literary version of *A-Ya*, published in 1985 (fig. 11). The image at once
underscores the importance of the Russian cultural mythologies of the
poet to Prigov's practice (literary and artistic), situates him in the act
of self-publishing, and places him in a liminal position between the vi-
sual artworks that surround him—including pieces from his *Tin Cans*
series—and the site of writing that he occupies. Prigov presents him-
self in dark glasses, as he does throughout the series of photographic
portraits taken at this time in the artist's apartment-based studio. In-
appropriate to the working writer or artist in the internal environment
of his studio, the glasses suggest that the self-image is as artificial and
posed as the icon-like picture above his head and so might be taken as
another of his many works featuring Prigov himself.[43]

Conspicuous in this and other photographs in the series is one of
his *Poemographs* featuring a large "АЯ," which appears here in the
upper center of the image. Recalling the title of the magazine *A-Ya*
(or in Cyrillic, *A-Я*), in which the photograph was published, Prigov's
"АЯ" image plays between the individual self-presentation of the

Figure 11. Photographer unknown, Dmitri Prigov in his apartment (typing), n.d. Photograph, 17.6 x 12.5 cm. Published in *A-Ya* literary edition 1 (1985):84. *A-Ya* Archive, Norton and Nancy Dodge Collection of Nonconformist Art from the Soviet Union, Zimmerli Art Museum at Rutgers University, P-071.003.018. Reproduction photo by Peter Jacobs. Reproduced with the permission of the Estate of Dmitri Prigov.

portrait and the encyclopedic range from the first letter of the Cyrillic alphabet to the last—suggesting a totalizing cultural system as comprehensive as Belinsky's "encyclopedia of Russian life." At the same height and directly above Prigov is what looks like a self-portrait. The composition, reinforced by the geometric arrangement of rectangular works on the wall behind, ties Prigov to his self-image and to the "АЯ" *Poemograph* to his right. The image focuses attention on the photograph as self-portrait through the interplay of the portrait image on the wall behind and the shadow Prigov casts on the same wall. The self-portrait and various reiterations of self in the image are further highlighted by the "АЯ," which could be translated as "but

I" and so read as a further insistence on or reiteration of the self in the linguistic realm. This continuous insistence "but I" circumvents the *a*-to-*z* totality of any one system by enabling another to intervene.

Just as the title of the journal *A-Ya* juxtaposes the Roman and Cyrillic letter *A* with the distinctively Cyrillic *Я*, the presentation of Prigov's image in this Russian émigré journal underscores how he operates at the intersection of multiple media and languages. Published on the cusp of perestroika, in the first and only literary *A-Ya*, the image highlights the relationship between literature and the visual arts even as it reestablishes the divide and connects it again to the cross-cultural context. Whereas the bilingual Russian-English art magazine clearly appealed to a Western art audience, the literary magazine contained no translations. It was aimed at a Russian-speaking literary audience at a time when the majority of that audience remained almost completely indifferent to contemporary art.[44] The combination of image and text reinforces the interplay between artist and writer in the presentation of Prigov at his typewriter in his artist's studio. It also underscores his use of the cultural status of the poet in Russia in his rearticulation of Western conceptualist art. Further emphasizing the play between East and West, the "АЯ" *Poemograph* is one of a pair, the other of which is the mirror image "RA," which was also published by *A-Ya* in 1985, in a chapbook of Prigov's *Poemographs*.[45] Produced by using the Roman but not Cyrillic letter *R*, it renders the pair "RA" and "АЯ" a figure for opposition and equivalence between Russia and the West. Prigov straddles *A* and *Я*: the cross-culturally comprehensible image and the culturally and linguistically located text. He combines multiple systems of repetition and opposition—each as infinitely extendable as the uses of an alphabet—in encounters that, as he said in 1989, "no single language can encompass . . . entirely."[46]

PERESTROIKA

As the Soviet Union began to reform, Prigov turned increasingly to the question of how conceptual art itself might be rearticulated at the intersection of competing languages and cultural systems. In a 1986–87 interview conducted for the never-realized second issue of the literary *A-Ya*, Prigov recalled the East-West cultural distinction implied by the term *sots-art* and by Groys's influential essay on Moscow conceptualism: "Western conceptualism arose as a reaction to a reifying culture and to Pop Art with its fetishizing of the object. . . . When it entered our part of the world, conceptualism discovered the total absence of any idea of the object and its inherent qualities or of any hint whatsoever of fetishization. In our culture the sphere of the actual object has traditionally been confused with its naming and the inherent qualities of the object confused with the emotive force of its naming."[47] Cultural difference here provides Prigov with a fetishized object for conceptual play. The fetishization of the word as such and the fetishization of Russian cultural difference allow Prigov to claim that Russian art is really ahead of "Western conceptualism," which "should be more rightly termed *protoconceptualism*."[48] Like Russian theorist Mikhail Epstein, who claimed priority for Russian postmodernism in the lexicon that became increasingly dominant in the latter half of the 1980s in Russia and the West, Prigov echoes Cold War competition over who is most advanced. His tongue-in-cheek avant-gardist appeal to progress in art transforms the impoverishment and political restrictions of the Soviet space into a strength, just as he had earlier insisted that his typescript samizdat works, including the *Poemographs*, were diminished by publication in a glossy Western magazine. Prigov also implicitly refers to the hyperbolic claims for precedence in Russian modernism and to the innovative outsider position that artists from Russia, such as the Russian Futurists, adopted in the modernist period, and that they have continued to perform.[49]

At the same time, Prigov undermines this neat opposition between East and West by arguing that "no single idea arising in the sphere of culture can lay claim to the possession of ultimate truth." He implies that one should be wary of the assured, scholarly way he defends the opposition by describing his own metacommentary on his writing in the prefaces that frequently frame his work as "pretending to reassure with something like the customary scholarly . . . interpretation," and as "clothing" his texts in "philosophical discussion."[50] Instead, Prigov presents the East/West binary as itself a discursive system available for conceptual play, noting in the same interview his interest in archetypal constructions of the kind "us—them," "here—there," "friend—foe."[51] The first two are present in the dichotomy between Western conceptualism and Russian conceptualism. The third is also implicit in the Cold War framing of this opposition, frequently invoked elsewhere in his writing, as in his first *Azbuka* and in his poetic cycle "Reagan's Image in Soviet Literature."[52] More directly, the opposition is undermined by his simultaneous claims that in Russia "the actual object has traditionally been confused with its naming" and that conceptualism and other imported concepts "relate to their Western kin only in name."[53] The former point suggests that relating "only in name" is in fact the only kind of relation in "objectless" Russia, so that the terms of the opposition undermine the opposition itself, a paradox embodied in his АЯ-RA *Poemographs*, which present Roman and Cyrillic scripts as mirror images of each other and transform the letter or word into a fetishized cultural object and vice versa.[54] Likewise, by reproducing and intersecting the languages of Russian national identity, avant-garde innovation, and Cold War competition, Prigov's discussion of the differences between Western and Russian conceptualism sets up "weird, sometimes illicit, connections that contravene accepted norms" of the kind that he believes conceptualism establishes.[55]

An untitled poem published in 1990, just a year before the collapse of the Soviet Union, presents the conceptualist poet as staging a similarly strange set of parallels and connections at the intersection between the lyric assertion of singularity—"but I"—and national concepts and ideologies themselves in flux at this moment of geopolitical change:

> В Японии я б был Катулл
> А в Риме был бы Хоккусаем
> А вот в России я тот самый
> Что вот в Японии—Катулл
> А в Риме—чистым Хоккусаем
> Был бы

> In Japan I'd be Catullus
> But in Rome I would be a Hokusai
> But in Russia I am the one
> Who in Japan Catullus
> But in Rome a pure Hokusai
> Would be[56]

The poem employs a seemingly simple substitution: I would be [national poet/artist A] in country B, and [national poet/artist B] in country A. This structure suggests a serial form resembling those found in many of Prigov's works. Further pairings of artists, poets, and nations might include England's Shakespeare and Alexander Pushkin, whose central position in Russian culture is explored in many of Prigov's works. The poem connects this potentially serial form to the discursive systems of Russian thought and literature: its implicit claim to a privileged position between East and West reproduces a commonplace strategy from the Eurasianists to Osip Mandelstam's modernist use of multiple masks.

Yet the poem is complicated by contradictions, inexact parallels, noncorrespondences, and awkwardly forced grammatical parallelisms and oppositions, all of which undermine its apparently machine-like model of endless substitution and its conformity to this Russian cultural commonplace. The lyric subject asserts a world-encompassing yet unoriginal ambition, claiming uniqueness only by modeling himself on others whose positions are themselves not entirely parallel. Catullus's reputation in Japan is unlikely to be exactly the same as Hokusai's in Rome, and neither are they parallel figures within their own countries. Whereas Catullus is seen within the Western tradition as a classic of Latin lyric poetry, Hokusai's cultural prominence within Western art is largely a product of his Western, especially French, nineteenth-century reception and contrasts with his much lower reputation within Japan.[57] Italy in any case would be more properly parallel to Japan, unless we are to read this as a reference to the Rome of antiquity, in which case talk of Hokusai would be absurdly anachronistic. In fact, by switching to the instrumental case for Hokusai (*Khokkusaem*), the poem implies this distinction. The instrumental case suggests an indefinite, undefined subject—a conceptual Hokusai who might have lived in Rome two thousand years ago—in contrast with the definiteness of the nominative, historically actual Catullus.[58]

Like the lack of grammatical parallelism between Catullus and Hokusai, the subjunctive verbal form contributes to the grammatical awkwardness of the poem. It emphasizes that the situation described in the poem is one of pure potential, in which propositional and possible states exist outside or surround and unsettle any statements of truth, correspondence, or reality. (See the way the, "*byl by*," "would be," of the second and last lines surrounds the copula, "am," here.) The propositional, potential state appears outside the poetic form, because the conditional *byl by* in the last line breaks the poem's regular meter, a device so common in his poetry that it is sometimes called the "Prigov line."[59] As in Prigov's hyperbolic description of the Policeman who is visible from every present position, the lyric subject here becomes an abstract, indefinite, and all-encompassing archetype no longer tied to his actual location in Moscow or Russia, an abstraction that leads to an absurd, confused end. In each case, the claim to global fame is undercut. Just as the poem doesn't fit into its form, the "I" fits nowhere, as underlined by his awkward assertions about his own position.

But Prigov's undermining of self-creation and nation also acts as a form of supra-self-creation that appeals to the very imperialist notions it seems to dissolve. The allusion to Pushkin and the direct references to Catullus and Hokusai humorously self-aggrandize the poet and artist Prigov who claims to encompass them all. Alluding to his country's imperial status—its capital envisaged as the third Rome and its borders stretching from Europe to Japan—Prigov figures Russia as the home of conceptual play not through a strict serial template but through a series of false oppositions. He thus highlights parallel systems of world literature and world art that do not easily map onto one another. The poem insists on continuous interplay between such systems effected by a person who stands at their intersection—who asserts "but I" against the *a*-to-*z* comprehensiveness of any single world-encompassing view.

Like Pushkin, whose international fame is no rival for Hokusai's, Prigov in his work of the 1970s and 1980s depended on his local context: on the Russian cultural status of the poet and samizdat literary culture. He therefore faced a barrier to engagement with the international art market, unlike those artists who relied primarily on visual material and recognizable signs. Although a few of Prigov's *Poemographs* were published in the first issue of *A-Ya* in 1979, most had to wait for the first and only literary edition of the journal. Other works were excluded entirely, reflecting the tension between Prigov's increasingly frequent literal and artistic border-crossing and his reliance on the linguistic and cultural particularity of Russia for his conceptual play.

Prigov's work highlighted the difficulty of translation across cultures and languages, a difficulty that became increasingly apparent as the exchange value of contemporary Russian art increased in the perestroika era. For example, Grisha Bruskin's *Fundamental'nyi leksikon* (*Fundamental Lexicon*; 1986) sold for almost half a million dollars at the 1988 Sotheby's auction in Moscow. Although Bruskin was not considered part of the movement by some other Russian conceptualists, his work's use of clichéd Soviet images became a figure for Russian conceptualism after Sotheby's chose *Fundamental Lexicon* for the cover of its sales catalog.[60] Like Zhang Hongtu and Kosolapov, Bruskin made a play of his work being both easily understood and exotically Eastern, thus emphasizing its tradability: concept as commodity. Prigov's texts likewise highlight exchange value and translation, but as in his trade with Catullus and Hokusai, they utilize particular elements of Russian culture, language, and literature. They emphasize differing values and unequal and multiple systems of exchange—problems Prigov confronted directly in the 1990s in the face of the transformation of Russian literature and the collapse of its cultural centrality in the new, post-Soviet era.

AFTERLIFE

In 1989, changes unfolding in Eastern Europe marked the end—and burial—of an era. In August, soon after the historic Polish elections, Prigov attended the conference "Language—Consciousness—Society." Organized by the Leningrad-based group Poetic Function, of which Dragomoshchenko was a member, the conference brought together Russian sociologists, scientists, and writers, and also drew participants from abroad, including Hejinian and other US poets. One of these poets, Kent Johnson, recalls how during the conference he was presented with a curious object: "I have a gift for you, said Dmitri Prigov, and he handed me a manila envelope. . . . I opened the envelope and peered inside. . . . I pulled out seven, no, nine small stapled bundles, each with a typed word or three on the outside. . . . Ah, he said, They are Little Coffins of Poems, and inside each is a poem, but these little coffins may never be opened, for this would be of course disrespectful to the deceased."[61] Another of these poets, Michael Davidson, similarly describes a "small packet, stapled on all sides, containing, [Prigov] says, fragments of his poems torn into tiny confetti." For Davidson, this packet was a metaphor for both the torn-up city filled with "trenches and potholes" and the "change of weather," the shift in political climate that enabled writers previously divided by the Iron Curtain to meet. Writing alongside Davidson in the book *Leningrad*, Hejinian interpreted Prigov's gift in two contexts—Soviet censorship and social animosity to poetry: "If the state tore up the poems, the cultural context is one in which poetry represents a challenge and a conflicting picture of power. If the people tore the poems, the cultural context has turned poetry into litter." Hejinian's interpretation suggests that the work appealed to a particular image of dissident Soviet literature abroad and yet could also be read in a proto-post-Soviet context.[62] Situated on the borderline between such cross-cultural readings, at the intersection of poetry and contemporary art, and at a

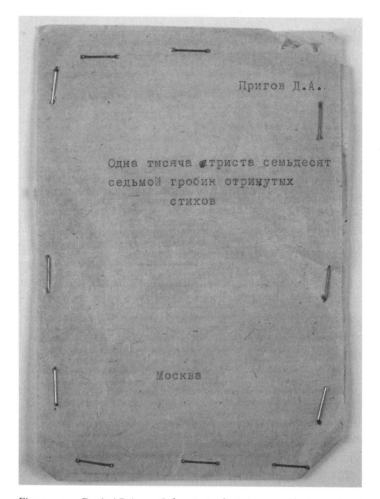

Figure 12.   Dmitri Prigov, *Odna tysiacha trista sem'desiat sed'moi grobik otrinutykh stikhov* [The one thousand three hundred and seventy-seventh little coffin of rejected verse], n.d. Paper, staples, typescript text, 14.7 x 10.5 cm. Photo courtesy of the Moscow Museum of Modern Art. Reproduced with the permission of the Estate of Dmitri Prigov.

moment of historical transition, Prigov's *Grobiki otrinutykh stikhov* or *Little Coffins of Rejected Verse* (fig. 12) emphasized the belatedness of poetry and samizdat in the face of the stagnation and demise of the Soviet Union, while also functioning as a commentary on late-Soviet samizdat culture.

Kent Johnson was to edit an anthology of Russian poetry in English translation, *The Third Wave,* conceived at the time of the conference but only published after the collapse of the Soviet Union. In the prefatory piece to his work in this volume, Prigov lists the *Little Coffins,* along with the *Poemographs,* as examples of how "just as conceptualism in the fine arts was marked by a strong verbalization of visual space, a similar process occurred in literature: texts were often transformed into three-dimensional, manipulable objects, so that many of them could be defined as a particular type of art only by virtue of the author's directly designating them so."[63] The *Little Coffins* comprise stapled paper packages containing Prigov's "rejected verse," either on a whole sheet of paper or in confetti-like strips.[64] The packages with their hand-typed covers resemble samizdat books. And in their size, they mirror especially Prigov's many small-format samizdat publications, which he termed *Mini-buks,* though of course the *Little Coffins* cannot be opened and read without damaging their encasement. Numbering in their thousands, Prigov's *Little Coffins* parody the exuberant textual excessiveness of samizdat culture—the "graphomania" that Prigov celebrates and parodies in his own vast poetic output (he aimed to produce 24,000 poems by the year 2000, one for each month of the two millennia).[65] Yet the package-books are sealed and coffin-like, suggesting the burial of Russian culture in samizdat under the system of Soviet censorship that condemned many texts to the death of nonpublication.

While satirizing and celebrating Soviet samizdat culture, the *Little Coffins* gained new currency in the late-Soviet moment when the conduits of exchange between Russian and Western contemporary art and literature broadened from isolated initiatives such as *A-Ya.* They came to stand for the burial of Soviet culture as a result of the liberalization of publishing. They also represented Prigov's own rebuilding (perestroika) and rearticulation of that culture through works that appealed to the exchange value not of words on the page, but of contemporary art operating within a globalized market system. Davidson finds in the *Little Coffins* "signs of community, in many cases, among total strangers," so expressing, like Hejinian, the dream of a transnational poetic collectivity that would unite East and West under the utopian signs of Russian modernism. But as Davidson also wryly notes, Prigov's card was "written in roman characters, as though for Western export." Seen in this light, the *Little Coffins* are the ultimate globally marketable local product for a poet whose work would otherwise be limited to a Russian audience, since one cannot—and in fact must not—read them.

The *Little Coffins* suggest a parallel between the subsuming of local particularities in a new global system and the negation of authorial agency. As with much of Prigov's work—and many recent English-language conceptual texts—they are characterized by a template structure that can produce a potentially endless volume of material. These serial conceptual writings highlight the comprehensiveness of structures or systems imposed by theoretical thinking, suggesting a totalizing treatment of linguistic material that seems to reduce the author to a cog in the linguistic machine. The sealed packages underscore the apparent death of the author by condemning the poet's words to the graves or coffins of the work's conceptual design, and sealing the local, belated poetic product within the globally marketable packaging of contemporary art.

But positioned between Soviet samizdat culture and the international art market, the *Little Coffins* stand at the intersection of multiple systems and so offer the possibility of an afterlife such as that proposed by the responses of the three US poets. In their very undead form and parasitic relation to their "deceased" verse, the *Little Coffins* evoke Benjamin's concept of "afterlife" or *Nachleben*. Conforming to this concept, the post-Soviet afterlife of the *Little Coffins* interrupts the given, by stressing the continuous reworking of historical understanding at a moment of historical, social, and geopolitical change.[66] The *Little Coffins* come to be read as addressing globalization, reframing their earlier examination of the fetishized samizdat text as a figure for the fragility of human life, the obsession with the poet's or artist's every word, and the figurative and literal death of the poet within the Russian literary tradition.[67] The buried samizdat poem outlives the samizdat text in the post-Soviet era by becoming a kind of calling card for Prigov's position at the juncture of late-Soviet dissident culture, Soviet ideology, post-Soviet Russian nationalism, and the global art market.

Underscoring the burial of samizdat culture and the end of the esteemed cultural status of the poet, Prigov foresaw at this time the "complete disappearance of Russian literature as a significant sociocultural phenomenon," describing this national transformation, in the world historical terms of the moment, as "a global catastrophe."[68] Prigov linked cultural catastrophe to cross-cultural exchange in his 1995 book *Iavlenie stikha posle ego smerti* (*The Appearance of Verse after Its Death*). Like the *Little Coffins*, this book seemingly presents the results of how, in Prigov's words, those "writers fighting for Europeanization of Russia, that is, as we know a priori, the writers possessed by quite noble and progressive impulses . . . are digging their own graves."[69] The title cycle "23 iavleniia stikha posle ego smerti" ("23 Appearances of Verse after Its Death"), dated 1991, clearly associates the end of the Soviet Union with the "death" of poetry, while undercutting such apocalyptic thinking through absurdist humor. The title cycle begins with what is described as "a poem that deeply affected me in my childhood, although it was written 50 years later."[70] Other poems are presented as translations, as in the case of a poem said to be an impromptu translation from the English by a friend who "did not understand a word" of what he was reciting.[71] Such translations of incomprehensible languages and rewritings of imagined pasts propose an afterlife for poetry rearticulated and transformed by Russia's changed relations to the wider world and to its own history.

Like the *Little Coffins*, which stage the death of poetry through its transformation into contemporary art, *The Appearance of Verse after Its Death* as a whole underscores the intersection between the Russian literary tradition and the international marketplace by mixing text with a series of Prigov's drawings. Each drawing is attributed to a different artist and a different language and sometimes a different script: "Deutsch" by Kandinsky, "Chinese" by Miró, "Japanese" by Bosch (fig. 13), and so on. These drawings, all dated 1993, present the language or nationality in white on dark crosshatch. The crosshatch style, ubiquitous in Prigov's art, combines here with the crosshatching of names and languages producing intersecting lines of unexpected combinations that signal the new and confusing relationship between Russian culture and a rapidly globalizing world.

Prigov's post-Soviet work of the 1990s emphasizes such exchanges and substitutions and links them to both the new capitalist situation and cross-cultural comparison. For example, *Ischisleniia i ustanovleniia (Calculations and Determinations*; 2001) presents prose equations and indexes of value such as the following: "If the quality of taste of a watermelon is taken as 1, then a herring must also be given a 1. Red caviar from 1.1 to 0.8. Brown bread 0.8. When it is slightly toasted it reaches 0.89. But toasted and then cooled down makes it immediately a 0.7."[72] These playful lines focus on value systems with exchangeable units as in commercial transactions. They take commensurability and exactitude to absurd levels.

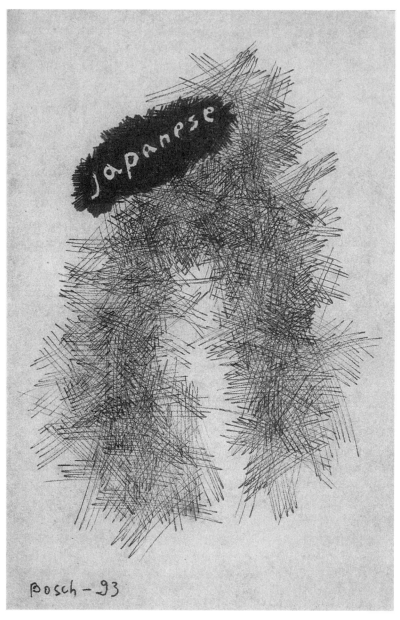

Figure 13.   Dmitri Prigov, illustration from *Iavlenie stikha posle ego smerti* [The appearance of verse after its death] (Moscow: Tekst, 1995), 27. Reproduced with the permission of the Estate of Dmitri Prigov.

Figure 14. Dmitri Prigov, Natalia Mali, and Andrei Prigov (PMP Group), performance still from *V storonu otsa* [Toward the father], 2003. Reproduced from the exhibition catalog *PMP-pozitiv; ili, Rekonstruktsiia po kasatel'noi / PMP-Positive; or, Tangential Reconstruction* (Moscow: Gosudarstvennyi tsentr sovremennogo iskusstva / National Centre for Contemporary Arts, 2004). Reproduced with the permission of Natalia Mali, Andrei Prigov, and the Estate of Dmitri Prigov.

Focusing on comparison and commensurability, Prigov frequently produces intersections between national culture and quantifiable values that can be exchanged. For example, "If the value of Russian literature is defined as 1, then Chinese reaches 0.99. German gets to 0.89. English to 0.87. French literature 0.785. Spanish and Italian each get 0.75. I reach 0.31."[73] "Raschety s zhizn'iu" ("Accounts with Life") implies a link between the application of numerical values, exchange, and an international comparative perspective, listing meals consumed in museums in various cities, the cost of these meals, and their value in other senses. One meal costs 15 gilders but the "feeling" is worth "around 60 gilders."[74] Unlike the strict blandness of earlier pieces that employ financial accounts, such as his *Savings Book*, this work presents Prigov as a globetrotting international artist by tracing his visits to various galleries around the world.[75] In this way, the exchange of Soviet ideology for the global marketplace replaces one world-encompassing system ("To the West and to the East looks the Pliceman")

Figure 15.   Dmitri Prigov, Natalia Mali, and Andrei
Prigov (PMP Group), photograph of the performance
Obliteriruiushchee omovenie [An obliterating ablu-
tion], 2004. Ink-jet on canvas. Reproduced from the
exhibition catalog *PMP-pozitiv; ili, Rekonstruktsiia
po kasatel'noi / PMP-Positive; or, Tangential Recon-
struction* (Moscow: Gosudarstvennyi tsentr sovre-
mennogo iskusstva / National Centre for Contempo-
rary Arts, 2004). Reproduced with the permission of
Natalia Mali, Andrei Prigov, and the Estate of Dmitri
Prigov.

with another (marks, gilders, krones, dollars, and pounds). But as
always in his work, by applying such a system to an absurd extent,
Prigov stresses its failure to encompass the world.

Late in his life, Prigov worked increasingly on the borderlines
between media, linking photography, video, live performance, and

poetry through the figure of Dmitri Prigov himself.[76] Recalling his use of the transcendent Russian poet hero in his 1970s work, in a performance featured in a 2004 exhibition of the Prigov Family Group (later renamed PMP Group), Prigov becomes a literal icon, whose portrait is worshipped by his son, Andrei Prigov, and Andrei's wife, Natalia Mali (fig. 14). In a video performance included in this same exhibition, he takes an embodied, though heavenly, form: he has his feet bathed like Christ while dressed as a Bosch-like angel-monarch (fig. 15). The angel garb exemplifies the way Prigov frequently transgresses gender norms.[77] But the poet is also cast in the role of father to the family that includes his son and daughter-in-law.[78] The person Prigov and the poet Prigov symbolize authority and power, reinforced through conventional gender and generational relations. By combining the figures of poet, angel, and father, Prigov produces an intersection between national literary and religious traditions and the consolidation of the conservative concept of family as nation in Russia, which was crystallized in the year following the performance by the founding of the nationalist youth movement Nashi (Ours).

Prigov reinforces the relationship between authoritarianism and poetic authority, evident in Soviet-era works such as his policeman poems and his first *Azbuka*, in the performance video *Narod i vlast' sovmestno lepiat obraz novoi Rossii* (*The People and the State Together Are Building an Image of the New Russia*), also featured in the 2004 Prigov Family Group exhibition. In this performance, Prigov, wearing an officer's hat, builds a clay model, assisted by his half-naked son (fig. 16). The video combines Prigov's most famous poetic persona, the policeman, with the authoritarian nationalism of the "new Russia." If with "the abolition of censorship and disappearance of real policemen . . . the conceptual Policeman also becomes obsolete," then both conceptual and real policemen return in the 2000s, the latter most notably in the guise of former KGB officer Vladimir Putin.[79]

The work "Stikhi dlia Dzhordzhika" ("Verses for George"), which concludes the exhibition catalog, reinforces Prigov's return to his 1970s and 1980s theme of the special cultural status of poetry in Russia, but here again the theme is rearticulated in the new historical moment, taking on an afterlife shaped by the post–Cold War era of globalization. "Verses for George" comprises the opening lines of some of the most well-known Russian poems repeated verbatim except that in each case the subject or addressee is replaced by the word *Dinozavr*, or

Figure 16.   Dmitri Prigov, Natalia Mali, and Andrei Prigov
(PMP Group), video still from *Narod i vlast' sovmestno
lepiat obraz novoi Rossii* [The people and the state together
are building an image of the new Russia], 2003. DVD, 8
minutes. Reproduced with the permission of Natalia Mali,
Andrei Prigov, and the Estate of Dmitri Prigov.

"Dinosaur," as in the opening lines of Pushkin's masterpiece *Eugene
Onegin*: "My Dinosaur has most honest principles" (*Moi Dinozavr sa-
mykh chestnykh pravil*).[80] The effect is of course extremely humorous,
and as a result Prigov used it as a performance piece.[81] The humor is
increased because "Dinozavr" with its three syllables creates a clumsy
break in rhythm from the mainly iambic lines, a stylistic signature of
Prigov's verse.[82] In his foreword to "Verses for George," Prigov pres-
ents the work as marking the post-Soviet shift in the cultural status
of poetry. He frames the verses as his solution to the problem of how
to teach his nephew the classics of Russian poetry in an era of global
popular culture, symbolized here by his nephew's "dinosaur mania,"

an affliction that, Prigov emphasizes, crosses national, religious, and ideological boundaries.

Just prior to the exhibition, Prigov had emphasized in an interview how the cultural position of poetry had been replaced by rock and pop stars, so that people no longer knew "hundreds if not thousands" of poems by heart. "Efforts to move into boundary zones—performance or visual—which could provide the best opportunities for the expansion of [poetry's] audience—have not been accepted by the literary milieu (still inevitably wedded to the culture of the nineteenth century) and have simply been absorbed by the musical and visual communities because of their current domination of mass culture."[83] The dinosaur poems exemplify the kind of performance works unlikely to be accepted by many in the literary establishment. They also emphasize Prigov's insistence in the interview that the problem is not exclusively Russian but pervasive "throughout the world"—a view that itself ironically recalls the universal pretensions of the literary tradition apparently realized in his rewriting of Russian literary classics for a global audience.[84]

And yet the dinosaur poems tell a somewhat different story. "Verses for George" is the only part of the exhibition catalog for which an English translation is not provided. Rather than marking the erasure of local traditions in the face of a global system, the work depends on the intersection between the universal ambitions of the Russian literary tradition and the apparently universal appeal of dinosaurs to young children. "Verses for George" acts as an untranslatable symbol for the father and the fatherland, figured through the poet passing on tradition to the next generation, even as it intersects with the global phenomena of dinosaur mania and contemporary art.

For all the renewal of poetry after its apparent death in the dinosaur poems, when I interviewed Prigov in Moscow in 2006, just a year before his own death, he insisted that poetry itself was passé, that he produced not poems but "contemporary art," shifting to English to express the term.[85] In another late piece that recalls the themes of the Prigov Family Group exhibition, the video "opera" *Rossiia* (*Russia*; 2004), Prigov returns to his relation to Western conceptualism to emphasize this renunciation of poetry (never actually realized), again marking the encounter between national traditions and global art. Accompanied by a soundtrack of slow-tempo, quasi-romantic piano music, the short film comprises Prigov's attempts to make a cat say the word "Rossiia" or "Russia" to comic effect. The film concludes when Prigov is joined by his son, and the two then sing "Russia" to-gether. The piece alludes to *Interview with a Cat* (1970) by Marcel Broodthaers, who, like Prigov with his *Little Coffins*, had staged his transformation from a poet to a visual artist by turning his books into sculptural work that rendered them unreadable. Where Broodthaers talks to his cat about conceptual art, however, Prigov combines West-ern conceptual art practice with repetitive nationalist ideology.[86]

Prigov's return to the subject of Russian nationalism and Western conceptual art coincides with the revival of conceptualism not as an artistic but as a literary practice in the United States. Led by writ-ers such as Kenneth Goldsmith (like Prigov, a sculptor-turned-poet) and hailed by influential critics such as Marjorie Perloff as the new twenty-first-century poetics, conceptual writing became the most influential avant-garde poetry of the first decade of the new millen-nium. Yet for all that Goldsmith and Perloff insist that conceptual poetry builds on historical precedents from various countries and adopts a principled "unoriginal" or "uncreative" approach, neither cites Prigov's precedent.[87] Perloff's omission of Prigov perhaps re-flects her assertion in the early 1990s that his conceptualism de-pended on the romantic concept of "psychological depth" and so was "almost the antithesis of the conceptualism of our sixties and seventies, which rejected the notion of hidden meaning outright." Her distinction in turn derived from Groys's Cold War–inflected opposition, which was mapped out over two decades before the rise of US conceptual writing.[88] When in his introduction to the 2011 anthology of conceptual writing *Against Expression* (coedited with Goldsmith) Craig Dworkin mentions Prigov's example, it comes as no surprise therefore that he does so only to warn that it "should not to be confused" with conceptual writing.[89] This is despite the fact that Dworkin, like Groys some thirty-four years earlier, cites Men-ard's act of copying "word for word and line for line" as an exem-plary forerunner of conceptual practice.[90]

The binary opposition between Russian and Western conceptual-ism continues to resonate today, despite its being playfully parodied in many of Prigov's works and undermined by the myriad connec-tions and parallels between his and recent US conceptual writing. Despite Perloff's claim that conceptual writing reflects a new "inde-terminacy . . . of location" in the age of the Internet, the opposition demonstrates the persistence of national difference and Cold War–derived East/West binaries in the discourse of globalization.[91] As

Prigov's work and US conceptual writing illustrate, no reproduction or repetition—even when "word for word"—is ever quite the same: the afterlives of a text, an image, or a person are manifold. Meaning always depends on location, on a context that changes from place to place and from one historical moment to the next. Yet as conceptualist strategies of repetition and appropriation underscore, neither is that local context ever entirely separate from intersections with other contexts, places, and times.

Prigov's work offers a model for reading the contemporary world that depends on neither absolute sameness nor total strangeness, on neither local difference nor global culture, but on a complex cross-hatching of various traditions and discursive systems, each with local associations and global ambitions. Prigov highlights, as he puts it, "the absurdity of the total ambitions inherent in the desire . . . to capture and describe the entire world."[92] He questions both reading strategies that seek to transcend the discourses with which they play, and those that emphasize their complete enmeshment in an all-encompassing system. He negotiates among various systems through which the world might be read, including the familiar binaries of similar and different, original and derivative, traditional and modern, extinct and newborn, belated and advanced, East and West, living and dead. Prigov estranges any one national position or global vision, generating many lines of languages, media, economies, ideologies, and histories whose singular points of intersection are ultimately undefined.

CHAPTER SIX

Charles Bernstein
and Broken English

The skips on the record which our pounding feet accentuate, making
the needle dance out of synch to the rhythm our bodies seem to want to
keep . . . —keep us honest.

—CHARLES BERNSTEIN, "The Conspiracy of 'Us'"

. . . . Terrorism
in the defense of free enterprise is no vice; violence
in the pursuit of justice is no virgin. This is
what distinguishes American and Canadian verse . . .
. . . .
Half the world thinks the night will never end
while another half sweats under the yoke of unrelenting
brightness. It's time to take our hats off
and settle in. The kettle's on the stovetop, the
centuries are stacked, like books, upon the shelf.
Bunt, then buzz.

—CHARLES BERNSTEIN, "Being a Statement on Poetics for the New Poetics
Colloquium of the Kootenay School of Writing,
Vancouver, British Columbia, August 1985"

Charles Bernstein is perhaps best known for the satirical mode that
this second epigraph exemplifies. Nevertheless, he is often read as a
serious commentator on literary studies and its recent global turn, an-
ticipated here by his application of the language of Cold War–era in-
ternational relations to poetry. Satire and seriousness are not uncom-
mon bedfellows, but the attribution of a serious statement to a given
satire is always the product of interpretation, of how one reads. Al-
though his essays have made a major contribution to the comparative
and transnational turn in US literary and cultural studies, Bernstein
himself warns against a reduction of his satirical or other variegated

styles to direct statement by repeatedly insisting on the importance of the mode of communication—or poetics—to the message conveyed.[1] Bernstein's writing emphasizes the place of rhetoric in thinking comparatively and cross-culturally and in addressing the relation of literature and culture to globalization. From his essays on Ezra Pound in the 1980s and on global poetics in the 1990s and 2000s to his response to the invasion of Iraq by the United States and its allies in 2003, he underscores not just the what but the *how* of literature, comparison, and history. Addressing the changes wrought between the late–Cold War era and the post-9/11 world, his work stages the interplay between political statement and poetic diversion. He invites and promotes readings that stress social, historical, and political location and those that emphasize a text's transcendence of its location through what he calls "commonness . . . in . . . partiality."[2]

Bernstein's writing foregrounds the rhetorical dichotomy that continues to dominate comparative thought: the binary between commonness and strangeness that shapes the way we understand both our recent past and our current era. On the one hand, his texts address the dichotomy between aesthetic and ideological readings of contemporary literature and culture. On the other hand, they tackle the related problem of the loss of affect in the distant reading practices that a global perspective seems to entail. Unlike the other writers considered here, Bernstein does not seek alternatives to these binaries but plays with and exacerbates them, insisting on their inescapability for a writer based in New York, at the heart of the world's geopolitical, economic, and cultural system.[3] Even so, Bernstein does offer a response to these entrapping dichotomies. His writing invites a mode of reading that operates between these two approaches, or what he terms "frames," deploying each to unsettle the other, to reveal its blind spots and assumptions.[4] This frame switching in turn produces moments of resonant dissonance—an "out of synch" dance—between the global distance of a superpower and the affective immediacy of a song of resistance.

GLOBAL FEELING

In a number of essays from the 1980s to the 2000s, Bernstein reworks the modernist appeal to transnationalism and dialect to propose a new global poetics based on nonstandard English. In Bernstein's framing, the Second World War and Auschwitz in particular provoke this comparative, spatial turn. These atrocities lead to a rejection of Enlightenment humanism, and with it notions of rationality and the universal subject. For Bernstein, to acknowledge the war entails the "death of . . . rationality as such."[5] What was already present in radical and dialect modernisms—in the "discovery of the entity status of language" and the "flattening of the Euclidian space of representing"—develops after the Second World War into "a more conscious rejection of a lingering positivist and romantic orientation toward, respectively, master systems and the poetic Spirit or Imagination as transcendent."[6] For Bernstein, this break necessitates a comparative, cross-cultural turn in poetry, a desire for "forms that find ways out of the Western Box."[7] Bernstein here refers to Charles Olson's writing on Mayan culture, through which Olson hoped to escape the "Western Box" within which, in his view, Ezra Pound was trapped.[8] Bernstein follows Olson in describing a cross-cultural impulse in the avant-gardes canonized by Donald Allen's anthology *The New American Poetry, 1945–1960* (1960). According to Bernstein, this New American Poetry rejects "a monoculturally centric point of view" found in the modernist mode of comparison exemplified by Pound, who assumed a position of mastery in relation to his use of non-European sources.[9]

Bernstein's prime examples of the escape from the Western Box are Jerome Rothenberg's anthologies, to which he returns again and again, especially *Technicians of the Sacred* (1968) and *Shaking the Pumpkin* (1972). He describes these books as opposing the fixed identity of US literature through "a concerted assault on the primacy of Western high culture and an active attempt to find in other, nonwestern/nonoriental cultures, what seemed missing from our own."[10] More recently Bernstein cites Rothenberg's epic cross-cultural anthology *Poems for the Millennium* as the inspiration for his "99 Poets/1999" special issue of *Boundary 2*, which he in turn identifies as the starting point for his "Poetics of the Americas" essay and his follow-up piece "Our Americas: New Worlds Still in Progress."[11] The acknowledgement of cultural and historical others in these anthologies allows Bernstein to conceptualize the social as dialogue or conversation, rather than through fixed individual and group identity.[12]

While Bernstein praises the ideological critique implicit in Rothenberg's anthologies, he also draws on their emphasis on the unassailable alterity of poetry. Bernstein's early correspondence with Rothenberg evidences their interest in collectives and identities, especially their common Jewish heritage. It also exhibits their belief in the transcendent power of the word, showing that as a young poet in the mid-1970s, Bernstein was drawn to Rothenberg's *Technicians of the Sacred* for its emphasis on orality and the world-creating possibilities of all languages.[13] Rothenberg developed these ideas (which he termed "ethnopoetics") further through his journal *Alcheringa*, which in 1975 featured one of the first introductions to the emergent Language writing: a group of "language centered" texts selected and presented by Ron Silliman.[14] Corresponding with Rothenberg around this time, Bernstein connected Rothenberg's work to his own interest in transcribing recorded voices and their shared interest in the Jewish tradition, especially the Cabbala, which Bernstein associated with his view of the world-creating power of language: "my interest is in [the Cabbala] as poetry as myth, word as complete incarnation of structure of reality."[15] In his letters to Rothenberg, Bernstein cites the radically democratic and nonhierarchical implications of Rothenberg's *Technicians of the Sacred* and its introduction in particular. But Bernstein's appeal to a mystical-religious conception of language also indicates a more ambivalent attitude toward the appeal to other traditions, which he shares with Rothenberg and antecedents such as Pound. This ambivalence is evident in Rothenberg's "Pre-face" to *Technicians of the Sacred*. In the "Pre-face," Rothenberg disavows the use of the word "primitive" to describe the non-Western texts in the anthology, while simultaneously emphasizing the term in order to claim a special place for these poetries.[16] In this respect, Rothenberg continues a modernist tradition of appealing to the non-European other through the paradoxical rhetoric of the "mask of authenticity," in which the attributes of another culture are simultaneously adopted and distanced.[17] The title of Rothenberg's anthology itself underscores this tension between artifice ("technicians") and religious transcendence ("sacred"), between the particularity of different traditions and a universalizing and hegemonic conception of them as the "primitive" sources of the Western anthologist's transcendent, transcultural vision.

Bernstein's much noted refusal of fixed identity can be read as developing out of Rothenberg's, Olson's, and Pound's visions of a global poetics, even as he defines himself against their legacy. In language that he would reprise in his essays on Pound, Bernstein criticizes Olson's search for archaic, authentic origins, when "we can see in such worlds from which we are cut off only projections of ourselves writ large." Nevertheless, he approves of Olson's attempt "to

create a collaged 'hyperspace.'" Bernstein argues that Olson's attempt
failed because of his commitment to archaic origins and "one side of
a . . . dichotomy." He implies that he himself seeks to take up Olson's
"undone business" through an approach free from origins and com-
mitted to working both sides of each dichotomy, rather than stressing
seriousness over humor, or assurance over confusion.[18]

With his "vision of global culture, a poetry 'of a fundamental
human nature,'" Rothenberg offers Bernstein his most consistent
model, one that better seems to realize his vision of a "collaged 'hy-
perspace.'" Rothenberg perhaps more than any other poet exempli-
fies the continued attraction of transcultural or global poetics in US
post–Second World War avant-garde poetry.[19] His transculturalism
differs from Pound's and even Olson's in that his work as an antholo-
gist gives voice to multiple authors and traditions without subsuming
them under the name of a single writer. Yet he nevertheless maintains
a commitment to a transcultural poetics built upon a belief in a uni-
versal element of human culture. Such transcendent visions entail, as
in Pound, the subservience of various traditions to the anthologist's
or poet's master plan, so that in many of Rothenberg's anthologies,
"the usual markers of poetic identity drop away in the face of the
transitivity he produces by his disembedding of the poems from their
usual locations."[20] This effect has been central to new developments
in English-language avant-garde poetics over the last few decades and
to Bernstein's writing in particular.

Bernstein's centrifugal pull toward endlessly widening differ-
ence cannot avoid entirely the centripetal desires for poetic essence
or "fundamental human nature" in Pound, Olson, and Rothenberg.
Bernstein's historical account of the development of a multicultural
poetics similarly leads to an explicitly global vision and comparative
practice, which he calls "*ideolectical,* implying dialogue, dialogic,
ideology, ideolect, dialect, and dialectic." He explains that he uses
"the term first to talk about nonstandard English practices from the
point of view of African-American dialect poetry . . . moving from
there to the nonstandard, or what I would call ideolectical practices
of Gertrude Stein or Louis Zukofsky." Bernstein's dialectical and ide-
olectical poetries explicitly provide for comparison "on the basis of
this idea of nonstandardization involving examples from quite sep-
arate traditions."[21] Exchange with those who are different, foreign,
outside becomes for Bernstein the basis of an international commu-
nity of poetry, albeit one that would escape fixed identity.

Bernstein's global vision parallels comparative literature's disciplinary turn during the same period from Eurocentric and diachronic conceptions of comparison to those based on spatial contiguity and simultaneity. His account of ideolectical poetics hinges on differentiating his and Rothenberg's positions from their shared debt to the hierarchical, Eurocentric transnational modernism of an earlier era, associated especially with Pound, and from the homogenizing pressures of our current era of globalization. Likewise, contemporary comparative literature frames itself in relation to and against its rationalist, Eurocentric history and the current wave of globalization. The establishment of the discipline of comparative literature in the nineteenth century coincided and was intertwined with a project to bring together all knowledge within a grid-like hierarchical system.[22] This globally ambitious comparative literature has been revived recently "partly in response to the concerted critique of Eurocentrism over the last twenty years, and partly in response to the exigencies of the rapid pace of globalization in contemporary life."[23] While sharing a similarly global ambition, the new comparative literature differs from its nineteenth-century precursor in that it coincides with a critique of the earlier grid-like conception of knowledge as the basis of comparison. Instead, it emphasizes a spatial poetics of "sheer extensiveness" in which literatures are contiguous rather than equivalent in a way that neither reduces particularities "to equivalent forms nor induces a paralyzing incommensurability."[24]

Both Bernstein and those who wish to practice comparative literature on a global scale have, however, attracted criticism for their ideological complicity in the very modes of thinking that they disavow. The new global spatialization of comparison and Bernstein's comparative turn coincide with the rise of the rhetoric of multiculturalism and globalization and therefore encounter the same problem as the postcolonial theory from which they in part emerge. The global space of comparison "coincides with what is variously called late capitalism or globalization whose generalization of exchange value neutralizes the ideological resistance and the political consequence claimed for . . . culture."[25] The situation is, of course, further complicated for both comparative literature and Bernstein's new and newer American poetry by the particular position of the United States as the world's economic, cultural, and military superpower. For example, Wai Chee Dimock's spatialized reading of US literature "through other continents" and "deep time" does not clearly differ from modernist modes of spatialization and mastery.[26] Indeed, Dimock's stress on the relevance of Iraq's ancient and medieval past to the 2003 US-led invasion resembles Olson's turn to ancient Sumerian civilization with the same troubling insistence on the simultaneity of past and present.[27]

Bernstein's distinction between dialectical and ideolectical poetries—which itself recalls Rothenberg's distinction between "primitive" and supposedly nonprimitive poetries—seems to look back to the modernist binary between modernism and modernity in its "nostalgic wish for a return to formalism that turns out to conceal a disavowed identity politics."[28] More generally, comparative approaches predicated on distinctions between Europe and non-Europe, ideolect and dialect, or center and periphery easily become caught up in an entrapping dynamic: that is, a dynamic where difference itself becomes undifferentiated and the power relations involved in identificatory processes are ignored, as in Bernstein's discussions of writers like Kamau Brathwaite.[29]

Such criticisms of Bernstein and global comparison reflect a "fundamental" anxiety surrounding the ideological basis of cross-cultural thinking and the difficulty of differentiating new approaches from the homogenizing imperative of globalization and from critical antecedents who failed "to do justice to true alterity."[30] The anxiety is also evident in the way that contemporary theorists of global and transnational poetics are compelled to address and differentiate themselves from Pound.[31] The various ways that critics deal with these concerns highlight a dichotomy between the "theological and ideological styles of reading" dominant in literary and cultural studies today.[32] Theological readings are deeply mistrustful of any attribution of use value to literature, while ideological readings reduce literature to "its role in either obscuring or accentuating social antagonisms."[33] Both modes of reading are evident in the field of contemporary avant-garde poetry: some scholars favor an ideological hermeneutics of suspicion and others defend contemporary avant-garde poetry for its literary value in aesthetic terms.[34] The new comparative literature and Bernstein's global rhetoric seem to alternate between these binary positions. They present a utopian model of radical particularity and alterity in which the "literary" provides a privileged realm of resistance through its insistence on irony and endless figuration. But they are also subject to a symptomatic, suspicious, ideological reading, which argues that such notions of resistance conflate and so erase differences to produce exchangeable products within the process of capitalist globalization.

Yet in Bernstein's writing, the hermeneutics of suspicion, with its rhetoric of mastery and guarded borders, itself functions as a source of figuration, poetic play, and even affect. Refusing to allow an easy reading solely on either level, his poetics stresses the rhetorical structures not only of persuasion, ideology, and artifice, but also of affective absorption and "global feeling."[35] Read suspiciously, Bernstein's essays on Pound in the 1980s and on transnational poetics in the 1990s and 2000s illustrate this rhetorical continuity from the them-and-us oppositions of Cold War poetics to the appositional, multicultural rhetoric of the post–Cold War era. This continuity becomes more visible after 9/11 and is correspondingly accentuated in his response to the 2003 US-led invasion of Iraq. His writing neither opposes nor resolves the polarized approaches to comparative literature and global poetics. Instead it exacerbates the interplay between ideological critique and a theological belief in strangeness and difference. Through this oscillation, however, it also stages affectively the continuous movement between nearness and distance in global comparison, literature, and history.[36]

SUSPICIOUS READING

The problems of cross-cultural comparison and their relationship to the hermeneutics of suspicion are exemplified by Bernstein's preoccupation with Pound. In his readings of Pound, Bernstein argues for and against both theological and ideological hermeneutics of suspicion. He rejects the suspicious control and defense of literature as a realm of authorized culture and both propounds and rejects a hermeneutics of suspicion as the reading of literature for its ideological impulses. In this way, he invites each mode of reading and generates the third he implicitly advocates: one founded on a strangeness that eludes both confining approaches.

In his two essays on Pound, "Pounding Fascism" (1985) and "Pound and the Poetry of Today" (1986), Bernstein addresses Pound's fascist ideology and what he sees as its central role in *The Cantos*. In the first essay, he attacks the "special pleading" that has allowed critics to ignore or partition off Pound's fascism from his poetry. He argues that Pound has become a figurehead of modernism precisely because of his fascism. Pound's "fatherly voice of authority," according to Bernstein, supports the Eurocentric, hierarchical view of culture found in notions such as the "Core Curriculum."[37] Bernstein claims that although

Pound sought in *The Cantos* to assert a totalizing cultural authority transnationally and transhistorically—to express "a predetermined Truth of a pancultural elitism"—he actually ended up producing a poetry that resists such notions of authority. Pound's poetry exhibits "a compositionally decentered multiculturalism," in which radical particulars do not cohere. Bernstein describes how Pound in his *Cantos* sought "to create a work using ideological swatches from many social and historical sectors of his own society and an immense variety of other cultures." For Bernstein, "This complex, polyvocal textuality was the result of [Pound's] search—his unrequited desire for— deeper truths than could be revealed by more monadically organized poems operating with a single voice and a single perspective." Bernstein's Pound thus aimed to create a centripetal poetics that would draw all culture of value into its vortex to make an essential world or global poetics of "deeper truths." But according to Bernstein, this desire in fact led to its opposite: a centrifugal, "collage" poetics of nonessential multiplicity and difference—Pound's famous failure to make his work cohere.[38] *The Cantos*, in Bernstein's words, was ultimately "not the mastertext of modernism but the wreck of Enlightenment rationalism."[39] Pound's failure was his success.

Bernstein's apparently straightforward argument strongly invites if not demands a hermeneutically suspicious ideological reading through its own structure of internal self-contradiction. In his championing of Pound's technique, Bernstein ironically reinscribes the division between Pound's political thinking and his artistic practice even as he attacks this division as the source of an ongoing, deeply troubling, ideologically motivated misreading of Pound. Bernstein seems to conduct his own "special pleading" in order to present Pound's *Cantos* as the masterwork of an alternative anti-Enlightenment, antirationalist modernism or postmodernism. Likewise, Bernstein's concept of collage threatens to become merely another representation of literature as a realm outside ideology, of unlimited signification, like Roland Barthes's "infinity of language" or Umberto Eco's elaboration of Charles Peirce's idea of "unlimited semiosis."[40]

This hermeneutically suspicious reading of the essay is itself anticipated in Bernstein's advocacy of such a reading of Pound's poetry. Bernstein makes the case for the value of a hermeneutics of suspicion by following Robert Casillo's reading of *The Cantos* for their fascism, concluding that "to understand a work requires interrogating its motivations and social context."[41] Here Bernstein openly invites a reading of the essay's contradictions in its negotiation between an interpretive reading practice that would carefully guard against the uncovering of ideological motivations and one that would insist upon an ideological reading. Read in this way, Bernstein appears to perform what he describes: "some work may usefully evade any single social or political claim made for or against it because of the nature of its contradictions, surpluses, and negations."[42] By producing this self-contradiction, this estrangement from itself, Bernstein describes and enacts the self-extension—the common strangeness or "commonality and difference"—that literature can produce.[43]

Bernstein heightens this poetics of self-contradiction in the second essay, "Pound and the Poetry of Today." Here he reads Pound's *Cantos* as anticipating an alternative poetic practice that, while it runs directly counter to Pound's ideology, is the true "paradise" of his poetry—a paradise that Bernstein identifies with Rothenberg's *Technicians of the Sacred*.[44] Yet this utopian vision of post-Poundian poetics invites the questions Bernstein raises in his first essay. In his second Pound essay, Bernstein echoes the centric, dominating element in Rothenberg's *Technicians of the Sacred*, which builds a universal poetics on a them-and-us, primitives-and-moderns binary. He characterizes Pound's poetry as a liberatory, centrifugal "collage poetics," rather than the centric "montage" poetics for which Pound consciously aimed. For Bernstein, Pound's example leads to a "hyper- and hypo-American collage," a claim that apparently undermines his own argument that Pound's collage poetics led to the diffusion of a nationalist poetic ideology.[45] Bernstein presents, in his words, an "attempt to critique Poundian panculturalism with decentered multiculturalism" that participates in the very panculturalism to which it is opposed.[46] Reversing his reading of Pound, Bernstein reproduces the centric authority he claims to resist.

This reading is, however, again only a step toward opening up a reading of self-difference, of common strangeness—of how the essay renders something else not directly but indirectly in its very performative self-undermining. If the dominant literary-theoretical hermeneutics of suspicion, both theological and ideological, enforce a position of false objectivity by asserting a distrustful distance between scholarly analysis and immediate affective response or lay interpretation, Bernstein's essays on Pound mobilize these contrary strategies of reading simultaneously and in self-contradictory ways. By moving between "uncompromising wariness and hypervigilance" of Pound's fascism and a celebration of how his "polyvocal textuality" resists ideological reduction, Bernstein disrupts the distance and objectivity that these approaches were supposed to guarantee.[47] Recognizing this in "Pounding Fascism," Bernstein writes of the impossibility of a calm response to Pound by noting how the problem is not outside but "within oneself." "It is not," Bernstein says, "that it is prudent to fight fire with fire, but that one burns."[48] The incendiary nature of the situation suggests Bernstein's anger as a Jew and alludes to the destructive results of fascism in Europe in the murder and literal incineration of millions. In this way, the distancing strategies of the essay underscore the distancing of the Holocaust in Pound scholarship, as well as the inevitable problem of distancing in writing about its enormity. Through these multiple layers of distancing, however, the essay also makes a claim for the affective immediacy of the burning and so for the disavowal of objectivity in thinking, writing, and reading. This move also invokes the very politics of identity that Bernstein repeatedly rejects.

A decade after his essays on Pound, in "Poetics of the Americas" (1996), Bernstein returns to the same themes but in the context of globalization and multiculturalism rather than the culture wars and Cold War poetics of the 1980s. He links his attack on fixed individual and group identities to the rejection of essentialist notions of both the global and the local, or what he calls the "universalizing humanisms of internationalism and the parochialism of regionalism and nationalism." Instead, he describes a poetics that would transcend national borders without eliding difference:

> The impossible poetics of the Americas does not seek a literature that unifies us as one national or even continental culture. . . . Rather, [it] insists that our commonness is in our partiality and disregard for the norm, the standard, the overarching, the universal. Such poetry will always be despised by those who wish to use literature to foster identification rather than to explore it.[49]

Bernstein bases his claim for a "global poetics" on the very rejection of any singular poetics, of "the overarching, the universal," just as he asserts a conception of individuality and community that rejects the fixity sometimes associated with both these terms.

While the claim for "commonness . . . in our partiality" would seem to be radically inclusive of all poetries, the essay undermines this inclusivity by referring specifically and exclusively to the Americas. Bernstein presents not only the contradictory notion of commonness in partiality, but also the contradiction of inclusiveness tied to that well-known plank of US national ideology—so-called American exceptionalism. Moreover, this contradiction is itself part of US literature and culture—as in Whitman's claim to "contain multitudes" within a single "I" and the related founding national motto of "out of many, one." The motto "e pluribus unum" is of course most widely known for its appearance on US currency, which is in turn a critical element in the international system of trade and financial exchange associated with a homogenizing form of globalization.[50]

Reflecting these contradictions, some have criticized Bernstein's encompassing of diversity in "Poetics of the Americas," arguing that the essay presents the range of different poetries it cites "in univocal terms" through the "abstraction or relativizing of motives for discrepant uses of language."[51] Read in this way, Bernstein's transnational vision seems to ignore the "differences *between* national imaginaries" and the inescapable role that identity plays in our lives, illustrating the persistent "imaginations of a global avant-garde community" that allow "even mid- to late-twentieth-century discourses on cultural relativisms . . . to be read comfortably alongside unspoken assumptions in postmodern poetics that its overall project does or should transcend such boundaries."[52]

Yet these ideological critiques do not do full justice to the performative nature of this and other essays by Bernstein, though they again form a crucial step in opening the essay up to performative reading. Read performatively, the essay does in fact highlight the particularities of the US national imaginary through the emphases on exceptionalism and unity in diversity. Moreover, Bernstein makes extensive performative use of the tension between the liberating and the destructive homogenizing possibilities of a transnational poetics and his own problematic position as a US poet. Indeed, the use of the term "Americas" invokes precisely this duality. On the one hand, it challenges the use of "America" in the singular, when it is commonly taken as a synonym for the United States, much to the annoyance of the United States' North, Central, and South American neighbors. Instead, Bernstein's "Americas" asserts a more pluralistic, transnational outlook. On the other hand, as a US poet asserting a single, albeit impossible and multiple, poetics of the Americas, Bernstein performs the kind of homogenizing, transnational domination associated with US-based multinationals and the projection of US imperial power over the two continents of the Americas and beyond.

Bernstein's playful performance of the very positions he criticizes is particularly evident in a passage from the essay that highlights the issue of totalization as it transitions America from singular to plural:

> The problem here is twofold: the totalization of "America" and the globally dominant position of the U.S. Since the U.S. is the dominant English language (as well as Western) nation in the political, economic, and mass-cultural spheres, its monopolizing powers need to be cracked—from the inside and outside—as surely as one version of England's grip on our language's literature needed to be loosened in the nineteenth century and early twentieth century. The same logic that led to the invention of American, as distinct from English, literature now leads to the invention of, on the one hand, a non-American-centered English language literature and, on the other, a poetics of the Americas.[53]

By calling simultaneously for both "a non-American-centered English language literature" and "a poetics of the Americas," Bernstein implies the opposite of what he seems to claim. By undermining the notion of a unitary and hegemonic US literature through the call for a poetics of the Americas, he proposes a US-based "poetics of the Americas" that through its very openness would absorb not only "non-American-centered English language literature" but all other literatures as well. "America" becomes the United States through a US-centered discussion of a "Poetics of the Americas," and this more pluralistic conception of US literature then enables Bernstein's reassertion and enhancement of the "globally dominant position of the U.S." This position here extends beyond the geographic boundaries of the Americas to encompass, at the very least, the entire English-speaking world. In proposing a solution to the stated twofold problem, Bernstein actually redoubles it.

Bernstein's essay subsumes the particular poetries of the Americas under a global notion of "commonness in . . . partiality" in a process that resembles the way a generalized "elsewhere" tends to replace local particularities of language and culture in the reception of poetry in translation in the English-speaking world. The translated poem "comes to us as existing elsewhere" since it is assumed that "no matter how good the translation, there is an original that is always still better."[54] Bernstein's conception of "partiality" extends this notion of a generalized elsewhere and otherness to include not just poetry written in other languages but all nonstandard dialect or ideolect poetries. Exemplifying a theological mode of reading, Bernstein's claim for the literature of partiality's value depends on its common unassailable alterity, which is absolutely disconnected from its particular use value and location.

In "Poetics of the Americas," Bernstein plays between two possibilities for a global poetics. On the one hand, he emphasizes a generalized otherness or "elsewhere." On the other, through his use of US hegemonic rhetoric, he subsumes this "elsewhere" under economically and geopolitically determined "global structures of value," and performatively draws attention to the unequal terms of trade on which this system of value is based.[55] Bernstein's latter more properly globalized and homogenizing vision returns us to Stephen Owen's description of a possible "new identity for lyric poetry . . . not dependent on any particular national language"—a poetry produced by "common global structures of value" that mean "much of the world must play the game by rules . . . that are not of their making and in whose making they have no say." Such a poetics would remove all local particularity, so that "regional variation is replaced by a national style" analogous to the national cuisines found in a "food court" in a mall.[56] Yet Bernstein's own work has consistently opposed this kind of generic local color. Indeed, he has described some forms of multicultural poetics in terms that strongly resemble Owen's analogy of the food court, pointing out how local color often conceals a fundamental sameness. Bernstein argues that "works selected to represent cultural diversity are those that accept the model of representation assumed by the dominant culture in the first place." He demonstrates his point by giving a number of culturally specific variations on the theme of the line "I see grandpa on the hill / next to the memories I can never recapture."[57]

In "Poetics of the Americas," however, global homogeneity and generalized difference not only compete but also intertwine. Bernstein writes, "everywhere the local is under fire from the imposed standard of a transnational consumer culture and undermined by the imperative to extract it and export it as product."[58] Here Bernstein presents the imperatives of transnational trade as opposing the particularities of place, people, and culture and so the kind of poetics he advocates. But simultaneously, he writes approvingly of the Americas being "transected by innumerable overlaying, contradictory or polydictory, traditions and proclivities and histories."[59] Postcolonial studies "has capitalised on its perceived marginality while helping turn marginality itself into a valuable intellectual commodity."[60] Likewise, in opposing international poetic transactions to "transnational consumer culture," Bernstein ends up presenting poetry as just another kind of import-export business. Drawing on his frequently noted deployment of the rhetoric of business, fashion, and rapidly shifting poetic styles, Bernstein oscillates between the assertion of and resistance to US hegemony, enacting the circulation of money, goods, and styles in our increasingly globalized world.[61]

"Poetics of the Americas" points toward the creeping suspicion in literary and cultural studies that the structures of Enlightenment thinking will continue to divide the world into the West and the rest so long as this division is insidiously perpetuated even when seemingly opposed. From the romantic appeal to the folk, through modernist appeals to the so-called primitive, to the notion of hybridity in postcolonial theory, attempts to oppose a binary system of black and white rationality and order end up producing another dichotomy.[62] The turn to otherness, hybridity, partiality, and difference lies not outside this larger binary system but within it. In the tradition of the manifesto, Bernstein's essays highlight this system by acting out "both an affirmation of and a challenge to universalism" through the inescapable oscillation of their arguments between sameness and difference.[63] Yet at the same time, they also question this opposition through a playful poetics of self-contradiction.

My hermeneutically suspicious ideological approach here seems to produce a theological reading of Bernstein's poetics as a self-reflexive, self-sufficient aesthetic object that enacts the disruptive otherness for which it calls. Like Bernstein's poetics of "commonness . . . in . . . partiality," this theological reading insists on the performative qualities of these essays, on their affective immediacy, particularity, and partiality. Yet the self-reflexivity of these essays performatively underscores the complicity of these texts in the structures of global power they seek to oppose. They both invite and resist a political, ideological reading with its suspicious, anti-affective distancing of textual immediacy. Bernstein's Pound and Americas essays imply a connection between these oscillating readings and the concept of a global poetics. Through his appeals to a "multicultural poetics" or a "poetics of the Americas," Bernstein suggests that it is easy enough to conceive or know that the global totality exists, but that, as Jameson argues, one cannot engage with this totality at the level of "existential experience."[64] The global scale of comparative literature and of

Bernstein's poetics confront the annihilation of affect through comparison's "normative and generalizing activity."[65] Yet where contemporary literary and cultural studies remain locked between theological and ideological approaches, Bernstein's transnational poetics is more productive. Oscillating between global totality and local particularity, his writing generates singular affective encounters between these poles that emerge out of the ashes of their own destruction.

WHAT ARE YOU FIGHTING FOR?

The events of September 11, 2001, and the bellicose response of the United States raised the stakes in the competition between global distance and affective immediacy and between ideological and theological readings. In the United States, politicians appealed to the awful horror of the destruction of the Twin Towers in reviving the them-and-us rhetoric of the Cold War and giving free reign to the security services' suspicious readings for signs of the enemy. In his 2006 collection *Girly Man*, Bernstein responded with a widely noted shift to a seemingly more direct and accessible style.[66] Like Bernstein's essays, many of the poems seem to reach for the affective immediacy resisted in his earlier writing. This surface belies, however, a more distanced poetic, an affective dead zone that functions as a biting counterpoint to the poems' apparently accessible and personal style. Just as his Pound and Americas essays explore the interplay between ideological and theological readings in comparison and global poetics, so *Girly Man* highlights the related tension between the creation and negation of lyric affect.

Girly Man addresses the problem of affect perhaps most obviously through the inclusion of pieces written in the immediate post-9/11 period, in which Bernstein's persona-mask seems to slip to produce the "formulas that Bernstein has elsewhere attacked in his writing on writing."[67] In the context of *Girly Man*, however, what seems at stake in all these poems is the use of these formulas for transparency, directness, and simplicity. Bernstein highlights these formulas in the "Let's Just Say" sequence, alluding to William Carlos Williams's rhetoric of directness in "This Is Just to Say," and including what he claims to be "a totally / accessible poem" that is "all about / communication. / Heart to heart."[68]

The opening poem of "Let's Just Say" and of *Girly Man* as a whole, "In Particular," deploys apparently direct, simple language, while equally undermining its own claim to mimetic representation and affect through its emphasis on the exchangeability of the language employed. The poem performs the mundane everyday acts of group identification, which Bernstein would presumably associate with fostering identity rather than exploring it, the very position he seeks to oppose in "Poetics of the Americas." It presents in standard English the conventional racial, gender, and social divisions that his poetics of nonstandard individual particularity would seem to oppose. The poem begins with those most basic of reductive race and gender divisions: black and white, man and woman:

> A black man waiting at a bus stop
> A white woman sitting on a stool[69]

The poem continues for about one hundred lines with various forms of group identification, especially nationalities: "A Filipino eating a potato / A Mexican boy putting on shoes." With its invocation of multiple nationalities and of the "particular," the poem can be read as addressing the issues of group and individual identity and the related problems of transnational linkages and globalization. At one level, the poem presents a kind of "food court" of types analogous to the "food court" of world poetry described by Owen. The poem provides the reader with the particularities of a given individual and, simultaneously, undermines this notion of particularity. Through syntactic parallelism (A [human subject] + [predicate]) and nonspecific and sometimes hilarious descriptions, the poem invites the reader to replace one term of identification with another, say, "A Mexican" with "A Montenegrin" or "A Christian lady" with "A Chinese mother."[70] The poem places identity in circulation, presenting a United Colors of Benetton image of the world, in which local color is united through exchangeability (as in global fashion and trade), conventionalized identities, an analogously homogeneous application of standard English, and a repetitious syntactic form.

The poem's conclusion further emphasizes the exchangeability of its terms by providing an almost exact inversion of the opening two lines:

> A white man sitting on stool
> A black woman waiting at bus stop[71]

Yet there is one important and striking difference, easily lost in a quick scan but unmistakable when read aloud. The final two sentences lack the indefinite article *a* before their final nouns. This article is central to the poem: it begins each new line and so appears in visually arresting columns of *A*s down each page. Of course, the omission of the article in these final two lines draws the reader's attention to this indefinite article all the more. The indefinite article contradicts the title's claim to particularity, underscoring that these are not particular people but indefinite, generalized types. The omission of the indefinite article also moves the poem a step away from standard English, hinting more generally at what is missing from the poem—namely, particularity and diversity of language, especially the languages of the various peoples described.

Through this small omission that points to a much larger one, and by placing identity in circulation, the poem also undermines the fixed identities used to market "local color" or "Chinese food" in a US mall.[72] Like "Poetics of the Americas," "In Particular" dialectically employs exchange value, especially the exchange of terms naming a national or ethnic group, to highlight and undermine such notions of identity. And like "Poetics of the Americas" too, by performing the language of the dominant culture and drawing attention to this performance, the poem stresses what is left out.

In the third section in *Girly Man*, entitled *World on Fire*, Bernstein further explores the tension between ideologically suspicious distancing and affective proximity, moving from the ground zero of anti-affect in the opening section to a more complex engagement with lyric enunciation. *World on Fire* immediately follows the September 11 cycle "Some of These Daze" in *Girly Man* and was first published as a chapbook in 2004, when it was clearly located in the context of the US invasion of Iraq. The title of the cycle refers to the popular song "I Don't Want to Set the World on Fire," which, in the version recorded by the Ink Spots, became a hit after the Japanese bombing of Pearl Harbor in 1941.[73] Most of the poems from *World on Fire* draw on popular songs of the 1930s or 1940s. The one exception is "Broken English," the title of a well-known song by Marianne Faithfull:

BROKEN ENGLISH

What are you fighting for? The men move

decisively toward the execution chamber.
Joey takes aim but muffles his fire.

Overhead, the crescent moon cracks
the unbroken sky. A moth beats its wings
against the closed door—intransigence its

only lore. *What are you fighting for?* The sirens

cry wolf to the obedient masses who sway,
hysterical, in synch to the boys
on the back streets and the ladies of mourning.

Brushing up fate pixel by pixel, burnishing
dusk: the sum of entropy and elevation.

Tony takes it in his intestine, the sharp
pain in his body like ripples
in a sand dune, his face exquisitely detached

from any sign of the sensation. *What are
you fighting for?* The market plunges, savings

slip away like a greased pig in a taffy
pull. Sometimes the easiest thing is just to stop
thinking about it. Then it can just think you.

Depending on the angle of incline and the rate

of decomposition. Wives to each other, husbanding
the fear that feeds upon itself and its prey.
Doesn't that count for something, even

in these pitched accommodations?

What are you fighting for?

What are you fighting for?[74]

The title "Broken English" immediately introduces the problems of comparison posed and explored by Bernstein in his other writings. "Broken English" refers not only to Faithfull's 1979 song but also to the dialects and nonstandard English that he suggests in "Poetics of the Americas" furnish a pluralist model of commonality and comparison. As part of *World on Fire*, "Broken English" claims a place within this global space of comparison in difference. Just as this pluralist model represents for Bernstein the "political reversal of Poundian centrism," so the appeal to English here acknowledges how imperialism and racial theory inadvertently produced a plural, hybrid notion of English and Englishness.[75]

Like Bernstein's Americas and Pound essays, "Broken English" suggests a tension or "fight" between theological and ideological readings. "What are you fighting for?" also poses the question: what are you reading for? "You" might read the poem as an isolated literary object protected from the world of the "war"—the rhyme word for "fighting for" in Faithfull's song, but a word that the poem is unable or unwilling to enunciate. Yet the poem also invites an ideological reading that asks what the poem itself is fighting for: does it expose or merely reinforce the workings of power on a global scale from Auschwitz gas chambers ("execution chamber") to desert warfare in Iraq ("like ripples / in a sand dune")? The question echoes Bernstein's insistence in "Pounding Fascism" that "It is always revealing to ask of a work: what does it serve and how?"[76] For instance, the word "war" maintains an overwhelming ghostly presence in the poem through its very absence. Its absence invites a symptomatic reading of the poem as an expression of a schizophrenic postmodern subjectivity unable to articulate a direct political critique—as in Jameson's reading of fellow Language writer Perelman's "China."[77] Yet neither the theological nor the ideological reading defines the poem and the "fight" over interpretation that it provokes. Rather, the poem and fight are about the problem of reading itself. Like Derek Jarman's music video *Broken English*, produced to accompany the release of Faithfull's song, Bernstein's poem deploys a collage poetics of geographical and historical sweep (from "sand dune" to "taffy / pull") that invites a consideration of how the reader should traverse discontinuities in language and in the world. The poem implies that both "pitched" battles and "accommodations" are problematic and so suggests the inadequacy of readings that, on the one hand, seek to accommodate the poem's diverse material into a single ideological message and, on the other hand, insist on the text's irreducible resistance.

The poem negotiates the loss of affect in the face of the global scale of comparison by thematizing the absence or failure of sensation: "men move / decisively toward the execution chamber"; "his face exquisitely detached / from any sign of the sensation." The lack of feeling here echoes Faithfull's song: "Cold, lonely, puritan." Like Faithfull's song, Bernstein's poem uses detached language to describe a violent act apparently undertaken without emotion, without feeling, without hesitation ("decisively"). The poem describes murder, broken bodies, in language that is itself broken, disconnected from its affective content. Bernstein's text abounds in clichés such as "takes aim," "sharp / pain in his body," and "The market plunges," performing the disconnection between feeling and expression that it describes.

Like Faithfull's song, however, Bernstein's poem produces affect out of this failure, out of the totalizing figure of "broken English" and its borrowed refrain. Ironically, the poem's emotional impact emerges from the discrepancies between sensation and expression. These discrepancies parallel the apparent lack of emotional response from the addressee in Faithfull's song: she carries on after losing her father, husband, mother, and children.[78] In both Faithfull's punk-inflected song and Bernstein's "Broken English," the absence of emotional response is what moves the reader, an effect that relies on this oscillation between affective engagement and generalizing, detached distance.

The poem enacts this problem of "enunciation," as Bernstein puts it, through the tension between generality and particularity, between an eternal lyric present and a historically and autobiographically defined position.[79] Faithfull's song describes a generalized war, underscored by Jarman's footage of the Second World War and the Vietnam War, but it also refers autobiographically to Faithfull's broken voice on her return to recording after an extended absence. Faithfull's voice and detached performance employ the genre of punk rock to oppose both the hypermasculinity of this genre and her 1960s representation as a hyperfeminine object of male desire. The song also marks a public, social shift in attitude toward the possibility of political change between the late 1960s and the late 1970s. It registers a corresponding turn from a utopian desire for personal liberation to a more dystopian view of human nature—a change enacted in the contrast between Faithfull's songs of the 1960s and the rough, broken voice with which she announces her comeback in "Broken English."

Bernstein's poem also connects autobiography to world historical changes, highlighting the problematic relationship between the intimate affective nearness of the lyric and the generalizing anti-affective distance of the song's global scale and sense of historical repetition. Bernstein's use of Faithfull's 1979 song connects autobiographically to his punk-like response to the previous generation of US avant-garde writers, such as Ginsberg and Olson, at the same historical moment through his editing with Bruce Andrews of the roughly stapled journal $L=A=N=G=U=A=G=E$ (1978–81). Equally, Bernstein's poem addresses the contemporary war in Iraq even as he conveys a general-ized sense of the "world on fire" that alludes both to the Second World War and to the Vietnam War. Bernstein and other Language writers often frame the development of their poetics and their response to earlier avant-garde writers around these two conflagrations.[80] Born in 1950, Bernstein frequently cites the Second World War as the lo-cus of his personal and poetic origins. As he emphasizes in discuss-ing "Broken English," he grew up in the shadow of this war, whose aftermath led to the new post-Poundian poetics he describes in essays such as "The Second War and Postmodern Memory." In addition to the use of wartime standards in *World on Fire*, he underscores this war's importance in a number of poetic works, such as the libretto *Shadowtime*, which centers on Walter Benjamin's final days. Draw-ing on Faithfull's foregrounding of temporal indeterminacy ("Could have come through anytime"), he emphasizes a Benjamin-like sense of historical repetition through the poem's reiterated refrain. He im-plicitly asks whether the 2003 US attack on Iraq is merely a rehash of, in Faithfull's words, the "old war" of 1991, or for that matter of 1969, or 1941.

The cover of *Girly Man* also suggests a connection to Benjamin among a historical pastiche of references (fig. 17). The illustration is a detail from Susan Bee's *Fleurs du mal*, depicting a man, who, recall-ing the classic image from *King Kong* (1933), holds a young Marilyn Monroe–like woman in his massive hand. Although "the mad doc-tor holding the woman is from a B movie poster," in the context of the painting's title and Bernstein's book, and with his small round glasses and moustache, he also resembles Benjamin.[81] Bernstein here suggests a parallel between his own reassemblage of historical frag-ments, especially in *World on Fire*, and Benjamin's great project on nineteenth-century Paris in which Baudelaire's poems played such an important role. At the same time, the image highlights gender and ra-cial stereotyping in its presentation of the woman as a vulnerable sex object and its depiction of the gorilla as a proxy for the racial other under the ethnographic gaze.[82] On the one hand, this recalls the mi-sogyny of male modernist writers such as Baudelaire and their objec-tification of women in their work: the reddish hair of the woman in the image in particular recalls Baudelaire's "À une mendiante rousse" ("To a Red-Haired Beggar Girl"), a poem Bernstein has himself trans-lated and written about as exemplary of such objectification.[83] On the other, it alludes to the Nazi's genocidal racism against the Jews,

Figure 17.   Susan Bee, detail from *Fleurs du mal*,
2003. Mixed media and collage on linen, 147 x
91 cm. This detail was used as the cover image
for Charles Bernstein, *Girly Man* (Chicago: Uni-
versity of Chicago Press, 2006). Reproduced with
the permission of Susan Bee.

which Benjamin sought to flee, raising further questions about iden-
tity politics and Bernstein's use of African-American popular music
in *World on Fire*.

"Broken English" also stages this problem of affect and anti-af-
fective distance, of personal, lyric enunciation, and generalized pub-
lic address, in another way. The poem intertextually juxtaposes
the anti–Vietnam War song "I-Feel-Like-I'm-Fixin'-to-Die Rag" by
Country Joe McDonald (performed at Woodstock in 1969) to Faith-
full's "Broken English" released a decade later.[84] The poem and two

Figure 18.   Still image of Country Joe McDonald and the Fish, from *Wood-stock: Three Days of Peace and Music*, directed by Michael Wadleigh (1970; Burbank, CA: Warner Home Video, 1994), DVD.

songs share the refrain "What are you fighting for?" In this way, the poem addresses the problem of the protest lyric and presents a clear dichotomy between, on the one hand, a specific protest framed in terms that stress authenticity and the possibility of change and, on the other, a negative, ill-defined sense of rebellion that stresses inauthenticity and complicity. The contrast appears most clearly in the difference between the images of McDonald and Faithfull associated with each song (figs. 18 and 19). In the first image, from the 1970 *Woodstock* feature film, Country Joe McDonald is presented singing live to a massed audience of 300,000 (as he points out during his performance), a crowd who responds to his call to sing along. The second image is from Jarman's music video, one of the first to accompany a single. The music video emphasizes artifice and the distance between singer and listener, as opposed to the emphasis on immediacy and togetherness in the Woodstock film: it presents Faithfull not singing at all but playing a video game. Heightening the mediation, Jarman shoots (a pun that is felt in this context) her face as a reflection in a video-game screen. She appears apparently uninterested in addressing, or even looking at, another human being. Instead, she engages in a game of war. The difference between the two films is also one between the naturalistic, documentary montage of *Woodstock* and Jarman's antinaturalistic montage enframed by the opening and

Figure 19.   Still image of Marianne Faithfull, from *Broken English: Three Songs by Marianne Faithfull*, directed by Derek Jarman (Island Records, 1979). Image sourced from the Television New Zealand Archive.

closing shots of Faithfull. *Woodstock* conveys the experience of a live performance by interspersing shots of McDonald and the crowd, who clap and sing along. Jarman's film juxtaposes rapidly changing images ranging from Nazi propaganda films to dance hall scenes, to a Vietnamese monk's self-immolation, shifting from one place and time to another at a bewildering speed. Jarman presents a global, indeterminate amalgam of war, destruction, and propaganda that cannot easily be opposed because it is everywhere, conveying the confusion in Faithfull's question "What are you fighting for?"

Bernstein's posing of the same question exploits the gulf between the two songs that he echoes. His references would seem to track a familiar historical change analogous to the shift Perloff identifies from the utopian postmodernism of the 1970s to Jameson's and others' dystopian Marxist analysis of postmodernity in the 1980s.[85] Bernstein's poem seems at first glance closer to McDonald's clearly oppositional mode in its engagement with the specific situation of a US military invasion of another country. Equally, it recalls McDonald's lyrics in its allusion to the "market" (McDonald refers to "Wall Street" and its complicity in the war machine). Yet the poem's distancing strategies, the unidentified source of the drive to destruction—seemingly just identified as "it," as in "it can just think you"—and the negative presentations of the collective endeavor ("obedient masses"), contrast with the clear culpability attributed to "Uncle Sam," "Wall Street," and the "generals" in McDonald's lyrics. In these respects, Bernstein's poem recalls the threatening impersonality of the temporally indefinite, unnamed subject of the lines in Faithfull's lyric "Could have come through anytime, / Cold, lonely, puritan"—the last word of which, in Faithfull's drawn out rendering, has the ghostly inevitability of "pure return."

By thematizing the disconnection between sensation and expression, Bernstein's poem undermines its apparently strong and direct antiwar message and the generality/particularity binary on which the rhetoric of the conventional war poem is constructed. Just as the parataxis resists a single reading, various forms of resistance and breaking are thematically prominent in the poem, including "fighting," "fire," "muffles," "cracks," "beats its wings / against the closed door," "intransigence," "slip away," "stop," "decomposition." This resistance is reinforced by enjambment and détourning, by various failures to supply the anticipated word or phrase, as in "pitched accommodations" instead of pitched battles. Distancing thus provides a way to "break English" in a positive sense: to undermine its structures and conventions so as to oppose the rhetorical status quo. In another sense, it *opposes* broken English: the English produced, for example, by "the Bush administration's abuses of language."[86]

Like suspicious practices of close reading, however, detachment also threatens to produce numbing conformity and so is equally suspect in "Broken English." Detachment not only resists the abuses of language: it is also a product of those abuses. In an interview, Bernstein discusses the poem in relation to how "martial power requires detachment from feeling." Detachment "makes a person prey to forces beyond themselves."[87] The separation from or inability to express "sensation," the poem implies, might be dangerous: might allow a country "just to stop / thinking about it" and go to war—let it "just think you." It is part of the rational order and racial supremacism that, for Bernstein, led to the death camps and Hiroshima, as well as to contemporary atrocities in Iraq, as the image of the unthinkingly "obedient masses" suggests.

Around the time of writing and publishing *World on Fire*, Bernstein engaged in a debate about the relation of poetry to political protest. Bernstein criticized the Poets against War movement (founded in response to the US invasion of Iraq) and called instead for "an approach to politics, as much as to poetry, that doesn't feel compelled to repress ambiguity or complexity nor to substitute the righteous monologue for a skeptic's dialogue."[88] In this statement, Bernstein again mobilized the very rhetorical moves that he claimed to be undermining, provoking a critical response from other avant-garde writers. Kent Johnson described Bernstein's "moral decree" as being "astonishingly blind to the ironies of its own arrogance," while David Baptiste-Chirot compared Bernstein to George Bush: both ask their "listeners to make a choice—you're either with us or against us."[89] Yet such suspicious readings are entirely to the point—they are what Bernstein's texts repeatedly demand. By performatively adopting the rhetorical modes he claims to oppose, Bernstein destabilizes their certainties and points to their complicity. In some texts, this play is humorously obvious, as in his recent recantation of his poetics: "I was wrong, I apologize and recant. I altogether abandon the false opinion that only elitist and obscure poetry should be praised. I abjure, curse, detest, and renounce the aforesaid error and aversion. And I now freely and openly attest that the best way to get general readers to start to read poetry is to present them with broadly appealing work, with strong emotional content and a clear narrative line."[90] Yet the same poetic play is operative throughout his poetics, as in the affective lyric intensity and anti-affective distancing of "Broken English," conveyed partly through his intertextual references to "broadly appealing work, with strong emotional content."

Whether Bernstein perpetuates or dismantles the structures or frames of thinking he puts into play is left in doubt. Alluding to this uncertainty, Bernstein has written about his use of irony as perpetual circulation or exchange: "With irony, you're left with some sense of authoritative distance from whatever's being mocked or ironized, especially in the modernist form. I'm interested in coming back around so that you're actually where you were if it wasn't ironic. You've gone through this humorous turn, but it's self-cancelling in the sense that you're not remaining at a distance from it, nor are you ridiculing it. On the contrary, you've gone through a kind of comic spin cycle."[91] Bernstein's poetry, his statements on global poetics, and his acts as a poetic global trader could all be read as a kind of "comic spin cycle" comprising competing centrifugal and centripetal forces.

When Bernstein resists the authoritative "distance" of irony, he recalls Barthes's insistence on textual play rather than ironic authority.[92] But Bernstein puts another spin on the theological celebration of the limitlessness of the text. In Bernstein's spin cycle, the circulation of terms—the assertion of one totalizing whole in opposition to another totalizing whole—draws attention to the paradoxes and inevitable exclusions of a transnational or global poetics. By refusing distance, Bernstein's assertions and performances of a global poetics are at once ironic and sincere, distancing and affective, emphasizing—as in the title of his best-known essay/poem—both "artifice" and "absorption."[93] Bernstein invites both ideologically suspicious and defensively theological readings and so articulates the implicated position of poem, writer, and critic within the global circulation of capital and the uneven structures of modernity, modern art, and global power.

Bernstein highlights the importance of poetics—the rhetorical structures or frames that shape habits of thought and literary criticism, be they ideological interrogations or theological defenses of the aesthetic. By drawing attention to these rhetorical structures, his writing suggests a comparative mode of reading that if not escaping this binary of commonality and strangeness would at least challenge its certainties. Neither side of the binary, as Bernstein's poetics underscores, is a privileged guarantor of aesthetic or political praise or damnation. Commonness suggests what might be seen from an ideological, hermeneutically suspicious perspective as normative and totalizing, the source of unthinking notions of nationalism or "global feeling." But commonness also connotes everyday particularity and so the refusal to overlook everydayness in favor of the transcendent otherness or strangeness of the theological aesthetic. Commonness in this sense might renew attention to the affective possibilities and common experiences of reading, rather than suspiciously distancing the reader from them. At the same time, through his appeals to a universal nonstandard, Bernstein invites the thoroughgoing ideological critique to which strangeness has been subject for its transcendent appeal to otherness and its corresponding negation of the common, the everyday, the particular within a generalized play of difference. Yet in Bernstein's writing, strangeness, difference, and otherness remain necessary for unsettling totality, countering automatization, and insisting that things might be another way—the "bunt" and "buzz" against the darkness and "brightness," the "night" and day dichotomies that would break the world in "half."[94]

To follow Bernstein's incessant motion between commonness and strangeness in this way is to experience the entrapping jaws of the dialectic. Repeated in Bernstein's writings across the historical changes of the last few decades, the dialectic is revealed as "just an old war, / Not even a cold war." Yet Bernstein's "spin cycle" also seeks to disarm the dialectic through an image of everyday domesticity with a touch of comedy: instead of a revolutionary resolution of oppositions, we are left with just another revolution of the washing machine.[95] Or, if we listen closely, the turntable. For if, as Bernstein claims, "doubt can cause cessation," then by refusing dialectic resolution, his writing insists on the perpetual dissonance of the skipping needle as a source of poetic affect and as a counterpoint to perpetual war.[96]

Conclusion

More and more I have the sense of being present at a point of absence where crossing centuries may prove to be like crossing languages.

—SUSAN HOWE, *That This*

We think we are undergoing daily renewal, when in fact we are only sacrificing to forgotten ancestors.

—HAUN SAUSSY, *Great Walls of Discourse and Other Adventures in Cultural China*

Can one take captives by writing—
"Humans repeat themselves."

—LYN HEJINIAN, *The Guard*

On 20 March 2003, the New Zealand state broadcaster interrupted its regular schedule to announce that US-led forces had entered Iraq. Obviously prepared for the inevitable news, the announcer immediately switched to Marianne Faithfull's "Broken English." Like Bernstein, the radio station repeated this old song to protest an event that was itself a reprise of a war that twelve years earlier had helped mark the end of the Cold War. Faithfull's song likewise repeated and transformed the refrain of a 1960s antiwar anthem. In the cracked voice introduced by Faithfull's comeback album, "Broken English" tracked a collective and personal narrative from 1960s utopianism to 1970s militant radicalization and faithlessness. Faithfull dedicated the song to the antinuclear campaigner turned militant, or "terrorist," Ulrike Meinhof, prefiguring but also unsettling its use as an antiwar anthem a quarter of a century later. Equally prophetically, she anticipated the replacement of the "Cold War" with its rhyming partner: "an old war."

It is tempting to take such recurrences, or historical rhymes, between the Cold War world and today as evidence that history comprises progressive developments on a theme, new battles in the same "old war"—reproductions of sameness and difference across time and space, languages and cultures. Elsewhere, Bernstein reworks Walter Benjamin's "On the Concept of History," where Benjamin writes of Paul Klee's *Angelus Novus* blown backwards into the future by the storm of progress.[1] Benjamin's angel of history has himself, of course, been frequently reprised, and not just by Bernstein. He reappears most strikingly in the late 1980s and early 1990s, the very transitional, millennial, "end of history" moment to which this book has repeatedly returned. Benjamin's angel informs many works from the period including Tony Kushner's *Angels in America* (1990–92), Wim Wenders's *Der Himmel über Berlin* (*Wings of Desire*; 1987), and Laurie Anderson's *Strange Angels* (1989).[2] In reworking Benjamin's angel, all three—like Faithfull a decade earlier—confront their late–Cold War moment and the problem of repetition. Kushner entitles the barely post–Cold War second part of his epic play *Perestroika*, or "rebuilding" in English translation. Wenders returns the angel to Benjamin's divided hometown of Berlin. There, in an album released less than a month before the fall of the Wall, Anderson, who contributed music to Wenders's film, finds "Hansel and Gretel . . . alive and well" before allowing Hansel to repeat almost verbatim Benjamin's description of the angel of history, though with the twist that history is now "his story."[3]

Benjamin's angel suggests the catastrophe that accompanies but is concealed by a linear view of history: the hell of endless repetition. For Benjamin, recognizing the human propensity toward repetition means escaping the illusion of progress. With the seeming collapse of the polarized oppositions of East and West, communism and capitalism at the end of the Cold War, Benjamin's angel provided a timely reminder that, as this book has repeatedly demonstrated, such oppositions have not gone away. Rather, the "old war" continues in the binary between the local and the global, or in a return to its older variant, the particular and the universal.

Are we locked in repetition—"sacrificing to forgotten ancestors"— or confronting a fundamentally new historical moment, "a point of absence where crossing centuries may prove to be like crossing languages"?[4] Instead of arguing for or against either position, I suggest that the question itself needs to be reframed. As Susan Howe's half-rhyming dichotomy between "present" and "absence" implies, each position represents a pole in the opposition between sameness and

difference that dominates attempts to think our current era histori-
cally (a product of the past, or a premonition of the future?) and spa-
tially (global or local?). Benjamin's stress on the perpetual reproduc-
tion of the new in modernity itself illustrates the pervasiveness of the
commonness/strangeness binary. While helping us recognize the on-
going power of conceptual structures and historical dynamics that
we thought we had overcome, his insight holds us captive to another
form of the same dichotomy.

"Humans repeat themselves." Such habitual ways of thinking and
writing can "take captives," as Hejinian suggests in the opening lines
of *The Guard*, her first attempt to use her experience of what I have
called "Russian estrangement" to cross the divisions of the Cold
War.[5] Read alongside the poem's later references to "a picture," the
opening lines echo the words of Wittgenstein: "A *picture* held us cap-
tive. And we couldn't get outside it, for it lay in our language, and
language seemed only to repeat it to us inexorably." We cannot escape
these repetitions in language: the "tracing . . . over and over again"
of what seems to be "nature" but which is in fact "merely . . . the
frame through which we look at it."[6] Yet by "crossing languages," by
highlighting the contingency of any single frame, any one linguistic,
geographic, historical, or cultural position, we can come to recognize
such recurrences—including the commonness/strangeness binary—as
something other than an unmediated "picture" of reality and so be-
gin to read and write them differently.

Seen in this light, Hejinian's lines offer an alternative way to un-
derstand recurrence: not as repetition, but as, in Gertrude Stein's
sense, "insistence." For Hejinian, as for Stein, "there is no such
thing as repetition."[7] Each insistence transforms and is transformed
by the form and context of its presentation; it depends on a poet-
ics. By presenting the line "Humans repeat themselves" in quota-
tion marks, Hejinian highlights its status as a repeated phrase—a
version of the cliché "history repeats." In so doing, she transforms
a direct statement into an example that simultaneously describes
its own repetitiveness. She also anticipates the repeated words and
themes that are continuously recontextualized across the roughly
750 lines of this radically disjunctive poem. Thus the line highlights
its own transformation of the human propensity toward cliché and
historical repetition into the possibility of a singular poetics of in-
sistence. Repetitions can come to be seen as insistences in this way
when approached through the rhetorical strategies of continuous

reframing—the poetics—explored here: not just Hejinian's estranging of cliché and everyday life, but also Yang Lian's superimposition and constellation, Dragomoshchenko's co-response, Bei Dao's allegory and echo, Prigov's intersecting iterations, and the ideological and theological readings invited by Bernstein's insistent repetition of Faithfull's question—itself borrowed from another song—"What are you fighting for?"

Yet insistence is not confined to poetics: it is shaped by content and context, by each encounter with a new place and time. Bernstein's repetition of Faithfull's question depends on a series of shifts in historical context, in this case from the refrain of an upbeat anti–Vietnam War song, through a chillingly dystopian late–Cold War, punk-inflected, feminist response to armed conflict, to an attempt to oppose the 2003 US invasion of Iraq while not writing a straightforward protest poem. Likewise, Hejinian's first encounter with Russia and Dragomoshchenko in 1983 frames the line "Humans repeat themselves." In this context, the line not only highlights how we are held captive by conventional ways of writing and thinking, such as the opposition between East and West, but also attempts to bridge the Cold War divide through an appeal to our common humanity. Bei Dao's allegorical poetry is equally inseparable from the shifting meanings of the word *shijie* 世界 (world) and the historical events through which successive readings of his poems have been framed, including the Cultural Revolution, the incident of April 5, 1976, the 1978 Democracy Wall, the massacre of June 4, 1989, and the rise of globalization and a new global literature.

Insistences, then, are inextricable from the myriad of intersecting encounters that constitute history. As Prigov's conceptualist repetitions and appropriations underscore, no context is ever entirely separate from intersections with other contexts, persons, places, and times. A poem sealed in one of Prigov's *Little Coffins* and presented to a foreign poet in 1989 looks back to the samizdat culture born of Soviet censorship, repackages it for foreign export, and looks forward to the collapse of the Soviet Union and so to the death and afterlife of that culture. The literal encounter between two persons in the back and forth of letter writing becomes a figure for Dragomoshchenko's poetics of co-response between writer and reader, Russia and the United States. Likewise, through his reprise of the figure of the flâneur, Yang Lian stages the encounter between nineteenth-century Europe and late twentieth-century China, between Auckland

and Beijing, and between before and after June 4, 1989. In a series of collisions that recall Duoduo's reading of Baudelaire's "Le soleil" almost two decades earlier, his exile writing presents the insistent layering of encounters as the condition of modernity.

Each new insistence is an encounter that confronts and reshapes all the other instances and contexts: Benjamin, Bernstein, Meinhoff, Faithfull, the Second World War, the First and Second Gulf Wars. Like the afterlives of Faithfull's "Broken English," the insistences I have traced produce encounters across space, language, and culture—be it the flâneur who strides across centuries and continents; Russian modernist estrangement in Hejinian's postmodernist long poems; Chinese and US appeals to world literature in Bei Dao's poetry and its reception; or the rediscovery of conceptual poetry in the United States thirty years after it made its debut in Russia in the work of Prigov and others. Benjamin called an instance of such insistent encounter the "here-and-now"—the present including history, be it the now of my writing or your reading.

To think about our current era of globalization therefore means confronting questions of poetics as well as history: the rhetorical forms—the repetitions of sameness and difference, commonness and strangeness—through which we have come to understand the changes of the last few decades. Reprising but also reframing Benjamin's insights, I have proposed encounter and superimposition—insistence not repetition—as an alternative to historical dialectics, to a single modernity, a single comparative framework of commonness and strangeness, a single norm that sweeps all before it. To recall Howe's words, the half-rhyming dichotomy of "present" and "absence" is complicated by the repeated "crossing" of "centuries" and "languages"—by the insistent encounters among persons, cultures, places, and times. When seen through the many new encounters and poetries wrought by the passage from the Cold War world to our current era, history appears not as progress, mimetic translation, genetic development, nor wave upon wave of influence, of sameness and difference, but as insistence across space and time, language and culture. Comparison as encounter.

Although it might seem easy enough to recognize the central role that such encounters play in shaping our world, the burden of this book has been to insist that the study of literature and culture cannot simply pay lip service to our condition of common strangeness. Literal and imaginary travels, encounters, superimpositions, and constellations play a constitutive role in contemporary poetry and culture at large. These encounters do not leave the reader or writer unchanged, but repeatedly compel both to see the world anew. In acknowledging these encounters, I have also participated in them. I have invited an encounter by asking you, the reader, to walk with me through the streets of my Auckland childhood made strange through Yang Lian's eyes; traverse the intimate relationship between a Russian and an American poet estranged and abstracted through their imaginings of cross-cultural difference; and journey from underground writing to post–Cold War conceptions of world literature and global poetics. I have also augmented these encounters by bringing them together in this book, offering, in Baudelaire's words, my own "fantasque escrime" (fanciful fencing) to fuse my wandering images but also to acknowledge and question the patterns, or "les hasards de la rime" (the chances of the rhyme), through which we have come to know our era, the repetitions—the structures of sameness and difference—to which we are so prone.[8]

From China to Russia, from the 1970s to the post-9/11 world, the binary of commonness and strangeness is inadequate to the task that we now face: to address the "fanciful" encounters that constitute not only avant-garde poetry but also the multivalent poetics of contemporary culture and history at large. *A Common Strangeness* describes not just the various poetries that emerged from such encounters at a moment of historical flux, but also the comparative methods they might inspire. Such methods require forms to read and write our recent past and present that do not solidify into a totalizing system of sameness versus difference, commonness versus strangeness, theological versus ideological readings. To say that we have nothing in common but our strangeness seems to collapse our particular differences into the false plurality of totalizing Difference. Yet to insist on the commonplace of encounters between specific differences is to begin to recognize the complex, strange yet familiar experience of being in the world.

Unless otherwise noted, all translations are my own. For cases where I refer to multiple sources from a single archive, I supply any applicable box, folder, and page numbers in the note and full details of the relevant archive in the list of works cited.

INTRODUCTION

1. Jameson, "Postmodernism," 73–75.

2. Perelman, *Primer*, 60–61.

3. Jameson, "Postmodernism," 74.

4. For treatments of poetry in China in this way, see, for example, Mc-Dougall and Louie, *Literature of China*; Xudong Zhang, *Chinese Modernism*. For similar perspectives on Russian poetry, see, for example, Kahn, "Causework," 14; Cavanagh, *Lyric Poetry*.

5. On the equation of anticommunism with antimodernism in the 1950s, see Filreis, *Counter-Revolution*; on a similar attack on Language writing in the 1980s, see Sloan, "Crude Mechanical Access."

6. On the Cold War institutional histories of comparative literature and area studies, see Spivak, *Death of a Discipline*; Chow, *Age of the World Target*.

7. Judt frames his history of Europe since 1945 as an attempt, in the light of the changes that took place in 1989, to recover the complexity "blasted flat" by the Second World War and by the "new and less complicated continent" that was consolidated in the Cold War period. Judt, *Postwar*, 9. Yet despite Judt's note of optimism, "the struggle to recast Europe *after* the momentous upheaval of 1989 resulted in prefabricated structures from *before* the upheaval moving eastward and securing a future for themselves." Sarotte, *1989*, 201. On the importance of the symbolic and conceptual structures of the Cold War to post–Cold War history and international relations, see also Judt, "What Have We Learned"; Leffler, "Dreams of Freedom," 160–61. From the Korean perspective, the Cold War has never ended. Suzuki-Morris, "In Interesting Times."

8. On US Cold War poetics, see Davidson, *Guys Like Us*; Nelson, *Pursuing Privacy*. On post–Cold War poetics, see Monroe, "Avant-Garde Poetries."

9. Epstein, *Postmodern v Rossii*; Perloff, "How Russian Is It?" and *Radical Artifice*; Watten, "Post-Soviet Subjectivity"; Xudong Zhang, *Chinese Modernism*; Lo, "Writing the Otherness of Nature"; Chen, *Occidentalism*; McDougall, "Anxiety of Out-fluence."

10. On this transnational turn, see, for example, Mao and Walkowitz, "New Modernist Studies"; Friedman, "Periodizing Modernism" and "Planetarity"; Saussy, *Comparative Literature*; Hayot, "Asian Turns."

11. On this structure, see Hayot, "Asian Turns." For examples, see Bush, *Ideographic Modernism*; Chen, *Occidentalism*; Dimock, *Through Other Continents*; Dimock and Buell, *Shades of the Planet*; Hayot, *Chinese Dreams* and *Hypothetical Mandarin*; Huang, *Transpacific Displacement* and *Transpacific Imaginations*; Huk, *Assembling Alternatives* and "New Global Poetics?"; Mayhew, *Apocryphal Lorca*; Saussy, *Great Walls of Discourse*. A notable exception is Saussy's three-way discussion of modernism in "Mei Lanfang in Moscow."

12. The stress on diverse, localized manifestations of transnational or global modernism is widespread. See, for example, Hayot, introduction to "Modernisms' Chinas"; Nicholls, *Modernisms*; Noland and Watten, *Diasporic Avant-Gardes*; Perloff, *Futurist Moment* and *21st-Century Modernism*; Charles W. Pollard, *New World Modernisms*; Ramazani, *Hybrid Muse* and *Transnational Poetics*. For a totalizing notion of "supermodernity," see Augé, *Non-places*.

13. Chow, *Age of the World Target*, 76; Kadir, "Comparative Literature," 75; Spivak, *Death of a Discipline*, 73. On the problem with even a constitutively heterogeneous concept like "hybridity" as a global unit of comparison, see Huk, "New Global Poetics?"; Krishnaswamy, "Criticism of Culture."

14. It is perhaps no accident that Latour's critique of this dominant mode of binary thinking, *We Have Never Been Modern*, appeared in 1991. Indeed, its opening chapter includes a subsection entitled "1989: The Year of Miracles."

15. Examples of the enlarged scale of today's comparative approaches include Damrosch, "Rebirth of a Discipline," *How to Read World Literature*, and *What Is World Literature?*; Dimock, *Through Other Continents* (with its near-geological sense of time); Friedman, "Periodizing Modernism" and "Planetarity" (which together develop a temporally, geographically, culturally, and linguistically expansive account of modernism and modernity); Moretti, "Conjectures on World Literature" (where he advocates "distant reading" as a way to address the sheer volume of the world's literatures); and Spivak, *Death of a Discipline*, 71–102 (in which she introduces her notion of "planetarity").

16. The seemingly irreconcilable disjunction between knowing the world in its totality and individual experience was the very problem with which Jameson concluded "Postmodernism; or, The Cultural Logic of Late Capitalism." Jameson, "Postmodernism," 91–92. On this problem, see also

Jameson, *Geopolitical Aesthetic*; Jameson, *Seeds of Time*; Jameson, "Cognitive Mapping"; Melas, *All the Difference*.

17. For example, Perloff identifies as characteristic of twenty-first-century modernism Charles Bernstein's negotiation between "pure nominalism" and a global space of "information glut" and "sheer 'noise.'" Perloff, *21st-Century Modernism*, 178–80. Compare this to Spivak's call to "imagine ourselves as planetary subjects rather than global agents," so that "alterity . . . is not our dialectical negation," but "contains us as much as it flings us away." Spivak, *Death of a Discipline*, 73.

18. See Boym, "Estrangement as a Lifestyle."

19. Huk, *Assembling Alternatives*, 2.

20. Lionnet and Shih, introduction, 5.

21. On Pound's search for a global "essence of culture," see Huang, *Transpacific Displacement*, 86–92. Herd writes of Olson's intervention in 1950s international relations in "From Him Only." On Rothenberg's transcultural anthologies, see Middleton, "Transitive Poetics." Von Hallberg views Rothenberg's transnational vision as part of a broader turn to translation in post–Second World War US poetry. Von Hallberg, "Poetry, Politics, and Intellectuals," 171.

22. Yu argues that Perelman's "China" exemplifies an Asian turn among US avant-garde poets, which "took on a political edge" during that defining Cold War conflict, the Vietnam War. Yu, *Race and the Avant-Garde*, 63. "China" was, however, first published in 1980, five years after US forces had withdrawn from Vietnam, two years after Vietnam and China had themselves gone to war, and shortly after the United States had normalized diplomatic relations with China. Thus the transnational appeal of Perelman's title can be seen not only as engaging the binary oppositions of the Cold War but also as pointing to China's role (as "number three") in complicating them.

23. Monroe, "Avant-Garde Poetries," 95–96; Perloff, *Unoriginal Genius*, 123–45; Spahr, "Connected Disconnection."

24. For an overview of mainland Chinese poetry in the 1970s and 1980s, see Van Crevel, *Language Shattered*. For developments since that time, see Van Crevel, *Chinese Poetry*.

25. Golynko-Vol'fson, for example, highlights the increasing "demands of the global public sphere" in his insider's account of Russian poetry since the 1970s. Golynko and Pavlov, "Poetics of Intense Precision," 59.

26. On Sanskrit prosody in Chinese poetry as a marker of foreignness, see Klein, "Foreign Echoes," 192–246.

27. Shklovsky, *Theory of Prose*, 5; Shklovsky, "Iskusstvo," 12. In the same essay, "Art as Device," Shklovsky cites Tolstoy's depiction of a scene from the point of view of a horse, thus associating modernist estrangement with the radically estranging perspective of another species. Later in the essay he describes "poetic language" as having "the character of something foreign." Shklovsky, *Theory of Prose*, 7–8, 12; Shklovsky, "Iskusstvo," 14–16, 21.

28. For example, Bhabha's concept of hybridity emerges from poststructuralist theory, especially Derrida's notions of linguistic difference, in *The*

Location of Culture. Similarly, Kristeva conflates poetic strangeness with gender and cultural difference in her imagining of China. Chung, "Kristevan (Mis)Understandings." Many feminist scholars have criticized the reductive association of the "feminine" with avant-garde practice and linguistic differ-ence in poststructuralist theory. For an overview of such criticisms, see Ngai, "Bad Timing," 12–17.

29. See Derrida, "White Mythology"; Foucault, *Order of Things*; Barthes, *Empire of Signs*. On these three theorists and China, see Saussy, *Great Walls of Discourse*. See also Wolin, *Wind from the East*. Even Levi-nas, who wants to insist on the singular rather than collective other, depends on a contrast between the Greek and the Hebraic. Levinas, "Dialogue," 21. On Levinas's own complicating of this opposition, see Eaglestone, "Levinas, Translation, and Ethics"; and Eisenstadt, "Levinas versus Levinas."

30. This binary informs the structuralist/hermeneutic opposition that Culler argues characterizes twentieth-century literary theory. Culler, "Criti-cal Paradigms."

31. Shklovsky, *Theory of Prose*, 6; Shklovsky, "Iskusstvo," 13. Bürger discerns a similar dialectic in the avant-garde's "attempt to organize a new life praxis from a basis in art." Bürger, *Theory of the Avant-Garde*, 49. Rob-inson characterizes both Shklovsky and Brecht as "repersonalizing somatic formalists" in an attempt to bridge the apparent divide between their formal-ism and their stress on phenomenological experience. Robinson, *Estrange-ment*, xii.

32. Tynianov, "O literaturnoi evoliutsii."

33. David Der-Wei Wang, introduction, xxxiv; Boym, "Estrangement as a Lifestyle," 521; Shklovsky, *Third Factory*, 47. Compare this to Felski's Western feminist criticism of the avant-garde's and literary theory's attacks on the everyday. Felski, Introduction, 608–12; Felski, *Doing Time*, 77–98. While an important corrective, Felski's criticism does not fully recognize the historically and culturally contingent relation of estrangement to everyday life.

34. On the dominance of suspicious modes of reading in literary and cul-tural studies, see Felski, *Uses of Literature*; Felski, "After Suspicion." See also Bowlby's and Krishnaswamy's criticisms of scholars' appeals to world-transcending strangeness, from feminine difference to postcolonial hybridity. Bowlby, *Still Crazy*, 30; Krishnaswamy, "Criticism of Culture."

35. Blanchot, *Friendship*, 291; Blanchot, *L'amitié*, 328 (emphasis added). I draw here on Ffrench's reading of Blanchot's "common strangeness" as in-volving a "fundamental separation according to which what separates be-comes relation," not "a recognition of a common essence or property, of something that binds, but of a separation." Ffrench, *After Bataille*, 136–37. The distinction between speaking of and speaking to resembles that which Drichel draws between postcolonial politics and ethics. Drichel, "Regarding the Other."

36. Blanchot, *Infinite Conversation*, 48.

37. Mark 12:31; Levinas, "Prayer without Demand," 232.

38. Eagleton, *Walter Benjamin*, 69.

39. Due to the process of globalization that this book addresses, the interconnections among the six poets extend beyond national and linguistic affiliations. To name but a few further points of contact, Dragomoshchenko, Hejinian, and Prigov all participated in a conference in Leningrad in 1989; thanks to Hejinian, Dragomoshchenko and Bernstein have known each other for many years; Yang, who participated in the 2003 Third Moscow Poetry Biennale, performs with Prigov in Tarasov's *Sonatina for Percussion and Four Poets*; Dragomoshchenko was invited by Bei Dao to a poetry festival in Hong Kong in 2011; and Bernstein, Hejinian, and Yang have all published books with Green Integer Press.

40. Bernstein, *My Way*, 113–15.

CHAPTER 1. YANG LIAN AND THE FLÂNEUR IN EXILE

1. Gluck, "*Flâneur*," 78.

2. Shields, "Fancy Footwork," 66.

3. Walter Benjamin, *Arcades Project*, 336.

4. Goebel, "Benjamin's *Flâneur*," 378; Friedman, "Periodizing Modernism," 426. On Benjamin's theoretical encounters with non-Europe, see Bolle's *Physiognomik der modernen Metropole* and Bush's *Ideographic Modernism*, which examines the especially critical role played by China. On modernisms and modernities, see also Hayot: "every philosophical and literary modernism is itself subject to an internal, undermining comparative action, in which the 'foreign' always and in advance inhabits the 'native' national paradigm." Hayot, "Bertrand Russell's Chinese Eyes," 149.

5. Pensky, "Method and Time," 188.

6. Walter Benjamin, *Arcades Project*, 462.

7. Friedlander, "Measure of the Contingent," 12.

8. Friedlander, "Measure of the Contingent," 7.

9. On the poetics of citation and cross-reference in *The Arcades Project*, see Perloff, "Unoriginal Genius."

10. Walter Benjamin, *Selected Writings*, 4:343, 338, 343.

11. Walter Benjamin, *Selected Writings*, 4:339, 324, 343.

12. As Gluck implies, both Benjamin and Baudelaire present the flâneur via negation, under erasure and in exile from the very European metropolis that is his supposed home. While Benjamin associates the flâneur with Baudelaire's heroic act of separating himself from the crowd, he concludes "On Some Motifs in Baudelaire" with the assertion that Baudelaire was, finally, "no flâneur." Walter Benjamin, *Selected Writings*, 4:39, 342. Similarly, Baudelaire writes of "The Painter of Modern Life" that he "has an aim loftier than that of a mere *flâneur*." For Baudelaire, as for Benjamin, "modernity"—the painter of modern life's loftier aim—emerges through the negation of the flâneur. The flâneur and modernity—which Baudelaire associates with the "fugitive pleasure of circumstances" and "the ephemeral, the fugitive, the contingent," respectively—are both figured partly through their negation in favor of "the eternal and the immutable," to which "modernity" is opposed, but with which it is also, ironically,

equated as "the eternal [distilled] from the transitory." Baudelaire, *Painter of Modern Life*, 12.

13. Chow, *Age of the World Target*, 76; Kadir, "Comparative Literature," 75; Spivak, *Death of a Discipline*, 73.

14. Bowlby, *Still Crazy*, 8. "The *flâneur* as a man of pleasure, as a man who takes visual possession of the city, . . . has emerged in postmodern feminist discourse as the embodiment of the 'male gaze.'" Wilson, "Invisible Flâneur," 98. In similar terms, Shields describes the imperialist flâneur who treats "non-European Others" as "the fascinating objects of the *flâneur*'s writerly gaze." Shields, "Fancy Footwork," 62. Mary Louise Pratt likewise identifies in the flâneur an urban analogue to the European "interior explorer," though she also notes the use of the flâneur by non-Europeans to cast the imperial gaze back onto the imperial metropolis itself. Pratt, *Imperial Eyes*, 188–89.

15. Brooker connects the "dehistoricised or trans-historical" application of the flâneur to the figure's role as an "allegorical self-portrait of the postmodern critic him/herself." Brooker, "Wandering *Flâneur*," 124.

16. Yiyan Wang, "Venturing into Shanghai," 35. For another example of the application of the figure to Chinese modernist literature, see Yingjin Zhang, *City*, 225–29. For criticism of such applications, see Leo Lee, *Shanghai Modern*, 36–42. In questioning the place of the flâneur in Chinese literature of the 1930s and 1940s, Lee notes, "there was no Chinese concession in Paris" (37).

17. On the flâneur as a marker of attenuated male power, see Wilson, "Invisible Flâneur," 109. Similarly, Bowlby associates the ultimate failure of vision in "To a Passerby" and, especially, later in Proust with a recognition that the object of the male gaze is a "pure projection, pure fantasy," a recognition that creates the representational space necessary "for women to come along and walk in a way of their own." Bowlby, *Still Crazy*, 12–13.

18. Chow, *Age of the World Target*, 85. See Spivak, *Death of a Discipline*; Melas, *All the Difference*.

19. Chow, *Age of the World Target*, 88. Apter identifies this interplay between universality and particularity with a productive tension in contemporary comparative literature between "location-conscious" comparative modes and those committed to "'le grand écart' of cultural comparison," such as Badiou's leaping of "parallel universes that share no philological common culture," and even Said's and Spivak's very different "worldly dialectics." Apter, "'Je ne crois pas beaucoup,'" 56, 60–61.

20. Chow, *Age of the World Target*, 81.

21. Walter Benjamin, *Selected Writings*, 3:32; Foucault, *Order of Things*, xvi–xvii. On Foucault's use of an imagined China as a counterexample to Western knowledge, see Saussy, *Great Walls of Discourse*, 148. The flâneur's potential as a figure for the erasures involved in such interpretations is also suggested by the resemblance between Baudelaire's negation of vision in "To a Passerby" and De Man's emphasis on "the poem's essential blindness before it is reduced or overlooked in the act of interpretation." Baer, *Remnants of Song*, 137.

22. Stewart, *Poetry and the Fate of the Senses*, 3.

23. On Lu Xun and Xu Zhimo's translations, see Leo Lee, *Shanghai Modern*, 235–36. On Dai Wangshu's translations, see Gregory Lee, *Dai Wangshu*, 82–94. On Baudelaire in China, see, among others, Bien, "Baudelaire in China"; and Chen Yongguo, "Becoming-Obscure," 82–83.

24. Tamburello, "Ershi shiji houqi Zhongguo shiren." On underground reading, see Van Crevel, *Language Shattered*, 35–41; Xiaomei Chen, *Occidentalism*, 61–62; Song, "Glance at the Underground"; Song, "Wenge zhong de huangpi shu."

25. Tamburello, "Ershi shiji houqi Zhongguo shiren"; Van Crevel, *Language Shattered*, 43.

26. Van Crevel, *Language Shattered*, 36–37.

27. Bei Dao, "Translation Style," 61, 64.

28. Yang Lian, e-mail message to author, 14 February 2009.

29. Van Crevel, *Language Shattered*, 42.

30. McDougall, "Problems and Possibilities," 45.

31. While *menglong* 朦胧 literally denotes the obstruction of the moon's light, the dawn context suggests that the light obscured is the sun's, as in the variant 曚昽. Tamburello has even suggested that the term *menglong shi* 朦胧诗 might derive directly from Chen Jingrong's translation of the title of Baudelaire's "Le crépuscule du matin." Tamburello, "Ershi shiji houqi Zhongguo shiren." Although it is unlikely that Zhang Ming 章明, the orthodox critic who was the first to use the term *menglong* in relation to the new poetry, had Baudelaire in mind, the image is apposite both to *menglong* poetry's myths of origin and to its relation to the political and literary status quo in the 1970s. Zhang Ming, "Ling ren qimen," 53–54.

32. Quoted in Van Crevel, *Language Shattered*, 43.

33. Xiaomei Chen, *Occidentalism*, 6, 80, 5.

34. Saussy finds in Xu Zhimo's translation of Baudelaire's "Une charogne" half a century earlier a similar nonmimetic model of comparative literature "as a process of dissolution, of decay, of selective uptake," involving "infidelity" and "estrangement." Saussy, "Death and Translation," 127–28.

35. Baudelaire, *Œuvres complètes*, 83; Baudelaire, *Flowers of Evil*, 281 (modified translation).

36. Raser, "Barthes and Riffaterre," 62–63.

37. Raser, "Barthes and Riffaterre," 64; Walter Benjamin, *Selected Writings*, 4:320.

38. Walter Benjamin, *Selected Writings*, 4:41.

39. Walter Benjamin, *Selected Writings*, 4:319 (Benjamin's emphasis).

40. Walter Benjamin, *Selected Writings*, 4:319–20.

41. Walter Benjamin, *Selected Writings*, 4:19, 21.

42. Duoduo, "Gaobie," 386–87. The translations of Duoduo's "Farewell" and "Night of the North" are taken from Van Crevel, *Language Shattered*, 131 and 203–4, respectively.

43. Van Crevel, *Language Shattered*, 132.

44. Duoduo, *Duoduo shi xuan*, 143–44, 117–18.

45. Yingjin Zhang, *City*, 263–64; Leo Lee, "On the Margins," 221.

46. Wang, *High Culture Fever*, 181.

47. Yang, *Dahai*, 3–28, 57–68.

48. Xiaomei Chen, *Occidentalism*, 81. Chen contrasts Yang's and Jiang He's *xungen* poetry with *menglong* poetry's negative depiction or negation of the sun, as in Jiang He's earlier "black sun" and Bei Dao's imperative to "forget even the sun" (70–71, 76). A similar negation can also be found in Duoduo's poetry of the 1970s. See Duoduo's untitled poem beginning "Yi ge jieji de xue liu jin le" 一个阶级的血流尽了 ("There is a class whose blood has all flowed away"; published in Van Crevel, *Language Shattered*, 300). Even in the early 1970s, however, Duoduo's representation of the sun was arguably more complex, as, for example, in his Baudelaire-inspired association of the sun with the poet.

49. Yang, *Dahai*, 5, 7, 10.

50. Yang, *Dahai*, 8; Edmond, "Beyond Binaries," 165; Edmond, "Locating Global Resistance," 75.

51. Yang, *Dahai*, 59–60.

52. Edmond, "Locating Global Resistance," 77.

53. See Lo, "Writing the Otherness of Nature," 113; Barmé, *In the Red*, 275; Gregory Lee, *Troubadours*, 117–18; Edmond, "Beyond Binaries"; Edmond, "Locating Global Resistance," 73–79.

54. Wang, *High Culture Fever*, 217.

55. Wang, *High Culture Fever*, 215.

56. Walter Benjamin, *Arcades Project*, 10–11.

57. Edmond and Chung, "Yang Lian," 3–6.

58. Van Crevel and Lee also note continuities between post–June 4 exile literature and 1980s Chinese literature's sense of internal exile. Van Crevel, *Chinese Poetry*, 162–63; Leo Lee, "On the Margins," 225.

59. There is "no shortage of literary references to walking (*sanbu*) itself in Chinese poetry and fiction, both traditional and modern. But such literary walks often take place against or amidst a pastoral landscape." Leo Lee, *Shanghai Modern*, 39. Republican-era Chinese literary representations of the flâneur draw on the traditional figure of the scholar recluse, wanderer, or exile, but arguably present the figure as less detached and more infatuated with the modern urban world. Yiyan Wang, "Venturing into Shanghai," 47–49; Leo Lee, *Shanghai Modern*, 37; Shih, *Lure of the Modern*, 304; Yingjin Zhang, *City*, 225–29. The intellectual as a "solitary traveler" returns in post-Mao literature and film of the 1980s, but, prior to Yang's exilic writing, appears mainly in rural settings (although, as I have already noted of Duoduo's writing, the implicit confrontation between country and city is ever present). See Yingjin Zhang, *City*, 263–67.

60. The "Ghost Speech/Lies" sequence appears in Yang, *Guihua*, 1–86; and "Huanxiang zhong de chengshi," in Yang, *Dahai*, 335–93.

61. Yang, *Unreal City*, 88, 89; Yang, *Guihua*, 28, 29.

62. Yang, *Unreal City*, 75; Yang, *Guihua*, 16.

63. Walter Benjamin, *Selected Writings*, 4:26.

64. Yang, *Unreal City*, 34; Yang, *Dahai*, 333.

65. Yang, *Unreal City*, 91; Yang, *Guihua*, 32.

66. Yang, *Unreal City*, 88; Yang, *Guihua*, 29.

67. Walter Benjamin, *Selected Writings*, 4:23–24.

68. In "Le soleil" the streets are likewise deserted, but Benjamin argues that the poem contains a "phantom crowd" from which the embattled "poet, in the deserted streets, wrests poetic booty." Walter Benjamin, *Selected Writings*, 4:321.

69. Yang, *Unreal City*, 87; Yang, *Guihua*, 27.

70. Glad, preface, ix–x.

71. This generalized state of alienation exemplifies "exile literature" defined as a "state of mind" or aesthetic strategy, according to Van Crevel, *Chinese Poetry*, 147.

72. Yang, *Unreal City*, 67, 75; Yang, *Guihua*, 4, 15.

73. Yang, "To Touch the Border"; Yang, "Zhuixun."

74. Boym, "Estrangement as a Lifestyle," 528.

75. Walter Benjamin, *Arcades Project*, 356.

76. Walter Benjamin, *Selected Writings*, 3:39.

77. Baudelaire, *Œuvres complètes*, 85–87; Baudelaire, *Flowers of Evil*, 289–93. See also Baudelaire's "L'albatros," in which exile is the condition of the poet on earth. Baudelaire, *Œuvres complètes*, 9–10.

78. Edmond and Chung, "Yang Lian," 12; Yang, "To Touch the Border."

79. De Certeau, *Practice of Everyday Life*, 93. For criticism of the generalized use of the term "flâneur," see Brooker, "Wandering *Flâneur*."

80. Yang, *Unreal City*, 87; Yang, *Guihua*, 27–28.

81. Yang, *Unreal City*, 89; Yang, *Guihua*, 29.

82. Walter Benjamin, *Arcades Project*, 416.

83. Yang, *Unreal City*, 75; Yang, *Guihua*, 15.

84. The senses of touch and smell prevail in the rest of this description of the flâneur: "to catch the scent of a threshold or to recognize a paving stone by touch." Benjamin's emphasis on the nonvisual and nonlinguistic opposes conventional notions of "history," which he associates with "trumpery" in this passage. Walter Benjamin, *Arcades Project*, 416.

85. Yang, *Unreal City*, 75, 68; Yang, *Guihua*, 15, 5.

86. *Sanwen* 散文 is a traditional Chinese genre describing a "relaxed, irregular, and independent style, thus 'free prose,' or even 'essay.'" Nienhauser, *Indiana Companion*, 94. While initially used to designate a wide range of classical Chinese nonfiction prose, in the twentieth century the term became more closely identified with works akin to the English essay. David Pollard, preface, 11. It retains, however, associations with the broader classical understanding of the genre and the traditional emphasis on lyricism in Chinese prose. Consequently, even modern *sanwen* texts cannot always be categorized as essays and sometimes have closer affiliations with other Western genres. The modernist writer Zhou Zuoren 周作人, for example, advocated a lyrical prose or prose poetry form of *sanwen*, drawing on both the classical tradition and non-Chinese modernist prose poems by Baudelaire and others. Daruvala, *Zhou Zuoren*, 171.

Echoing this legacy, Yang writes of the "lyricism" (抒情) and "musical rhythm" (音乐节奏) of his *sanwen*. Yang, "Wode wenxue xiezuo," 163.

87. Baudelaire, quoted in Walter Benjamin, *Selected Writings*, 4:41; Yang, *Unreal City*, 69; Yang, *Guihua*, 5–6.

88. Walter Benjamin, *Selected Writings*, 4:40–41.

89. Yang, *Guihua*, 5; Yang, *Unreal City*, 69 (modified translation).

90. The "crude symbols" probably refer to the markings found on Banpo culture earthenware, which some have claimed prefigure Chinese writing. Yang elsewhere explicitly associates the history and language of China with "the pain of timelessness": "The 'history' of China is just like a square black Chinese character, which, time or tense notwithstanding, never changes." Yang, *Concentric Circles*, 12.

91. Walter Benjamin, *Arcades Project*, 356.

92. Gleber, *Art of Taking a Walk*, 11.

93. Yang, *Unreal City*, 80, 37; Yang, *Guihua*, 20; Yang, *Dahai*, 338.

94. Yang, *Guihua*, 16; Yang, *Unreal City*, 75–76 (emphasis in the original; modified translation).

95. Walter Benjamin, *Selected Writings*, 4:50.

96. Walter Benjamin, *Selected Writings*, 4:335–36.

97. Bowlby, *Still Crazy*, 19.

98. Spivak, *Death of a Discipline*, 42.

99. Yang, *Guihua*, 22–23; Yang, *Unreal City*, 82.

100. Yang, *Unreal City*, 82; Yang, *Guihua*, 22.

101. Yang, *Unreal City*, 81; Yang, *Guihua*, 21.

102. Yang, *Unreal City*, 82; Yang, *Guihua*, 22.

103. Yang, *Unreal City*, 67; Yang, *Guihua*, 4.

104. Walter Benjamin, *Selected Writings*, 4:335, 332.

105. Yang, *Unreal City*, 39; Yang, *Dahai*, 342.

106. Crang, "Rhythms of the City," 207.

107. Walter Benjamin, *Arcades Project*, 419.

108. Yang, *Unreal City*, 36; Yang, *Dahai*, 337.

109. Yang, *Unreal City*, 88; Yang, *Guihua*, 28.

110. Yang, *Unreal City*, 88; Yang, *Guihua*, 28.

111. Yang, *Unreal City*, 85; Yang, *Guihua*, 25.

112. Yang, *Unreal City*, 85; Yang, *Guihua*, 25.

113. Yang, *Unreal City*, 85; Yang, *Guihua*, 25.

114. Yang, *Unreal City*, 82; Yang, *Guihua*, 22.

115. Yang, *Unreal City*, 85; Yang, *Guihua*, 25.

116. Yang, *Guihua*, 26; Yang, *Unreal City*, 86.

117. Walter Benjamin, *Selected Writings*, 4:336.

118. Buck-Morss, *Dialectics of Seeing*, 308.

119. Yang, *Unreal City*, 81; Yang, *Guihua*, 21; Yang, *Dead in Exile*, 44. In China, the poem was further erased, by being retitled "Gei yi ge cusi de jiusui nühai" 给一个猝死的九岁女孩 ("To a Nine-Year-Old Girl Who Died Suddenly"). Yang, *Dahai*, 301. See Edmond, "Dissidence," 124–26.

120. Van Crevel, *Chinese Poetry*, 164.

CHAPTER 2. ARKADII DRAGOMOSHCHENKO
AND POETIC CORRESPONDENCES

1. See Hejinian's notebook, 7–15 June 1983 in the Lyn Hejinian Papers, box 47, folder 1. The notebook presents an account of Hejinian's trip to Russia based on her notes and recollections. It was probably written in June or July 1983, soon after she returned to the United States.

2. Reagan, Speech to the Annual Convention of the National Association of Evangelicals, Orlando, Florida, March 1983, reproduced in Donaldson, *Modern America*, 273–75; Rova Saxophone Quartet, *Saxophone Diplomacy*; Rogers, *Saxophone Diplomacy*.

3. Lyn Hejinian to Murray Edmond, 5–6 January 2000, private collection.

4. The preoccupation with such questions is everywhere in contemporary literary and comparative studies. Witness Felski's recent criticism of the tendency to approach texts as either isolated aesthetic objects or mere reflections of social and political power structures, and Chow's call for a comparative practice that moves between the particular and the universal while simultaneously exposing "the hierarchical frameworks of comparison . . . that have long been present as universals" and that "tend to subsume otherness." Felski, *Uses of Literature*, 4; Felski, "After Suspicion," 8–9; Chow, "Old/New Question," 303–4.

5. "I understand only now . . . I have not translated the name of this piece [The Corresponding Sky] completely accurately." Arkadii Dragomoshchenko to Lyn Hejinian, 19 October 1985, private collection. This and all subsequent quotations from Dragomoshchenko's letters to Hejinian appear in my translations. Dragomoshchenko's part of The Corresponding Sky, *Sky of Correspondences*, was published in samizdat as Dragomoshchenko, "Nebo sootvetstvii," and officially as Dragomoshchenko, *Nebo sootvetstvii*, and also appears in Dragomoshchenko, *Opisanie*. The work appears in Hejinian's English translation under the title *Description*.

6. Arkadii Dragomoshchenko to Lyn Hejinian, 1 June 1984, private collection.

7. Arkadii Dragomoshchenko to Lyn Hejinian, 26 October 1985, private collection (emphasis in the original).

8. As Sandler notes, Dragomoshchenko's writing frequently appeals to the tongue as both language and source of bodily eroticism, as in the line from *Ksenii* "Yes, certainly I feel the turf of your saliva with my tongue." Sandler, "Arkadii Dragomoshchenko, Lyn Hejinian," 35; Dragomoshchenko, *Xenia*, 140; Dragomoshchenko, *Ksenii*, 89.

9. Dragomoshchenko, "Shadow of Reading," 231.

10. Abrams, "Correspondent Breeze," 126. For further examples of Hejinian's and Dragomoshchenko's debt to romanticism, see Samuels, "Eight Justifications," 116–17; Sandler, "Arkadii Dragomoshchenko, Lyn Hejinian," 30; Wesling, review of *Redo*, 23.

11. Swedenborg claimed, "between the things which are of the light of heaven and those which are of the light of the world, there exist correspondences." Swedenborg, *Arcana Cœlestia*, 249 (entry 3337). The allusion to

vertical correspondence between earth and heaven in *Sky of Correspon-dences* is suggested not only by the title but also by the way Dragomosh-chenko's "cup" resonates with Hejinian's notion of "paradise" as the realm of perfect knowing and perfect correspondence between language and world. In her poem *The Guard*, completed soon after her first trip to the Soviet Union, the word "cuppings" acts like Dragomoshchenko's "cup" as a fig-ure for paradise in this sense. Edmond, "Closures of the Open Text," 258–60. Benjamin writes of how Baudelaire's poem appropriates and undermines Swedenborg's and the romantics' insistence on correspondences between earth and heaven: "The important thing is that *correspondances* encompass a concept of experience which includes ritual elements. Only by appropri-ating these elements was Baudelaire able to fathom the full meaning of the breakdown which he, as a modern man, was witnessing." Walter Benjamin, *Selected Writings*, 4:333. On the rejection of the "doctrine of vertical cor-respondences" in Baudelaire's poem, see also Culler, "Intertextuality and Interpretation," 123.

12. Baudelaire, *Œuvres complètes*, 11; Baudelaire, *Flowers of Evil*, 23.

13. Arkadii Dragomoshchenko to Lyn Hejinian, 21 March 1985, private collection.

14. Walter Benjamin, *Selected Writings*, 1:260.

15. Arkadii Dragomoshchenko to Lyn Hejinian, 26–28 June 1985, pri-vate collection (emphasis in the original).

16. Culler, "Intertextuality and Interpretation," 127; Eaglestone, "Levi-nas, Translation, and Ethics," 132; Levinas, "Ethics as First Philosophy."

17. Dragomoshchenko, *Description*, 21. Dragomoshchenko refers to Blanchot in Dragomoshchenko, "Shadow of Reading," 227–28; Drago-moshchenko, "Kraplenaia pamiat'," 3; Dragomoshchenko, *Fosfor*, 35, 224–25. See his translation of Blanchot's essay "Vzgliad Orfeia" ("The Gaze of Orpheus"). Russian translations of Blanchot were also published in the samizdat journal *Predlog* (1984–89), which Dragomoshchenko helped to establish. On the journal, see Dolinin et al., *Samizdat Lenin-grada*, 443–44.

18. Blanchot, *Infinite Conversation*, 47; Dragomoshchenko, *Descrip-tion*, 21; Blanchot, *Infinite Conversation*, 215, 212.

19. Chow, "Old/New Question," 303–4 (emphasis in the original).

20. Watten, *Constructivist Moment*, 318; Iampolski, "Poetika kasa-niia," 374. Ioffe and Pavlov also discuss Dragomoshchenko's response to this Kantian tradition. Ioffe, "Arkady Dragomoshchenko's Photography," 586–87; Pavlov, "'Poetry' vs. 'Literature,'" 561–63, 566.

21. Hejinian, *Guard*, 23; Arkadii Dragomoshchenko to Lyn Hejinian, 1 June 1984, private collection (emphasis in the original). The letter quoted in *The Guard* came from Czechoslovakia. It was one of a series signed "Fan Boy" or "Jazz Boy" and addressed to Hejinian's husband, the jazz musician Larry Ochs. Hejinian, *Language of Inquiry*, 63–64.

22. Barthes, *S/Z*, 10.

23. Dragomoshchenko, "Uzhin," 6.

24. Dragomoshchenko, "Uzhin," 46 (suspension points in the original).

25. Dragomoshchenko, "Uzhin," 9.

26. Arkadii Dragomoshchenko to Lyn Hejinian, 1 June 1984, private collection (emphasis in the original); Dragomoshchenko, *Description*, 21.

27. Dragomoshchenko, "Uzhin," 48–49.

28. Adding to these multilateral interconnections, Molnar was also the first to write about Dragomoshchenko and Hejinian's collaboration. Molnar, "Vagaries of Description."

29. On 8 June 1983, just two days before Hejinian arrived in the Soviet Union, a poetic evening took place in Moscow that has subsequently been mythologized by Epstein as the originating moment of "metarealism," "a particular stylistic tendency and . . . theoretical concept" in Russian poetry that Epstein associates with postmodernism and that he would later link to Dragomoshchenko. Epstein, *Postmodern v Rossii*, 2. The previous year in Leningrad, the young poet, critic, and editor Dmitry Volchek had founded the short-lived samizdat journal *Molchanie*, the forerunner of his better-known *Mitin zhurnal*, a leading outlet for Russian literary postmodernism in the 1980s.

30. Skidan, review of *Opisanie*. Ivanov claims that "anyone who wants to understand exactly what went on in literature in the second half of the 1980s and who wants a clear idea of how Soviet postmodernism began should be acquainted with this publication [*Mitin zhurnal*]." Ivanov, "V bytnost'," 195. As Kuz'min notes, in the late 1980s the editors of *Mitin zhurnal* came increasingly to focus the poetry section of the journal on a group of poets that included Dragomoshchenko. This favored poetry was characterized by the "linking of the Mandelstam-Vaginov tradition with the assimilation of English- and French-language stylistic, semantic, and compositional innovations of the first half of the twentieth century—from Pound to Breton." Kuz'min, "Literaturnyi periodicheskii samizdat," 210.

31. Volchek, "Interv'iu s Viktorom Krivulinym."

32. "Arkady must have written to you, Lyn, about his poetical evening in [the] Dostoyevsky Museum in December [1983] which turned into a real multimedia happening with music, acting, dancing, playback etc. Among the playback he used a cassette with the recording [of] your reading your own poetry during the broadcast. All in all it was nice but resulted in a kind of scandal." Alexander Kan to Lyn Hejinian, 30 January [1984], Lyn Hejinian Papers, box 5, folder 8. Molnar also recalls the event in a letter to Hejinian, noting that Dragomoshchenko's "notorious recital in December 1983 in the Dostoevsky museum . . . resulted in the club [Club-81] being henceforth banned from those premises." Michael Molnar to Lyn Hejinian, 13 February [1985], Lyn Hejinian Papers, box 27, folder 7.

33. Dmitry Volchek to Lyn Hejinian, 27 October 1985, Lyn Hejinian Papers, box 36, folder 28.

34. Dragomoshchenko, "Uzhin," 10, 18–19; Ostanin and Kobak, "Molniia i raduga."

35. This statement regarding aesthetic independence appears in the club's statutes, which were printed in the samizdat journal *Chasy* alongside a description of how the club was founded. Account of the establishment of

Club-81. Exactly why the KGB allowed the initiative to go ahead and whose idea it was to set up the club remain matters of some historical controversy. As Mikhailichenko documents, both the writers and the KGB officers involved claim it was their idea. Mikhailichenko, "Sbornik *Krug*," 236. As head of the KGB at the time of the club's establishment, Andropov may have had some role in the initiative as part of his concurrent campaign against Brezhnev supporters, including Grigory Romanov, the party boss of Leningrad and a member of the Politburo. Solovyov and Klepikova, *Yuri Andropov*, 164. In 1983, the Rova Quartet performed at the museum under the club's auspices after the Leningrad authorities refused to allow the concert to go ahead at the planned venue. Hejinian's diary entry from 14 June 1983, after Brezhnev had died and Andropov had assumed the position of General Secretary, supports the theory that the club served to undermine Romanov's authority: "The City Council of Leningrad, under the directorship of a powerful Party Member and member of the Politburo named Romanov, has refused to give permission for a concert, so an unofficial concert is to take place at the Dostoevsky Museum, which is where Club 81 meets. The Club is sanctioned by the KGB, which runs the Dostoevsky Museum." Hejinian, notebook, 7–15 June 1983, Lyn Hejinian Papers, box 47, folder 1.

    36. Ostanin and Kobak, "Molniia i raduga," 18. Dragomoshchenko later claimed, "I wasn't considered a dissident because I didn't know how to do it properly." Dragomoshchenko, quoted in Sakina, "Dragomoschenko,"241. Elsewhere, he describes how literature was for him a "tiny sanctuary of power" free from the social and political pressures of the late-Soviet period. Dragomoshchenko, "O iazyke piva." Dragomoshchenko's position maintained the notion of independence from official culture, which was "a consciously developed and defining myth of the Leningrad scene." Komaromi, "Unofficial Field," 605. See also Savitskii, *Andegraund*, 5; Ostanin, "Byt' vmesto imet'." Yet Dragomoshchenko departed from the views of more aesthetically conservative samizdat writers such as Viktor Krivulin and Boris Ivanov in emphasizing indifference rather than opposition. By contrast, Ivanov describes the samizdat writers of the 1970s and early 1980s as "a generation of authors who had *never* crossed the threshold of the . . . Writers' or Artists' Union, and who had never submitted their manuscripts to state, that is party, publishers." Ivanov, "V bytnost'," 196–97 (emphasis in the original). For more on the unofficial literary scene in Leningrad during this period, see Edmond, "Revistas, antologías y clubs."

    37. Perloff, "Russian Postmodernism"; Watten, *Constructivist Moment*, 320.

    38. Pavlov argues against the social and political framing of Dragomoshchenko's poetics. Pavlov, translator's preface. Berezovchuk describes Dragomoshchenko the social and cultural figure and Dragomoshchenko the poet as "two completely different people." Berezovchuk, "Kontseptsiia ritma," 206. Similarly, Iampolski discusses Dragomoshchenko's work as presenting the capacity of language in general to resist the establishment of place. Iampolski, "Poetika kasaniia," 361. Even Golynko-Vol'fson—who does discuss

Dragomoshchenko's poetry through its encounter with the American "other" and notes sociocultural differences between the two—emphasizes common understandings of language. Golynko-Vol'fson, "Ot pustoty."

39. Arkadii Dragomoshchenko to Lyn Hejinian, 4 September 1985, private collection (suspension points in the original).

40. Dragomoshchenko, *Opisanie*, 315.

41. Arkadii Dragomoshchenko to Lyn Hejinian, 1 June 1984, private collection.

42. Arkadii Dragomoshchenko to Lyn Hejinian, 1 June 1984, private collection.

43. Dragomoshchenko, *Nebo sootvetstvii*, 26–27; Dragomoshchenko, *Description*, 50 (modified translation; suspension points in the original).

44. Arkadii Dragomoshchenko to Lyn Hejinian, 21 March 1985, private collection.

45. Dragomoshchenko, *Description*, 79–80; Dragomoshchenko, "Primechaniia," 268–71; Dragomoshchenko, *Opisanie*, 15, 308–9.

46. Dragomoshchenko, *Opisanie*, 15.

47. Dragomoshchenko recalls this sense of the spatial and temporal dimensions of letters and their highlighting of the otherness of language in another, more recent literary work emerging from a long-distance correspondence, this time with the US-based Russian writer Margarita Meklina. Writing to Meklina, Dragomoshchenko imagines that "in letters there really exist inner possibilities for transitions, for another [*inoe*] taxonomy, for another [*inoe*] distribution of meanings across times and spaces." Dragomoshchenko and Meklina, *Pop3*, 199.

48. Blanchot, *Infinite Conversation*, 23. Bruns reads this passage from Blanchot as describing "a detour of language or a turning back or away from the movement of conceptual determination or the production of meanings, works, cultures, worlds." Bruns, *Maurice Blanchot*, 122.

49. Blanchot, *Space of Literature*, 216; Dragomoshchenko, *Nebo sootvetstvii*, 26; Dragomoshchenko, *Description*, 50.

50. Dragomoshchenko, "Primechaniia," 268; Dragomoshchenko, *Opisanie*, 308.

51. Dragomoshchenko, "Primechaniia," 269.

52. Skidan, review of *Opisanie*.

53. Dragomoshchenko, "Accidia," 216–21; Dragomoshchenko, *Description*, 83–90.

54. Arkadii Dragomoshchenko to Lyn Hejinian, 23–24 February 1984, private collection.

55. Sandler, "Arkadii Dragomoshchenko, Lyn Hejinian," 40.

56. Dragomoshchenko, "Accidia (Voina)."

57. Dragomoshchenko, "Accidia," 216; Dragomoshchenko, *Description*, 83 (modified translation).

58. Dragomoshchenko elsewhere describes the "boundless luminescence of the world . . . glimmering faintly in a fixed mirror," suggesting and unsettling mirror-like mimesis by connecting the mirror to a pun on *mira-zh*,

both "of this very world" and a "mirage." Dragomoshchenko, "I(s)," 127; Edmond, "Meaning Alliance," 556.

59. Perloff, "Russian Postmodernism"; Watten, *Constructivist Moment*, 303, 316–20.

60. Pavlov, translator's preface.

61. Perloff, review of *Leningrad*, 218–19; Iampolski, "Poetika kasaniia," 361–78.

62. Watten, *Constructivist Moment*, 303, 318.

63. Watten, *Constructivist Moment*, 295.

64. Iampolski, "Poetika kasaniia," 372–74.

65. Levinas, "Ethics as First Philosophy."

66. Dragomoshchenko, *Nebo sootvetstvii*, 52–53; Dragomoshchenko, *Description*, 93 (modified translation).

67. It seems reasonable to assume that Dragomoshchenko wrote "Nasturtium as Reality" with the idea that Hejinian would translate it. As part of the The Corresponding Sky collaboration initiated in May 1985, they had been sending poems to each other for over a year by the time Hejinian reported in a letter to him that she had received his "new" poem "Nasturtsia"—or what she translates in the letter as "A Nasturtium Like Reality." At this time, Hejinian's role as a translator of Dragomoshchenko's work was already well established: she wrote in the same letter that she and her cotranslator, Elena Balashova, had "a rough draft [translation] of half *The Corresponding Sky*" and suggested that the "Sun & Moon book" of Dragomoshchenko's poems in English translation (which would be published as *Description*) might include "both works." Lyn Hejinian to Arkadii Dragomoshchenko, 6 September 1986, private collection. Although Hejinian writes of The Corresponding Sky and "Nasturtium as Reality" as separate works here, Dragomoshchenko clearly thought of the latter as part of the former since he included it in *Sky of Correspondences* when it was first published that year. Dragomoshchenko's dedication of the poem to Hejinian, which appears in this original 1986 publication in *Mitin zhurnal*, supports the view that he wrote it with Hejinian and her translations in mind. Dragomoshchenko, "Nebo sootvetstvii."

68. Pushkin, *Polnoe sobranie sochinenii*, 4:274.

69. Mamin, *Okno v Parizh*. The film plays with cross-cultural misunderstanding and satirizes the importation of Western capitalism into the new post-Soviet Russia. For more on the film's connection to Pushkin and the Petersburg myth, see Chances, "Reflections."

70. Dragomoshchenko, "Nasturtsiia kak real'nost'."

71. Watten, "Post-Soviet Subjectivity."

72. Dragomoshchenko, *Nebo sootvetstvii*, 62; Dragomoshchenko, *Description*, 106 (modified translation).

73. Stewart, *Poetry and the Fate of the Senses*, 47.

74. Dragomoshchenko, "Shadow of Reading," 242.

CHAPTER 3. LYN HEJINIAN AND RUSSIAN ESTRANGEMENT

1. Hejinian, afterword, 105.

2. Hejinian, "Roughly Stapled."

3. Watten, *Total Syntax*, 1; Hejinian, "Roughly Stapled."

4. Michael Davidson, conversation with the author, 26 August 2003.

5. Hejinian's initial trip to Russia is documented in Hejinian, notebook, 7–15 June 1983, Lyn Hejinian Papers, box 47, folder 1. Correspondence and documents from these papers show that she made at least six subsequent trips to Russia: in 1985, 1987, 1989 (twice), 1990, and 1991.

6. On her poetics of translation, see Janecek, "Lin Khedzhinian"; Edmond, "Meaning Alliance."

7. Shklovsky, "Iskusstvo," 13. While I draw freely on translations by Lemon and Reis and by Sher, I have chosen to translate this passage myself in the interests of literalness and the preservation of ambiguities. Shklovsky, "Art as Technique," 12; Shklovsky, *Theory of Prose*, 6.

8. Matejka, "Formal Method," 285.

9. Erlich, *Russian Formalism*, 154.

10. Todorov, "Three Conceptions," 139.

11. Perloff, *Radical Artifice*. On estrangement as a device of mediation between art and life, see Steiner, *Russian Formalism*; Striedter, *Literary Structure*. Jameson also discusses what he sees as the "profound ambiguity" in Shklovsky's theory of poetic language, an ambiguity he identifies primarily in the tension between estrangement in content and form, the latter implying an autonomous aesthetic. Jameson, *Prison-House of Language*, 75–79.

12. Boym, "Estrangement as a Lifestyle," 515, 518.

13. Hejinian, *Language of Inquiry*, 161; Watten, *Constructivist Moment*.

14. Hejinian, *Language of Inquiry*, 301 (emphasis in the original).

15. Hejinian, *Language of Inquiry*, 301.

16. Hejinian, *Language of Inquiry*, 344.

17. Hejinian, *Language of Inquiry*, 301.

18. Hejinian, *Language of Inquiry*, 144, 344. Variations on these expressions, central to her definition of poetry, recur throughout Hejinian's essays. In *Language of Inquiry*, see, for example, "experiencing of experience" (3); "consciousness of life" (8); "consciousness of perception" (67); "experience of experience" (203); "thinking of thinking" (300); "experiences of our perceptions" (315); "experiencing experience" and "consciousness of consciousness" (344); and "*experience* of our experience" (345).

19. Hejinian, *Language of Inquiry*, 344, 95, 343.

20. Hejinian, *Language of Inquiry*, 345–46.

21. Hejinian's extension of estrangement to historical context resembles that made by Tynianov and that involved in Jameson's critique of Shklovsky's theory. See Tynianov, "O literaturnoi evoliutsii"; Todorov, "Three Conceptions"; Jameson, *Prison-House of Language*.

22. Hejinian, *Language of Inquiry*, 207.

23. Hejinian, *Language of Inquiry*, 201.

24. Perloff, "How Russian Is It?," 193.

25. Perloff, "Sweet Aftertaste," 122, 126.

26. Dworkin, "Penelope Reworking the Twill," 69, 62.

27. Samuels, "Eight Justifications," 116, 111–13.

28. Writing of *The Cell* (1992), a work composed in the late 1980s, during Hejinian's period of contact with Russia, Altieri suggests that Hejinian "dissolves fixed identity while preserving a range of values like individuality and intimacy which have derived from now outmoded depth-psychology versions of selfhood." Altieri, "Lyn Hejinian," 149. She focuses on "the subject's experience," even as she rejects dramatic climaxes "because the dramatic organization blinds the author to the most intimate features of repetition and change as life unfolds, and it greatly oversimplifies the play of voices that constitute self-consciousness within that unfolding." Altieri, "Lyn Hejinian," 150.

29. Hejinian, *Language of Inquiry*, 201–2.

30. Perloff, "How Russian Is It?," 193. Stephanie Sandler also discusses this contrast. See Sandler, "Arkadii Dragomoshchenko, Lyn Hejinian," 22–23.

31. Hejinian, *Language of Inquiry*, 202–3.

32. Fredman, "Lyn Hejinian's Inquiry," 63.

33. Hejinian, *Language of Inquiry*, 200.

34. Hejinian, *Language of Inquiry*, 158.

35. Hejinian, *Language of Inquiry*, 138; Shoptaw, "Hejinian Meditations," 60.

36. Nicholls, "Phenomenal Poetics," 243.

37. Nicholls, "Phenomenal Poetics," 241.

38. Perelman, "Polemic Greeting," 376.

39. Altieri argues that Language poetry both advocates a politics of identity and rejects identity. Altieri, "What Is Living." Watten also makes this point, while challenging the conclusions Altieri draws from it in some respects. Watten, *Constructivist Moment*, 116–18. For an account of one attack on Language poetry in the 1980s, see Sloan, "'Crude Mechanical Access.'"

40. Watten, *Constructivist Moment*, xviii.

41. Izenberg has addressed the social poetics of Language poetry partly in relation to their contact with Russia, identifying Language poetry's ethos of "collective life" with the collaborative book *Leningrad*. (On the poetics of collective voice in *Leningrad*, see also Silliman, "Task of the Collaborator.") Izenberg argues that the effect produced by Language poetry is one of "anaesthesis," rather than estrangement, suggesting that Language poetry texts such as *Leningrad* assert a universal human capacity to produce sentences. Izenberg, "Language Poetry," 135. Hejinian's poetics of estrangement suggests, however, that the sociality of her work is located precisely in the aesthetic, estranging quality of her poetry, a quality that Izenberg dismisses as largely irrelevant to Language poetry. For Hejinian, "aesthetic discovery is also social discovery." Hejinian, *Language of Inquiry*, 170. Moreover, where Izenberg argues that Language poetry "is not oriented toward . . . perception," Hejinian insists, following Shklovsky,

that the "function of art is to restore palpability to the world." Izenberg, "Language Poetry," 136; Hejinian, *Language of Inquiry*, 301. Far from emphasizing the universal everyday human capacity to produce language, therefore, Hejinian's poetics of estrangement stresses the extraordinary nature of poetic language.

42. For example, in a letter to Susan Bee and Charles Bernstein, Hejinian questioned why some Language poets refused to discuss subjectivity: "Why was the term subjectivity inadmissible, even as something to talk about? Self-expression is an obvious irrelevancy. But subjectivity? . . . What does it mean when one feels one 'doesn't have anything to say'? Who/what determines valid and relevant styles and topics of discourse? (This is the one that concerns me personally—and prompts my question about the topic subjectivity.)" Lyn Hejinian to Susan Bee and Charles Bernstein, 13 February 1983, Lyn Hejinian Papers, box 2, folder 10.

43. Lyn Hejinian to Ron Silliman, 21 January 1982, Lyn Hejinian Papers, box 7, folder 6.

44. Vladimir Kucheriavkin to Lyn Hejinian, [November] 1983, Lyn Hejinian Papers, box 5, folder 11.

45. Lyn Hejinian to Vladimir Kucheriavkin, 7 November 1983, Lyn Hejinian Papers, box 5, folder 11.

46. Nicholls, "Phenomenal Poetics"; Edmond, "Locating Global Resistance."

47. Hejinian, *Language of Inquiry*, 196.

48. Hejinian, *Guard*, 30.

49. Hejinian, *My Life* 1987 ed., 156.

50. Hejinian, talk on US poetry given in Leningrad, 28 May 1985, Lyn Hejinian Papers, box 53, folder 15, audiocassette.

51. Hejinian, notebook, 24 August 1984–July 1985, Lyn Hejinian Papers, box 47, folder 6, page 90 (emphases in the original).

52. Hejinian, *Language of Inquiry*, 202.

53. Hejinian, notebook, 24 August 1984–July 1985, Lyn Hejinian Papers, box 47, folder 6, page 91.

54. Lyn Hejinian to Ilya Kutik, 8 June 1990, Lyn Hejinian Papers, box 24, folder 9 (emphasis in the original).

55. Lyn Hejinian, e-mail message to author, 15 January 2005.

56. This talk was published under the same title in Hejinian, *Language of Inquiry*, 59–82. In the preface to the published version, Hejinian herself notes the influence of her second trip to Russia on the essay and compares it to the influence of her first trip on *The Guard*. Hejinian, *Language of Inquiry*, 59.

57. Lyn Hejinian to Michael Molnar, 6 September 1985, Lyn Hejinian Papers, box 27, folder 7.

58. Hejinian, "Person," 179–80.

59. See Edmond, "Meaning Alliance."

60. Lyn Hejinian to Michael Molnar, 8 June 1987, Lyn Hejinian Papers, box 27, folder 8.

61. Davidson et al., *Leningrad*, 34 (emphasis in the original).

62. Davidson et al., *Leningrad*, 35.

63. Davidson et al., *Leningrad*, 99.

64. Davidson et al., *Leningrad*, 104–5.

65. Shklovsky, "Iskusstvo," 20.

66. Hejinian used the title *This Time We Are Both*, which derives from the title of a painting by Arkadii's son, Ostap Dragomoshchenko, as the opening line of *Oxota*, and "We are both" as the final line preceding the book's "Coda." She also intended to use it as the title of the book *Leningrad*. Hejinian, *Oxota*, 11, 290; Lyn Hejinian to Katerina Dobrotvorskaia, 15 June 1990, Lyn Hejinian Papers, box 16, folder 23.

67. Davidson et al., *Leningrad*, 120.

68. On the distinction, see Boym, *Common Places*, 29–40.

69. Davidson et al., *Leningrad*, 148.

70. Hejinian, "On *Oxota*," 67.

71. Perloff, "How Russian Is It?," 188. Perloff probably has in mind Shklovsky's article "Pushkin and Sterne: *Eugene Onegin*." For a discussion of this article, see Hodgson, "Viktor Shklovsky."

72. McHale, "Telling Stories Again," 261.

73. McHale, "Weak Narrativity," 164–65.

74. Watten, *Total Syntax*, 24; Shklovsky, "Iskusstvo," 13.

75. McHale, "Telling Stories Again," 262.

76. Hejinian, *Language of Inquiry*, 209–10.

77. Hejinian, *Oxota*, 270.

78. Hejinian, *Oxota*, 173.

79. Hejinian, *Oxota*, 268.

80. Hejinian, *Oxota*, 11; Davidson et al., *Leningrad*, 104.

81. Boym, "Estrangement as a Lifestyle," 517–18.

82. Hejinian, *Language of Inquiry*, 210.

83. Boym, *Common Places*, 84.

84. In his suicide poem, Mayakovsky famously wrote: "Liubovnaia lodka razbilas' o byt" (The boat of love has smashed against the daily grind). Mayakovsky, *Bedbug*, 236–37 (modified translation).

85. Hejinian, *Language of Inquiry*, 301.

86. Watten, *Total Syntax*, 15.

87. Boym, *Common Places*, 31; Boym, "Estrangement as a Lifestyle," 518.

88. Buck-Morss, *Dreamworld and Catastrophe*, x–xi.

89. Boym, "Estrangement as a Lifestyle," 517.

90. Watten, *Total Syntax*, 15.

91. Boym, "Estrangement as a Lifestyle," 518.

92. Boym, "Estrangement as a Lifestyle," 518.

CHAPTER 4: BEI DAO AND WORLD LITERATURE

1. On the use of Bei Dao's poetry in the April–June 1989 Tiananmen protests and their aftermath, see McDougall, "Problems and Possibilities," 49.

2. Bonnie McDougall, e-mail message to author, 4 December 2010. Mc-
Dougall, who lived in Beijing and knew Bei Dao in the early 1980s, adds that
"it is increasingly hard now to imagine just how closed that world was."

3. Owen, "What Is World Poetry?," 28–32.

4. Spivak notes the relationship between the geopolitical turn to global-
ization and the shift toward global perspectives within comparative litera-
ture and area studies in *Death of a Discipline*, 1–4. Examples of this global
turn include Damrosch, *What Is World Literature?*; Huk, "New Global Po-
etics?"; and Saussy, *Comparative Literature in an Age of Globalization*.

5. Jones, "Chinese Literature," 176, 186, 189. Chow makes essentially
the same point about the practice of comparative literature as a whole as
it develops from Goethe's notion of *Weltliteratur*. Chow, *Age of the World
Target*, 71.

6. Jones, "Chinese Literature," 189.

7. Damrosch, abstract for the seminar "Comparative World Literature,"
American Comparative Literature Association 2009 Annual Meeting. (I pre-
sented an earlier version of a part of this chapter in Damrosch's seminar.)
Owen's notion of world poetry would seem closer to what Damrosch else-
where calls, in contradistinction to world literature, "a notional 'global lit-
erature' . . . unaffected by any specific context whatever." My broader defini-
tion here draws on Damrosch's description of world literature as "all literary
works that circulate beyond their culture of origin, either in translation or in
their original language," "not an infinite, ungraspable canon of works but
rather a mode of circulation and of reading." Damrosch, *What Is World Lit-
erature?*, 25, 4–5.

8. Jones, "Chinese Literature," 190.

9. Jameson, "Third-World Literature," 71–72, 67.

10. Fukuyama, "End of History?," 3, 5; Owen, "What Is World Poetry?,"
32.

11. Walter Benjamin, *Arcades Project*, 211; Cowan, "Walter Benjamin's
Theory of Allegory," 110.

12. Jameson, "Third-World Literature," 73.

13. Yeh argued that Owen was "imposing another hegemonic discourse,
one that is based on traditional poetry, on modern Chinese poetry." Yeh,
"Chayi de youlü," 95. (My thanks to Rey Chow and Michelle Yeh for helping
me obtain a copy of Yeh's unpublished English translation of the article, from
which I quote here.) Criticizing the way Owen's review works "to ghettoize
Chinese literature," Zhang Longxi insisted that the "barrier that needs to be
pulled down is the rigid opposition between China and the West." Zhang
Longxi, "Out of the Cultural Ghetto," 84, 97. Similarly, Chow described
Owen's position as "Orientalist melancholia" arising from an essentialized
and reified conception of China. This China is confined to the past and con-
trolled and defended by Western authorities such as Owen against the "in-
fidelity" of living representatives of a now impure Chinese culture. Chow,
Writing Diaspora, 1–6.

14. Yeh argued that while Owen bemoaned the lack of history in modern
Chinese poetry, in his review "the historical context essential to the writing

and reading of contemporary Chinese poetry is not taken seriously." Yeh, "Chayi de youlü," 96. Leo Lee argued that Bei Dao's Chinese was inflected by the particularities of his Beijing accent. Leo Lee, "Huli dong shihua," 204. Likewise, Dian Li detailed Bei Dao's use of idioms and allusions dependent on knowledge of traditional and contemporary Chinese culture. Li, *Chinese Poetry of Bei Dao*, 107–12.

15. Huang, *Transpacific Displacement*, 176–77.

16. De Man, *Allegories of Reading*, 5.

17. De Man, *Allegories of Reading*, 5; Chow, *Writing Diaspora*, 5. On the relationship of nationalism and cosmopolitanism to the emergence of comparative and world literature, see Damrosch, "Rebirth of a Discipline."

18. Spivak, "Translation as Culture," 17.

19. Chow, *Writing Diaspora*, 15.

20. "Supplementary figural superposition which narrates the unreadability of the prior narration." De Man, *Allegories of Reading*, 205.

21. On underground reading, see Van Crevel, *Language Shattered*, 35–41; Xiaomei Chen, *Occidentalism*, 61–62; Song, "Glance at the Underground"; Song, "Wenge zhong de huangpi shu."

22. Bei Dao, "Translation Style."

23. On the history of *Today*, see Van Crevel, *Language Shattered*, 63–68.

24. The first issue's English title was *The Moment*, though all subsequent issues and most of the extant copies of the first number, which was reissued in October 1979, bear the English title *Today*. Van Crevel, "Unofficial Poetry Journals."

25. Baum, *Burying Mao*, 63; *Jintian* bianjibu, "Zhi duzhe," 1–2. The editorial is attributed to the *Jintian* bianjibu (*Jintian* Editorial Board) and was most likely written by Bei Dao, Mang Ke, and other collaborators.

26. On Marx's use of Goethe's term in the *Communist Manifesto*, see Damrosch, *What Is World Literature?*, 3–4.

27. Espmark, "Nobel Prize," 150.

28. On the importance of the Nobel Prize in Literature to Chinese nationalism, see Lovell, *Politics of Cultural Capital*.

29. Bei Dao, *Bei Dao shi xuan*, 25–26; Bei Dao, *August Sleepwalker*, 33.

30. Damrosch, *What Is World Literature?*, 19–24.

31. See, for example, Van Crevel, *Chinese Poetry*, 26; Li, *Chinese Poetry of Bei Dao*, 17; McDougall, "Bei Dao's Poetry," 231.

32. The Chinese idiom "thunder out of a blue sky" (青天霹雳) describes a sudden and unexpected change.

33. *Jintian* bianjibu, "Zhi duzhe," 1.

34. On the dating of "The Answer," see Van Crevel, *Language Shattered*, 51n87, and Van Crevel, *Chinese Poetry*, 26n35. The connection of the poem to April 5, 1976, has lingered in accounts of the event. See Saussy's introduction to Bei Dao's 1999 Stanford Presidential Lecture. Saussy, "Bei Dao and His Audiences."

35. Li, *Chinese Poetry of Bei Dao*, 19.

36. Bei Dao, "Answer," 9; Damrosch, *What Is World Literature?*, 23.

37. Pozzana, "Distances of Poetry," 96.

38. Li, *Chinese Poetry of Bei Dao*, 16–17.

39. Van Crevel, *Language Shattered*, 51–52. In her introduction to *The August Sleepwalker*, McDougall alludes to the poem in describing Bei Dao's early poetry as "a revelation of the self inhabiting two unreal universes: a dream world of love, tranquility and normality, that should exist but does not, and a nightmare of cruelty, terror and hatred, that should not exist but does" (10).

40. Van Crevel, *Language Shattered*, 51; Van Crevel, *Chinese Poetry*, 26.

41. Zhang writes of allegorical interpretation, or what he terms "allegoresis," as "a strongly ideological interpretation, one that makes strenuous efforts to make the text fit in with a certain religious doctrine, a particular philosophical outlook, a moral teaching, an intellectual or political orthodoxy, over the resistance of the plain sense of the text." Zhang Longxi, *Allegoresis*, 152. See also Hayot's criticism of Zhang's conception of the "plain sense of the text." Hayot, review of *Allegoresis*, 124–26.

42. Cowan, "Walter Benjamin's Theory of Allegory," 110.

43. McDougall, "Poetry of Shadows," 3.

44. On the role of the Foreign Languages Press at this time in the wider context of the press's history, see McDougall, *Translation Zones*, 25–83.

45. McDougall, "Literary Translation," 22–23.

46. McDougall, introduction, 14.

47. For an account of the debate over modernism, see David E. Pollard, "Controversy over Modernism." See also Barmé, "Translator's Introduction." For the debate over artistic modernism as it extended throughout the 1980s, see Wang, *High Culture Fever*, 137–94. For an account of the debate over modernist poetry, see Van Crevel, *Language Shattered*, 71–76.

48. Chow, *Age of the World Target*; Bonnie McDougall to John Minford, 3 October 1985, Bei Dao Archive, box 403.

49. McDougall, "Bei Dao's Poetry" and "Zhao Zhenkai's Fiction." The special issue was *Renditions* 19–20 (1983).

50. Bonnie McDougall to John Minford, 19 December 1984, Bei Dao Archive, box 415.

51. Soong and Minford, *Trees on the Mountain*; Enright, "Fading or Blooming."

52. Lovell, *Politics of Cultural Capital*, 113–14; Bonnie McDougall, interview with the author, Hong Kong, 9 February 2008. The editor of the *Renditions* special issue, John Minford, was interested in the possibility of a Chinese author winning the Nobel Prize, as is indicated by a letter from Hansson to Minford in the summer of 1985, when Bei Dao first traveled abroad. In the letter Hansson responds to an apparent query from Minford about the possibility of a Chinese writer winning the Nobel Prize in Literature by noting that "the Swedish Academy . . . clearly want the prize to be as universal as possible & they are probably sensitive to criticism that small or non-Western languages are ignored" and that "Göran Malmqvist's election to the academy makes it pretty clear that a Chinese author is bound to get the prize within the next few years." Malmqvist, Hansson notes, "may have a rather strong emotional inclination to promote Chinese lit., e.g. by a Nobel prize award." Anders Hansson to John Minford, 13 June 1985, Bei Dao Archive, box 411.

53. Peter Jay first proposed to publish a collection of Bei Dao's poetry through his Anvil Poetry Press in early 1986 (at which time Michael March had already begun negotiating to publish the collection through Heinemann or Penguin). But McDougall and Bei Dao sought to accept Jay's offer and to speed up the publication process in early 1987 in response to the Anti–Bourgeois Liberalization Campaign, which had begun in January. Peter Jay to Bonnie McDougall, 13 March 1986, private collection; Bonnie McDougall to Michael March, 11 February 1987, private collection.

54. Hughes, *Selected Translations*, 199.

55. Peter Jay to Bonnie McDougall, 13 March 1986, private collection.

56. Owen, "What Is World Poetry?," 31.

57. Bei Dao selected "Hello, Baihua Mountain" from a range of possible poems to open his first officially published collection, *Bei Dao shi xuan* 北岛诗选 (*Selected Poems of Bei Dao*; 1986; revised and expanded edition 1987), and subsequently *The August Sleepwalker*, his first widely distributed book of poetry in English translation. Prior to these books, Bei Dao had experimented with various selections and loosely chronological orderings of his early poems in several self-published, mimeographed collections of his work. For example, *Mosheng de haitan* 陌生的海滩 (*Strange Shores*; 1978) begins with a poem dated 1973, followed by several dated 1972, including the first six poems in the *Selected Poems of Bei Dao*. *Strange Shores*, however, presents these six poems in a different order and intersperses them with other poems. In *Strange Shores*, "Hello, Baihua Mountain" appears third, after another poem dated 1972, entitled "Xing Guang" 星光 ("Starlight"). As this example illustrates, Bei Dao considered the selection and order of his poems to be significant and gave great attention to these aspects of his collections, including, as McDougall recalls, *The August Sleepwalker*. McDougall, interview with the author, Hong Kong, 9 February 2008.

58. Bei Dao, *Bei Dao shi xuan*, 2–3; Bei Dao, *August Sleepwalker*, 19.

59. Owen, "What Is World Poetry?," 31–32.

60. On the preservation of underground poems in the early 1970s, see Van Crevel, *Language Shattered*, 55–57.

61. The print run for Bei Dao's book is listed among the publication details at the end of *Bei Dao shi xuan*.

62. Owen, "What Is World Poetry?," 32.

63. Owen, "What Is World Poetry?," 31.

64. Walter Benjamin, *Arcades Project*, 21; Owen, "What Is World Poetry?," 28.

65. Bei Dao, *Bei Dao shi xuan*, 148; Bei Dao, *August Sleepwalker*, 110.

66. Owen, "What Is World Poetry?," 30.

67. Walter Benjamin, *Arcades Project*, 21–22.

68. McDougall notes that she was made aware of the personal referent of this and other poems while working with Bei Dao on translating his poetry. Bonnie McDougall, e-mail messages to author, 4 December 2010 and

29 July 2011. Bei Dao's removal of the poem's original dedication to a friend contrasts with his much more public and overtly political dedication of "Xuangao" 宣告 ("Declaration") to Yu Luoke 遇罗克, who was imprisoned and later shot during the Cultural Revolution. Bei Dao, *Bei Dao shi xuan*, 73.

69. McDougall explains her use of syntactic inversion here as an attempt to convey the inversion of the prepositional phrase 对于世界 (to the world) and the subject 我 (I) in the opening lines. Bonnie McDougall, e-mail message to author, 4 December 2010. Rather than rendering the lines as "To the world / I am always a stranger" (which would convey approximately the same feel to the English reader), however, McDougall adds another form of syntactic inversion not present in the Chinese (which maintains its neutral subject-verb-object word order) by translating the lines as "a perpetual stranger / am I to the world."

70. The *OED* references to "beloved" are all pre–twentieth century, whereas there are several late twentieth-century entries for "lover" in the relevant sense.

71. Van Crevel, *Chinese Poetry*, 179–80.

72. Owen, "What Is World Poetry?," 30.

73. Van Crevel, *Chinese Poetry*, 180.

74. Shklovsky, "Iskusstvo," 13.

75. Li, *Chinese Poetry of Bei Dao*, 21.

76. Damrosch, *What Is World Literature?*, 21.

77. Damrosch, *What Is World Literature?*, 24, 14.

CHAPTER 5. DMITRI PRIGOV AND CROSS-CULTURAL CONCEPTUALISM

1. Bann, introduction, 3.

2. Corris, "Invisible College," 12.

3. Barabanov, "Art in the Delta," 31. In one of their key *sots-art* works, the performance and sculptural piece *Kotlety "Pravda"* (*"Pravda" Burgers*; 1975), Komar and Melamid translated conceptual artist John Latham's 1966 dissolution of Clement Greenberg's *Art and Culture* into the Soviet ideological system by pulping an issue of the leading state newspaper, *Pravda*, and transforming it into "burgers," or *kotlety*. See Bann, introduction, 9. Komar and Melamid also emphasized their skeptical attitude toward the renewed Western interest in Russian modernists from Malevich (to whom the minimalism of the pulped *Pravda* ironically alludes) to constructivists such as Rodchenko and Tatlin. For Komar and Melamid, Russia's modernist avant-garde had laid the groundwork for Stalinist art, a view that Boris Groys would later forcefully articulate. Komar, "Conceptualism"; Groys, *Total Art*. Komar and Melamid's "conspicuous subversion of the historical avant-garde's social ambitions and formal strategies . . . clashed with both Western minimalists' admiration for the Soviet nonobjective tradition and Western conceptualists' fascination with the political radicalism of Soviet culture." Tupitsyn, "About Early Soviet Conceptualism," 103. For an example of the

gulf between Russian and Western views on political art at this time, see Joseph Beuys's interview with V. Bakchanyan and A. Ur, "Art and Politics," published in the bilingual Russian émigré arts magazine *A-Ya*.

4. Epstein, *After the Future*; Dobrenko, "Socialist Realism," 103.

5. Al'chuk, "Saund-poeziia." Fellow conceptualist writer Lev Rubinshtein also stresses the "global" nature of Prigov's project. Rubinshtein, "Professiia," 232.

6. On his use of seriality, see Janecek, "Seriality"; Janecek, "Seriinost'."

7. Prigov describes his own practice as involving "relationships between ideological, everyday, high culture, low culture, and other languages." Prigov, "Prigov kak Pushkin," 243. His emphasis on total semiotic systems reflects the role played by structuralism in the development of Russian conceptualism in the 1970s. Prigov quoted in Janecek, "Dmitry Prigov," 125. Andrei Zorin notes that during this period Prigov "worked with the structures of consciousness" that meant "the world of official Soviet culture felt to us like 'our home.'" Zorin, "Chtoby zhizn' vnizu tekla," 12–13.

8. Dworkin, "Zero Kerning," 16–17.

9. Prigov, "Preduvedomlenie avtora."

10. Levinson, *Box*, 1–2.

11. Catherine Ciepiela and Stephanie Sandler explore Prigov's use of "personas combining features of the masculine and feminine." Ciepiela and Sandler, "Telo u Prigova," 539.

12. Prigov's iterative poetics unites his position as an "'incorporeal' concept artist" with his role as a "'corporeal' practitioner of performance art" and with his "corporeal and material understanding of writing," combining the temporality of language and performance with the spatiality of sculpture, in which Prigov was first trained. Degot', "Prigov i 'miaso prostranstva,'" 50; Lutzkanova-Vassileva, "Reference, History, and Memory," 51; see also Kuritsyn, *Russkii literaturnyi postmodernizm*, 91–124.

13. Bakhtin, *Speech Genres*, 80; Bakhtin, *Problemy tvorchestva Dostoevskogo*, 143.

14. Prigov combines "sincerity and sham," uniting "burlesque and parody" with "intensity and seriousness" to call his own "parodic intent into question." Hirt and Wonders, "Dmitri A. Prigov," 141; Janecek, "Dmitry Prigov," 43. He seems to adopt an ironic distancing strategy but also to insist on humanist and traditionalist notions of individual artistic agency, provoking ongoing debate about how to read his work. See Golynko-Vol'fson, "Chitaia Prigova."

15. Bakhtin, *Problems of Dostoevsky's Poetics*, 181–204; Bakhtin, *Dialogic Imagination*, 419–22.

16. For example, Prigov, *Piat'desiat kapelek krovi*, 7; Prigov, *Sbornik preduvedomlenii*, 89; Prigov, *Sovetskie teksty*, 92; Prigov, "Kniga kak sposob nechitaniia," 61; Prigov, *Ischisleniia i ustanovleniia*, 46.

17. Hendershot, "Paranoia"; Ngai, "Bad Timing," 2, 6, 17. Like Ngai, Apter associates paranoia with globalization. She describes how "the

paranoid character of knowledge" reflects "the condition of subjective rivalry with intellectual globality," involving "the subject's jealousy of an alienating object—thought—that threatens to subsume or englobe it entirely." Apter, "On Oneworldedness," 372.

18. Bakhtin, *Speech Genres*, 80.

19. Barabanov, "Art in the Delta," 31. The quotations from Barabanov refer to Komar and Melamid's practice in the early 1970s, but are equally applicable to Prigov.

20. Prigov, *Sobranie stikhov*, 2:223, 4:43. The line "I s Iuga viden Militsioner" ("And from the South can be seen the Policeman") does not appear in the original 1976 version. Likewise, in 1976, *militsaner* was not capitalized, as it was in 1978 and subsequent publications. I follow the later version here. The translation is from Smith as adapted by Janecek, who also identifies the changes between the 1976 and 1978 versions. Smith, *Contemporary Russian Poetry*, 212; Janecek, "Dmitry Prigov," 49.

21. Prigov, *Sobranie stikhov*, 4:40.

22. Quoted in Obermayr, "Tod und Zahl," 230.

23. On the childlike and other stylistic elements of the poem, see Janecek, "Dmitry Prigov," 46–52.

24. See the reproductions from the *Book of Decrees* in Prigov, *Grazhdane!*, 200–201. Western conceptualist investigations of authorship and signature include Elaine Sturtevant's copies of other artists' works exhibited under her own name, and Sherrie Levine's rephotographing of images by masters of modern photography.

25. Groys, "Ekzistentsial'nye predposylki"; Borges, *Labyrinths*, 39. Groys only moved to Moscow and became familiar with the artists of Prigov's milieu after writing this essay. See Jackson, *Experimental Group*, 178–79. Prigov's numerous acts of verbatim or near-verbatim reproduction include his untitled manuscript of the opening lines of Pushkin's *Eugene Onegin* (complete with the author's emendations and signature); his performance piece "Mantra vysokoi russkoi kul'tury" ("Mantra of Russian High Culture"), in which he renders these same opening lines in various vocal styles; and his *Faksimil'noe vosproizvedenie (Facsimile Reproduction)* of his samizdat-style retyping of an entire section of *Eugene Onegin*.

26. Groys, "Moskovskii romanticheskii kontseptualizm," 4–5.

27. For other views of the poem, see Küpper, *Autorstrategien*, 151; Witte, "Katalogkatastrophen," 49–50; Tchouboukov-Pianca, *Konzeptualisierung*; Janecek, "Seriality."

28. Prigov, *Azbuki*.

29. Prigov, *Azbuki*.

30. Sandler, *Commemorating Pushkin*, 3.

31. Prigov, *Azbuki*.

32. Janecek, "Seriality," 8.

33. Mayakovsky, for instance, combined an excessive use of the first-person singular pronoun (his first book was entitled *Ia!*, or *I!*) with propaganda for the collective, as in his *Soviet Alphabet*. On Prigov's allusion to Mayakovsky's *Soviet Alphabet*, see Witte, "Katalogkatastrophen," 49.

34. On the connection to Marshak and other alphabet books and the changes in the symbolic meaning of the letter *ia* with the orthographic reform

of 1918, see Janecek, "Seriality," 12n11; Küpper, *Autorstrategien*, 146–48; Witte, "Katalogkatastrophen," 51.

35. Belinskii, *Polnoe sobranie sochinenii*, 7:503.

36. Prigov, Nikonova, and Sigei, "Perepiska," 271.

37. Prigov, "Dmitry Prigov," 52.

38. Bense, "Concrete Poetry," 73.

39. Tupitsyn, "About Early Soviet Conceptualism," 106.

40. Blok, *Izbrannoe*, 183–84. Prigov's poem is one of a pair, a mirroring that itself alludes to the reflection in a wine glass in Blok's poem. The other in the pair contains the same text but inverts its shape and so appears as an upright wine glass. Prigov, *Stikhogrammy*, n.p.

41. Dobrenko, "Byl i ostaetsia."

42. Prigov, "Preduvedomlenie avtora."

43. From around 1980, Prigov began referring to himself in the third person. He came to describe his project as involving the creation of an image of Dmitri Aleksandrovich Prigov. See Epstein, *After the Future*, 358n21; Janecek, "Dmitry Prigov," 120–21. Prigov's interest in the author's image is evident, for example, in his many works invoking Pushkin; in his *Bestiarii* (*Bestiary*) portrait series of famous writers, artists, and other figures all depicted in strange, monstrous forms; and in his playing himself in various performance works.

44. The editor of *A-Ya* encountered this indifference when he tried to interest prominent Russian writers such as Josef Brodsky. Responding to *A-Ya* editor Igor Shelkovsky's survey eliciting Russian writers' views on contemporary art, Brodsky replied that literature and contemporary art were "incompatible." Shelkovsky, "Zametki iz drugogo tysiacheletiia." In addition to Russian and English text, *A-Ya* sometimes included a French supplement. In the second issue, the editors of *A-Ya* underscored their focus on a Western audience by listing prices in four Western currencies and, in addition to its Paris editorial office, representatives in the United States, Italy, Switzerland, Japan, and Israel.

45. Prigov, *Stikhogrammy*, n.p.

46. Prigov, "Iskusstvo predposlednich istin," 18.

47. Prigov, "Conceptualism and the West," 12. The interview eventually appeared in English in the June 1989 issue of the US-based *Poetics Journal*, edited by Hejinian and Watten, a special issue that coincided with the Leningrad conference "Language—Consciousness—Society" and anticipated the momentous international events of that year with its focus on "Elsewhere."

48. Prigov, "Conceptualism and the West," 13.

49. See Oleg Kulik's guard dog performance in Zurich, which alludes to contemporary Russian art's uncertain position neither inside nor outside the Western arena of art. Kulik, *Reservoir Dog*.

50. Prigov, "Conceptualism and the West," 16, 15.

51. Prigov, "Conceptualism and the West," 14.

52. Prigov, *Azbuki*; Prigov, "From *Reagan's Image*."

53. Prigov, "Conceptualism and the West," 12–13.

54. Komaromi argues that this fetishization of the "object-sign" differed from the Western situation described by Baudrillard in that "nonconformist

ideology in the late Soviet Union was a belief in the 'pure' status of the cultural object." Komaromi, "Material Existence," 609. Prigov's practice highlights, however, precisely the impurities, the many intersections, underlying this myth of purity and so a more complex interrelationship between signs and how they are read cross-culturally. For readings that stress the impurities of samizdat culture and its interactions with official culture through Bourdieu's model of cultural capital, see Savitskii, *Andegraund*, and Komaromi, "Unofficial Field."

55. Prigov, "Conceptualism and the West," 12. The framing of this opposition is similar to that in the interview published by the ICA in 1989 (and probably conducted during his visit to London's ICA gallery in the spring of 1988). Prigov, "Everything You Ever Wanted to Know," 27.

56. Prigov, *Slezy geral'dicheskoi dushi*, 31.

57. Inaga, "Making of Hokusai's Reputation." Prigov's appeal to Hokusai here reflects his interest in European imaginings of Japan, as in his book *Tol'ko moia Iaponiia* (*Only My Japan*; 2001), the cover of which presents images of Mount Fuji, the sea, and boats in the style of Hokusai.

58. Hokusai's indefiniteness here recalls the role of "Japan" in the European imagination as a geographically specific figure for universal modernist art and placeless "transnational capitalism." Bush, "Unpacking the Present," 64. Japan plays a similar double role in *Only My Japan*, where Prigov writes: "as has been clear to everyone for a long time, I am not writing about Japan at all. And in any case, any unknown foreign land is simply the most convenient space for the development of one's own fantasies." Prigov, *Tol'ko moia Iaponiia*, 315.

59. Nicholas, "Dmitrij Prigov," 20; Zorin, "Al'manakh," 267.

60. Jackson, *Experimental Group*, 238.

61. Johnson, *Homage*, 92–93.

62. Davidson et al., *Leningrad*, 46.

63. Prigov, "What More Is There to Say?," 101.

64. The content of the *Little Coffins* varies. Johnson's description suggests that each contains a complete poem. Johnson, *Homage*, 93. Janecek confirms that his *Little Coffin* contains a verse draft on a crumpled but whole sheet of paper. Janecek, "Dmitry Prigov," 2n3. Yet according to Davidson, Prigov described the *Little Coffins* he gifted him as containing "confetti." Davidson et al., *Leningrad*, 46. Prigov's *Banka otrinutykh stikov* (*Tin Can of Rejected Verse*) also contains confetti-like fragments of rejected verse. Prigov, *Grazhdane!*, 156. Some *Little Coffins*, such as those held by the Zimmerli Art Museum, have been presented mounted on cardboard. There is also a variant that contains blank pages. Obermayr, "P-rigov wie P-uškin," 307n72.

65. As Boym notes, "the great imperial literary culture that Prigov the critic frequently recalls with nostalgia is recreated in his work through the themes of graphomania." Boym, *Common Places*, 209. Prigov's explanation of his goal of writing 24,000 poems by the year 2000 is quoted in Obermayr, "Tod und Zahl," 230.

66. Walter Benjamin, *Arcades Project*, 460. My interpretation of this passage draws on Andrew Benjamin, "Benjamin's Modernity," 112–13; and on Comay's relation of the term to Benjamin's stress on "redemptive refunctioning of the original through its . . . parasitical repetition." Comay, "Benjamin and the Ambiguities of Romanticism," 149.

67. Prigov describes how the "fragile and compromised material [of the samizdat text] carries precious content, a metaphor for human life" in an unpublished interview with Ann Komaromi. Cited in Komaromi, "Material Existence," 615. In Davidson's and Johnson's accounts, they are about to enter the House of Composers and look at Tchaikovsky's music manuscripts, so suggesting a parodic connection between the *Little Coffins* and the obsession with every scrap of paper produced by a great national writer or artist. On the figurative and literal death of the poet in modern Russian poetry, see Boym, *Death in Quotation Marks*.

68. Beliaeva-Konegen and Prigov, "Krepkogo vam zdorov'ia," 209, 207.

69. Beliaeva-Konegen and Prigov, "Krepkogo vam zdorov'ia," 209.

70. Prigov, *Iavlenie stikha*, 9.

71. Prigov, *Iavlenie stikha*, 13.

72. Prigov, *Ischisleniia i ustanovleniia*, 6.

73. Prigov, *Ischisleniia i ustanovleniia*, 6.

74. Prigov, *Ischisleniia i ustanovleniia*, 11.

75. Prigov continued to work in the genre of equations and comparison in his final years, as in his 2003 work "Tri grammatiki" ("Three Grammars"). For more on "Tri grammatiki," see Janecek, "Seriinost'," 505–12.

76. Golynko-Vol'fson, "Chitaia Prigova." For further examples, see Prigov's performance of himself in mid-2006 in the theatrical ballet *Al'fa-Chaika* (*The Alpha Seagull*), directed by Aleksandr Pepeliaev, and his participation in the popular Russian game show *Sto k odnomu* as the head of a team comprising Moscow artists. The game show episode was filmed on 15 May 2007, just two months before his death on 16 July. But, in another of Prigov's afterlives, it was only shown on Russian television on 16 September 2007, on the channel RTR.

77. Ciepiela and Sandler, "Telo u Prigova."

78. The Prigov-Mali-Prigov art collective later became known as PMP Group, but the 2004 exhibition catalog still emphasizes the original Prigov Family Group name. The words "Prigov Family Group" appear prominently on the cover of the catalog, so illustrating the dominance of the patriarchal and familial form that I am describing here. Prigov, Mali, and Prigov, *PMP-pozitiv.*

79. Boym, *Common Places*, 212. On Putin's authoritarianism and his mobilizing of populist nationalism, see, for example, Robertson, "Managing Society."

80. Prigov, Mali, and Prigov, *PMP-pozitiv*, n.p.

81. I witnessed Prigov give a lively rendition of the work as part of a performance at Harvard University on 19 February 2004.

82. Boym, *Common Places*, 209.

83. Prigov, "Uteshaet li nas eto ponimanie?"

84. Prigov, "Uteshaet li nas eto ponimanie?" Citing Prigov, St. Petersburg poet Aleksandr Skidan echoes his analysis of the effect of technology and globalization on poetry, noting the same shift to visual and performance art. Yet where Skidan sees poetry's "placelessness" as a bulwark against the "capitalist machine," technological reproduction, and visual and performance arts, Prigov appeals to this machine, in the form of global dinosaur mania, as a new source of placeless universalism. Skidan, "Poetry in the Age of Total Communication."

85. Dmitri Prigov, interview with the author, 19 July 2006.

86. Prigov and Studiia Muzei Anna Termen, *Rossiia*. Broodthaers's *Pense-Bête* (1964) comprised forty-four of his books of poetry embedded in plaster.

87. Perloff, "Unoriginal Genius"; Goldsmith, "Uncreativity." See also Goldsmith's frequently cited manifesto "Conceptual Poetics."

88. Perloff, "Russian Postmodernism." Perloff's interpretation of Prigov is based mainly on Epstein's account in his afterword to *The Third Wave*. Epstein's account in turn draws implicitly on Groys's seminal essay "Moscow Romantic Conceptualism."

89. Dworkin, "Fate of Echo," xlviiin2. See also Dworkin's *The UbuWeb Anthology of Conceptual Writing*, in which he includes precursor works by Vito Acconci, Joseph Kosuth, and Gertrude Stein, but not by Prigov. On his influential blog, Ron Silliman has repeatedly noted Prigov's omission from US discussions of conceptual poetics, 22 March 2006, 23 February 2006, 3 June 2009.

90. Dworkin, "Fate of Echo," xlv. In another parallel, Prigov and Goldsmith both insist that literature is fifty years behind the visual arts. In so doing, they echo Brion Gysin's fifty-year-old statement (first made in 1959) that "writing is fifty years behind painting." Prigov, "Uteshaet li nas eto ponimanie?"; Goldsmith, "Kenneth Goldsmith on Uncreative Writing"; Gysin, "Cut Ups," 131.

91. Perloff, "Unoriginal Genius," 231.

92. Prigov, "What More Is There to Say?," 102.

CHAPTER 6. CHARLES BERNSTEIN AND BROKEN ENGLISH

1. Bernstein is clearly an important influence on Yunte Huang's *Transpacific Displacement*, which seeks to open up US literary studies to transpacific readings. Huang studied at SUNY Buffalo under Bernstein and frequently cites his work, especially on Pound. Likewise, at the seminar "A New Global Poetics?" that I organized for the American Comparative Literature Association's 2007 annual meeting in Puebla, Mexico, both Romana Huk and I focused on Bernstein's essay "Poetics of the Americas" in our framing of the relationship between globalization and contemporary poetry. In the article that emerged from her paper, Huk notes that Bernstein in many ways anticipates Wai Chee Dimock's influential argument in *Through Other Continents* for a transnational approach to the study of US literature. Huk, "New

Global Poetics?," 761. See also the discussions of Bernstein in Huk, *Assembling Alternatives*, 3–4; and in Watten, *Constructivist Moment*, 111–18. For examples of Bernstein's insistence on the importance of poetics, see Bernstein, "What's Art," 605–7; Bernstein, "Comedy and the Poetics of Political Form," in Bernstein, *Poetics*, 218–28.

2. Bernstein, *My Way*, 115.

3. Bernstein's acute awareness of his position at the center of world economic and cultural power is evident, for example, in the title of his essay "In the Middle of Modernism in the Middle of Capitalism on the Outskirts of New York." Bernstein, *Poetics*, 90–105.

4. Bernstein, "What's Art," 607.

5. Bernstein, *Poetics*, 196.

6. Bernstein, *Poetics*, 200–201.

7. Bernstein, *Poetics*, 216–17.

8. Olson, *Mayan Letters*, 90. Olson refers specifically to Pound's *Guide to Kulchur*.

9. Bernstein, *Poetics*, 203. Bernstein elsewhere insists that Olson's move out of the Western Box remained incomplete because Olson "projects . . . phallocentric values onto the non-Western/archaic sources that were to be his escape route." Bernstein, *Content's Dream*, 328. For a defense of Olson against Bernstein's charge, see Herd, "From Him Only."

10. Bernstein, *Poetics*, 203.

11. Bernstein, introduction, 2; Bernstein, "Our Americas," 72.

12. On Bernstein's reconceptualization of community as an "uncommunity," or as "conversation," see Hart, "Taking the Unity out of Community"; Bernstein, "Community and the Individual Talent," 179, 185; Bernstein et al., "Poetry, Community, Movement," 206.

13. Charles Bernstein to Jerome Rothenberg, 28 April 1975, Charles Bernstein Papers, box 55, folder 2. I am grateful to Ann Vickery for drawing my attention to the Bernstein-Rothenberg correspondence in this context.

14. Silliman, "Dwelling Place."

15. Charles Bernstein to Jerome Rothenberg, 28 April 1975, Charles Bernstein Papers, box 55, folder 2.

16. See especially the note on his use of the word "primitive." Rothenberg, "Pre-face," xxv.

17. North, *Dialect of Modernism*, 67.

18. Bernstein, *Content's Dream*, 328, 333, 329, 333.

19. Von Hallberg, "Poetry, Politics, and Intellectuals," 171.

20. Middleton, "Transitive Poetics," 103.

21. Bernstein et al., "Poetry, Community, Movement," 205–6.

22. Chow, *Age of the World Target*, 76. In "Rebirth of a Discipline," Damrosch argues that there were conceptions of world and comparative literature in the nineteenth century more amenable to our own age but that they were subsequently largely ignored or forgotten.

23. Melas, *All the Difference*, xii. Critical texts in this spatial turn include Foucault, "Of Other Spaces"; Lefebvre, *Production of Space*; and Clifford, *Routes*.

24. Melas, *All the Difference*, 42. See also Chow's "post-European" and Spivak's "planetary" comparison: Chow, *Age of the World Target*, 71–92; Spivak, *Death of a Discipline*, 71–102.

25. Melas, *All the Difference*, 42.

26. Huk, "New Global Poetics?," 778.

27. On Olson's emphasis on Sumerian civilization as a point of origin for the West and a way of reforming Western civilization, and on his related interest in modern Iraq in the 1950s, see Herd, "From Him Only." I draw here on Robbins's criticism of Dimock for her implication that the moral and ethical claims on us of ancient and recent atrocities are the same. Robbins, "Uses of World Literature," 384–89. Compare this to Olson's erasure of temporal distance in his claim in "La Chute" that poetry, beginning with Gilgamesh, is "where the dead are." Olson, *Collected Poems*, 83.

28. Watten, *Constructivist Moment*, 116; see also Altieri, "What Is Living."

29. Chow, "Old/New Question," 295–98; Bernstein, *My Way*, 120–21. Huk makes a similar point about Bernstein in "New Global Poetics?" Homi Bhabha has demonstrated the inevitability of identificatory dynamics in postcolonial discourse. See especially Bhabha, *Location of Culture*, 57–93. On the unequal power relations involved in claims to a world or global poetics, see also Kadir, "Comparative Literature," 75; Spivak, *Death of a Discipline*, 73.

30. Bertens, review of *Comparative Literature*, 33.

31. For example, while Jahan Ramazani argues that Pound's poems "exemplify orientalist appropriation, exoticism, and misreading," he equally insists that "the intercultural crossings they enact are also self-divided, self-impeding, and self-critical." Ramazani, *Transnational Poetics*, 114.

32. Felski, *Uses of Literature*, 4.

33. Felski, *Uses of Literature*, 7.

34. Marjorie Perloff exemplifies this latter tendency, invoking Pound's and Eliot's modernist dictums of "the dance of the intellect," "language charged with meaning," and, more recently, the "individual talent" as the source of "genius," albeit "unoriginal," in the new, apparently placeless poetics of our digital, global age. I refer to the title of Perloff's book *The Dance of the Intellect*; her invocation of Pound's description of poetry at the end of *21st-Century Modernism*; and her essays "Avant-Garde Tradition and the Individual Talent" and "Unoriginal Genius."

35. Bernstein, *Poetics*, 9–89; Robbins, *Feeling Global*, 6. Bernstein's refusal to divorce a poetics of radical difference from a global, affectively engaged perspective is continuous with Robbins's argument for "uniting cultural politics"—often suspicious of the "view from above" and committed "to preserving and transmitting meanings that are observed from up close"—with "global or internationalist feeling." Robbins, *Feeling Global*, 9, 3, 174.

36. This affective engagement also differs from the third, "historical" mode of reading dominant in literary studies because it makes the critic "think through her own relationship to the text she is reading." Felski, *Uses of Literature*, 10.

37. Bernstein, *Poetics*, 121.

38. Bernstein, *Poetics*, 122–23.

39. Bernstein, *Poetics*, 126.

40. Barthes, *S/Z*, 6; Eco, *Role of the Reader*, 3. See Watten's diagnosis of a nostalgic desire for a return to modernist formalism elsewhere in Bernstein's work. Watten, *Constructivist Moment*, 116.

41. Bernstein, *Poetics*, 126.

42. Bernstein, *Poetics*, 126.

43. Felski, *Uses of Literature*, 19.

44. Bernstein, *My Way*, 165.

45. Bernstein, *My Way*, 163.

46. Bernstein, *My Way*, 162.

47. Felski, "After Suspicion," 29; Bernstein, *Poetics*, 123.

48. Bernstein, *Poetics*, 127.

49. Bernstein, *My Way*, 115.

50. Not only has Bernstein repeatedly insisted on his rejection of group, including national, identities, but one of his earliest essays on group identification, "The Conspiracy of 'Us'" (1979), hinted at the link between national collective identity and the poetry community that was his ostensible subject through the play on "US" as both collective pronoun and the "United States," a pun most visible in the original version, which was published with the heading in block capitals.

51. Watten, *Constructivist Moment*, 111–12.

52. Huk, *Assembling Alternatives*, 4, 2; Huk, "New Global Poetics?," 769–70, 775–76.

53. Bernstein, *My Way*, 114.

54. Owen, "Stepping Forward," 532–33. Von Hallberg makes a similar point about the reception of Czesław Miłosz in the United States. Von Hallberg, "Poetry, Politics, and Intellectuals," 175–82.

55. Owen, "Stepping Forward," 539.

56. Owen, "Stepping Forward," 533, 539, 536–37.

57. Bernstein, *Poetics*, 6.

58. Bernstein, *My Way*, 113.

59. Bernstein, *My Way*, 113.

60. Huggan, *Postcolonial Exotic*, viii.

61. On Bernstein's exploration of fashion and business, see Schultz, *Poetics of Impasse*, 184–211; McGuirk, "'Rough Trades'"; Nathanson, "Collage and Pulverization." Bernstein's titles frequently reference business and commerce as in "The Dollar Value of Poetry" and *Controlling Interests*.

62. See Young, *Idea of English Ethnicity*; Young, *Colonial Desire*; Latour, *We Have Never Been Modern*, 11–12.

63. Lyon, *Manifestoes*, 32.

64. Jameson, *Postmodernism*, 53.

65. Melas, *All the Difference*, 37.

66. See reviews of *Girly Man* by Devaney; Hicks; Peterson, "Either You're With Us and Against Us"; Tapper, "Technocrats of the Mind"; Thomas-Glass, "Accessibility of Obscurity."

67. Schultz, *Poetics of Impasse*, 210–11.

68. Bernstein, *Girly Man*, 7.

69. Bernstein, *Girly Man*, 3.

70. Bernstein, *Girly Man*, 3, 5, 3.

71. Bernstein, *Girly Man*, 6.

72. Owen, "Stepping Forward," 536.

73. Bernstein, "History/Lyric/Speech"; Seiler et al., "I Don't Want to Set the World on Fire"; Ink Spots, "I Don't Want to Set the World on Fire."

74. Bernstein, *Girly Man*, 47–48.

75. Bernstein, *My Way*, 162; Young, *Idea of English Ethnicity*.

76. Bernstein, *Poetics*, 126.

77. Jameson, *Postmodernism*, 28–31.

78. Faithfull, *Broken English*.

79. Bernstein, "History/Lyric/Speech."

80. For example, Bernstein, *My Way*, 66; Watten, "Turn to Language," 139–83.

81. Susan Bee, e-mail message to author, 4 July 2011.

82. On the relationship of *King Kong* to ethnographic cinema, see Rony, *Third Eye*.

83. Baudelaire, "To a Begging Redhead"; Bernstein, *Attack of the Difficult Poems*, 176–77.

84. Country Joe and the Fish, *I Feel Like I'm Fixin' to Die*; Wadleigh, *Woodstock*. I appreciate Lisa Samuels's drawing my attention to the song in this context.

85. Perloff, *Poetry on and off the Page*, 3–11.

86. This double reading of the title "Broken English" emerges from both Bernstein's and his interviewer Leonard Schwartz's comments in Bernstein, "History/Lyric/Speech."

87. Bernstein, "History/Lyric/Speech."

88. Bernstein, "Enough!"

89. Johnson, "Bernstein's 'Enough!'"; Baptiste-Chirot, review of *Lyric Poetry after Auschwitz*. Johnson's response also appears in his collection of poems *Lyric Poetry after Auschwitz*, which can in its entirety be read as an answer to Bernstein's views on antiwar poetry.

90. Bernstein, "Recantorium," 351.

91. Bernstein et al., "Poetry, Community, Movement," 206.

92. Barthes, *S/Z*, 45.

93. Bernstein, "Artifice of Absorption."

94. Bernstein, *Rough Trades*, 30.

95. Compare Brathwaite's disarming of dialectics, which he calls "another gun: a missile," by transforming it into "tidalectics": a circle that "moves outward from the centre to circumference and back again." Brathwaite, "Caribbean Culture," 42.

96. Bernstein, *Content's Dream*, 328.

CONCLUSION

1. Bernstein, *Shadowtime*; Walter Benjamin, *Selected Writings*, 4:392. As Bernstein's notes to the *Shadowtime* libretto stress, Benjamin's angel of history reprises not only *Angelus Novus* but also a poem inspired by

Klee: "Greetings from Angelus," written by Gershom Scholem almost two decades earlier for Benjamin's twenty-ninth birthday. Bernstein, "*Angelus Novus.*"

2. For more on the preponderance of angels in Western high culture of the 1980s and popular culture of the 1990s, see McHale, "What Was Postmodernism?"

3. "The Dream Before" from Anderson, *Strange Angels.*

4. Saussy, *Great Walls of Discourse*, 183; Howe, *That This*, 31.

5. Hejinian, *Guard*, 11.

6. Wittgenstein, *Philosophical Investigations*, 53 (entries 115 and 114).

7. Stein, *Writings*, 288; Hejinian, *Language of Inquiry*, 48.

8. Baudelaire, *Œuvres complètes*, 83; Baudelaire, *Flowers of Evil*, 281 (modified translation).

Abrams, M. H. "The Correspondent Breeze: A Romantic Metaphor." *Kenyon Review* 19, no. 1 (1957): 113–30.

Account of the establishment of Club-81 and the Club's statutes. *Chasy* 35 (1982): 292–97.

Al'chuk, Anna. "Saund-poeziia Dmitriia Aleksandrovicha Prigova v kontekste ego global'nogo proekta / The Sound Poetry of D. A. Prigov in the Context of His Global Project." In Prigov, *Grazhdane!*, 108–14.

Allen, Donald. *The New American Poetry, 1945–1960*. New York: Grove, 1960.

Altieri, Charles. "Lyn Hejinian and the Possibilities of Postmodernism in Poetry." In *Women Poets of the Americas: Toward a Pan-American Gathering*, edited by Jacqueline Vaught Brogan and Cordelia Chavez Candelaria, 146–55. Notre Dame, IN: University of Notre Dame Press, 1999.

———. "What Is Living and What Is Dead in American Postmodernism: Establishing the Contemporaneity of Some American Poetry." *Critical Inquiry* 22, no. 4 (1996): 764–89.

Anderson, Laurie. *Strange Angels*. Warner Brothers, 1989, compact disc.

Apter, Emily. "'Je ne crois pas beaucoup à la littérature comparée': Universal Poetics and Postcolonial Comparativism." In *Comparative Literature in an Age of Globalization*, edited by Haun Saussy, 54–62. Baltimore: Johns Hopkins University Press, 2006.

———. "On Oneworldedness: Or Paranoia as a World System." *American Literary History* 18, no. 2 (2006): 365–89.

Augé, Marc. *Non-places*. London: Verso, 2008.

Baer, Ulrich. *Remnants of Song: Trauma and the Experience of Modernity in Charles Baudelaire and Paul Celan*. Stanford, CA: Stanford University Press, 2000.

Bakhtin, Mikhail. *The Dialogic Imagination: Four Essays by M. M. Bakhtin*.

Edited by Michael Holquist. Translated by Caryl Emerson and Michael Holquist. Austin: University of Texas Press, 1981.

———. *Problems of Dostoevsky's Poetics*. Edited and translated by Caryl Emerson. Minneapolis: University of Minnesota Press, 1984.

———. *Speech Genres and Other Late Essays*. Edited by Caryl Emerson and Michael Holquist. Translated by Vern W. McGee. Austin: University of Texas Press, 1986.

———. *Problemy tvorchestva Dostoevskogo*. Kiev: Next, 1994.

Bann, Stephen. Introduction to *Global Conceptualism: Points of Origin, 1950s–1980s*, edited by Philomena Mariani, 3–13. New York: Queens Museum of Art, 1999.

Baptiste-Chirot, David. Review of *Lyric Poetry after Auschwitz: Eleven Submissions to the War*, by Kent Johnson, with "An Afterword Engaging Charles Bernstein's 'Enough!'" *Galatea Resurrects* 3 (August 2006). http://galatearesurrection3.blogspot.com/2006/08/lyric-poetry-after-auchwitz-by-kent.html.

Barabanov, Yevgeni. "Art in the Delta of Alternative Culture." In *Forbidden Art: The Postwar Russian Avant-Garde*, edited by Garrett White, 7–47. New York: Distributed Art Publishers, 1998. Published in conjunction with the exhibition of the same name, shown at the Art Center College of Design in Pasadena, CA, and the State Russian Museum, St. Petersburg.

Barmé, Geremie. *In the Red: On Contemporary Chinese Culture*. New York: Columbia University Press, 1999.

———. "Translator's Introduction." In *Trees on the Mountain: An Anthology of New Chinese Writing*, edited by Stephen C. Soong and John Minford, 44–48. Hong Kong: Chinese University Press, 1984.

Barthes, Roland. *Empire of Signs*. Translated by Richard Howard. New York: Hill and Wang, 1982.

———. *S/Z*. 1970. Translated by Richard Miller. London: Jonathan Cape, 1975.

Baudelaire, Charles. *The Flowers of Evil*. Translated by William Aggeler. Fresno, CA: Academy Library Guild, 1954.

———. *Œuvres complètes*. Edited by Claude Pichois. Vol. 1. Paris: Gallimard, 1975.

———. *The Painter of Modern Life and Other Essays*. Translated by Jonathan Mayne. 2nd ed. London: Phaidon, 1995.

———. "To a Begging Redhead." Translated by Charles Bernstein. *Golden Handcuffs* 1, no. 13 (Summer–Fall 2010): 31–33.

Baum, Richard. *Burying Mao: Chinese Politics in the Age of Deng Xiaoping*. Princeton, NJ: Princeton University Press, 1994.

Bei Dao 北岛. "Answer." In *A Splintered Mirror: Chinese Poetry from the*

Democracy Movement, translated by Donald Finkel, 9–10. San Francisco: North Point, 1991.

———. *The August Sleepwalker*. Translated by Bonnie McDougall. New York: New Directions, 1990.

———. Bei Dao Archive. Ch'ien Mu Library, Chinese University of Hong Kong.

———. *Bei Dao shi xuan* 北岛诗选 [Selected poems of Bei Dao]. 2nd ed. Guangzhou: Xin shiji, 1987.

———. *Mosheng de haitan* 陌生的海滩 [Strange shores]. Beijing: unofficial mimeograph publication printed by the author, [1978?].

———. "Translation Style: A Quiet Revolution." Translated by Wei Deng. In *Inside Out: Modernism and Postmodernism in Chinese Literary Culture*, edited by Wendy Larson and Anne Wedell-Wedellsborg, 60–64. Aarhus: Aarhus University Press, 1993.

Beliaeva-Konegen, Svetlana, and Dmitrii Prigov. "Krepkogo vam zdorov'ia gospoda literatory" [Wishes of good health to you, gentlemen-writers]. *Strelets* 70, no. 3 (1992): 205–12.

Belinskii, Vissarion. *Polnoe sobranie sochinenii* [Complete collected works]. 13 vols. Moscow: Akademiia nauk, 1953–1959.

Benjamin, Andrew. "Benjamin's Modernity." In *The Cambridge Companion to Walter Benjamin*, edited by David S. Ferris, 97–114. Cambridge: Cambridge University Press, 2004.

Benjamin, Walter. *The Arcades Project*. Edited by Rolf Tiedemann. Translated by Howard Eiland and Kevin McLaughlin. Cambridge, MA: Belknap, 1999.

———. *Selected Writings*. Edited by Marcus Bullock, Howard Eiland, Michael W. Jennings, and Gary Smith. Translated by Edmund Jephcott et al. 4 vols. Cambridge, MA: Belknap, 1996–2003.

Bense, Max. "Concrete Poetry." Translated by Irène Montjoye Sinor. In *Concrete Poetry: A World View*, edited by Mary Ellen Solt, 73. Bloomington: Indiana University Press, 1970.

Berezovchuk, Larisa. "Kontseptsiia ritma v poezii Arkadiia Dragomoshchenko: Neskol'ko predvaritel'nykh nabliudenii v zhanrovom moduse annotatsii" [The concept of rhythm in the poetry of Arkadii Dragomoshchenko: Some preliminary observations in the genre of annotation]. *Novoe literaturnoe obozrenie* 16 (1995): 205–20.

Bernstein, Charles. "*Angelus Novus*." A note citing Walter Benjamin's "On the Concept of History," linked from "*Shadowtime* Synopsis," by Charles Bernstein. June 2005. Electronic Poetry Center. http://epc.buffalo.edu /authors/bernstein/shadowtime/wb-thesis.html.

———. "Artifice of Absorption." In Bernstein, *Poetics*, 9–89.

———. *Attack of the Difficult Poems: Essays and Inventions.* Chicago: University of Chicago Press, 2011.

———. Charles Bernstein Papers. MSS 519. Mandeville Special Collections Library, University of California, San Diego.

———. "Community and the Individual Talent." *Diacritics* 26, nos. 3–4 (1996): 176–95.

———. "The Conspiracy of 'Us.'" In Bernstein, *Content's Dream*, 343–47. Originally published in *L=A=N=G=U=A=G=E* 8 (June 1979): n.p. Facsimile available at http://english.utah.edu/eclipse/projects/LANGUAGEn8.

———. *Content's Dream: Essays, 1975–1984.* Evanston, IL: Northwestern University Press, 2001.

———. "Enough!" E-mail to the Poetics List, State University of New York, Buffalo, 10 March 2003. Originally read on 9 March 2003 at the Bowery Poetry Club, New York, at the launch of *Enough: An Anthology of Poetry and Writing Against the War*, edited by Rick London and Leslie Scalapino.

———. *Girly Man.* Chicago: University of Chicago Press, 2006.

———. "History/Lyric/Speech." Interview by Leonard Schwartz. *Cross-Cultural Poetics*, episode 27. KAOS 89.3FM Olympia, WA. 15 March 2004. PennSound. http://writing.upenn.edu/pennsound/x/XCP.php. Transcribed as "Setting the World on Fire." *Jacket* 29 (April 2006). Archived by the National Library of Australia. http://nla.gov.au/nla .arc-10059-20061027-0000-jacketmagazine.com/29/schw-bernst.html

———. Introduction to "99 Poets/1999: An International Poetics Symposium." Special issue, *Boundary 2* 26, no. 1 (Spring 1999): 1–3.

———. *My Way: Speeches and Poems.* Chicago: University of Chicago Press, 1999.

———. "Our Americas: New Worlds Still in Progress." In Bernstein, *Attack of the Difficult Poems*, 65–72.

———. *A Poetics.* Cambridge, MA: Harvard University Press, 1992.

———. "Poetics of the Americas." In Bernstein, *My Way*, 113–37.

———. "Recantorium (a Bachelor Machine, after Duchamp after Kafka)." *Critical Inquiry* 35 (Winter 2009): 351–60.

———. *Rough Trades.* Los Angeles: Sun and Moon, 1991.

———. *Shadowtime.* Copenhagen: Green Integer, 2005.

———. "What's Art Got to Do with It? The Status of the Subject of the Humanities in the Age of Cultural Studies." *American Literary History* 5, no. 4 (Winter 1993): 597–615.

———. *World on Fire.* Vancouver: Nomados, 2004.

Bernstein, Charles, Bob Perelman, Jonathan Monroe, and Ann Lauterbach.

"Poetry, Community, Movement: A Conversation." *Diacritics* 26, nos. 3–4 (1996): 196–210.

Bertens, Hans. Review of *Comparative Literature in an Age of Globalization*, edited by Haun Saussy. *Recherche Littéraire / Literary Research* 24, nos. 47–48 (Summer 2008): 30–35.

Beuys, Joseph. "Art and Politics." Interview by V. Bakchanyan and A. Ur. *A-Ya* 2 (1980): 54–58.

Bhabha, Homi. *The Location of Culture*. London: Routledge, 1994.

Bien, Gloria. "Baudelaire in China." *Comparative Literature Studies* 22, no. 1 (1985): 121–35.

Blanchot, Maurice. *L'amitié*. Paris: Gallimard, 1971.

———. *Friendship*. Translated by Elizabeth Rottenberg. Stanford, CA: Stanford University Press, 1997.

———. *The Infinite Conversation*. Translated by Susan Hanson. Minneapolis: University of Minnesota Press, 1993.

———. *The Space of Literature*. Translated by Ann Smock. Lincoln: University of Nebraska Press, 1982.

———. "Vzgliad Orfeia" [The gaze of Orpheus]. Translated by Arkadii Dragomoshchenko. *Mitin zhurnal* 32 (1990). Available online at http://kolonna.mitin.com/archive.php?address=http://kolonna.mitin.com/archive/mj32/blansho.shtml.

Blok, Aleksandr. *Izbrannoe*. Moscow: Moskovskii rabochii, 1973.

Bolle, Willi. *Physiognomik der modernen Metropole: Geschichtsdarstellung bei Walter Benjamin*. Cologne: Bohlau, 1994.

Borges, Jorge. *Labyrinths*. New York: New Directions, 1964.

Bowlby, Rachel. *Still Crazy after All These Years: Women, Writing and Psychoanalysis*. London: Routledge, 1992.

Boym, Svetlana. *Common Places: Mythologies of Everyday Life in Russia*. Cambridge, MA: Harvard University Press, 1994.

———. *Death in Quotation Marks: Cultural Myths of the Modern Poet*. Cambridge, MA: Harvard University Press, 1991.

———. "Estrangement as a Lifestyle: Shklovsky and Brodsky." *Poetics Today* 17, no. 4 (1996): 511–30.

Brathwaite, Kamau. "Caribbean Culture: Two Paradigms." In *Missile and Capsule*, edited by Jürgen Martini, 9–54. Bremen: Universität Bremen, 1983.

Broodthaers, Marcel. *Interview with a Cat*. New York: Marian Goodman Gallery, 1995, compact disc. Originally released in 1970.

Brooker, Peter. "The Wandering *Flâneur*, or, Something Lost in Translation." *Miscelánea: A Journal of English and American Studies* 20 (1999): 115–30.

Bruns, Gerald L. *Maurice Blanchot: The Refusal of Philosophy.* Baltimore: Johns Hopkins University Press, 1997.

Buck-Morss, Susan. *The Dialectics of Seeing: Walter Benjamin and the Arcades Project.* Cambridge, MA: MIT Press, 1989.

———. *Dreamworld and Catastrophe: The Passing of Mass Utopia in East and West.* Cambridge, MA: MIT Press, 2000.

Bürger, Peter. *Theory of the Avant-Garde.* Translated by Michael Shaw. Minneapolis: University of Minnesota Press, 1984.

Bush, Christopher. *Ideographic Modernism: China, Writing, Media.* New York: Oxford University Press, 2010.

———. "Unpacking the Present: The Floating World of French Modernity." In *Pacific Rim Modernisms*, edited by Mary Ann Gillies, Helen Sword, and Steven Yao, 53–69. Toronto: University of Toronto Press, 2009.

Cavanagh, Clare. *Lyric Poetry and Modern Politics: Russia, Poland, and the West.* New Haven, CT: Yale University Press, 2009.

Chances, Ellen. "Reflections of Contemporary Russian Society, Culture, and Values in Iurii Mamin's Film, 'Window to Paris.'" In *American Contributions to the Twelfth International Congress of Slavists (Cracow), August–September 1998; Literature, Linguistics, Poetics*, edited by Robert A. Maguire and Alan Timberlake, 21–31. Bloomington, IN: Slavica, 1998.

Chen, Xiaomei. *Occidentalism: A Theory of Counter-Discourse in Post-Mao China.* 2nd ed. Lanham: Rowman & Littlefield, 2002.

Chen Yongguo. "Becoming-Obscure: A Constant in the Development of Modern Chinese Poetry." *Modern Language Quarterly* 69, no. 1 (2008): 81–96.

Chow, Rey. *The Age of the World Target: Self-Referentiality in War, Theory, and Comparative Work.* Durham, NC: Duke UP, 2006.

———. "The Old/New Question of Comparison in Literary Studies: A Post-European Perspective." *ELH* 72, no. 2 (2004): 289–311.

———. *Writing Diaspora: Tactics of Intervention in Contemporary Cultural Studies.* Bloomington: Indiana University Press, 1993.

Chung, Hilary. "Kristevan (Mis)Understandings: Writing in the Feminine." In *Reading East Asian Writing: The Limits of Literary Theory*, edited by Michel Hockx and Ivo Smits, 72–91. London: RoutledgeCurzon, 2003.

Ciepiela, Catherine, and Stephanie Sandler. "Telo u Prigova" [Prigov's body]. Translated by Evgeniia Kanishcheva. In *Nekanonicheskii klassik: Dmitrii Aleksandrovich Prigov*, edited by E. Dobrenko, M. Lipovetskii, I. Kukulin, and M. Maiofis, 513–39. Moscow: Novoe literaturnoe obozrenie, 2010.

Clifford, James. *Routes: Travel and Translation in the Late Twentieth Century*. Cambridge, MA: Harvard University Press, 1997.

Comay, Rebecca. "Benjamin and the Ambiguities of Romanticism." In *The Cambridge Companion to Walter Benjamin*, edited by David S. Ferris, 134–51. Cambridge: Cambridge University Press, 2004.

Corris, Michael. "An Invisible College in an Anglo-American World." Introduction to *Conceptual Art: Theory, Myth, and Practice*, edited by Michael Corris, 1–18. New York: Cambridge University Press, 2004.

Country Joe and the Fish. *I Feel Like I'm Fixin' to Die*. Vanguard, 1967, 33⅓ rpm.

Cowan, Bainard. "Walter Benjamin's Theory of Allegory." *New German Critique* 22 (1981): 109–22.

Crang, Mike. "Rhythms of the City: Temporalised Space and Motion." In *Timespace: Geographies of Temporality*, edited by Jon May and Nigel Thrift, 187–207. New York: Routledge, 2001.

Culler, Jonathan. "Critical Paradigms." Introduction to "Literary Criticism for the Twenty-First Century." Special issue, *PMLA* 125, no. 4 (2010): 905–15.

———. "Intertextuality and Interpretation: Baudelaire's 'Correspondances.'" In *Nineteenth-Century French Poetry: Introductions to Close Reading*, edited by Christopher Prendergast, 118–37. Cambridge: Cambridge University Press, 1990.

Damrosch, David. *How to Read World Literature*. Chichester, UK: Wiley, 2009.

———. "Rebirth of a Discipline: The Global Origins of Comparative Studies." *Comparative Critical Studies* 3, nos. 1–2 (2006): 99–112.

———. *What Is World Literature?* Princeton, NJ: Princeton University Press, 2003.

Daruvala, Susan. *Zhou Zuoren and an Alternative Chinese Response to Modernity*. Cambridge, MA: Harvard University Asia Center, 2000.

Davidson, Michael. *Guys Like Us: Citing Masculinity in Cold War Poetics*. Chicago: University of Chicago Press, 2004.

Davidson, Michael, Lyn Hejinian, Ron Silliman, and Barrett Watten. *Leningrad: American Writers in the Soviet Union*. San Francisco: Mercury House, 1991.

De Certeau, Michel. *The Practice of Everyday Life*. Translated by Steven F. Rendall. Berkeley: University of California Press, 1984.

Degot', Ekaterina. "Prigov i 'miaso prostranstva' / Prigov and the Meat of Space." In Prigov, *Grazhdane!*, 50–59.

De Man, Paul. *Allegories of Reading: Figural Language in Rousseau, Nietzsche, Rilke, and Proust.* New Haven, CT: Yale University Press, 1979.

Derrida, Jacques. "White Mythology: Metaphor in the Text of Philosophy." *New Literary History* 6, no. 1 (1974): 5–74.

Devaney, Thomas. Review of *Girly Man,* by Charles Bernstein. *Philadelphia Inquirer,* 18 February 2007.

Dimock, Wai Chee. *Through Other Continents: American Literature across Deep Time.* Princeton, NJ: Princeton University Press, 2006.

Dimock, Wai Chee, and Lawrence Buell, eds. *Shades of the Planet.* Princeton, NJ: Princeton University Press, 2007.

Dobrenko, Evgeny. "Byl i ostaetsia" [He was and remains]. *Novoe literaturnoe obozrenie* 87 (2007). http://magazines.russ.ru/nlo/2007/87/do17.html.

———. "Socialist Realism, a Postscriptum: Dmitrii Prigov and the Aesthetic Limits of Sots-Art." In *Endquote: Sots-Art Literature and Soviet Grand Style,* edited by Marina Balina, Nancy Condee, and Evgeny Dobrenko, 77–106. Evanston, IL: Northwestern University Press, 2000.

Dolinin, B. E., B. I. Ivanov, B. V. Ostanin, and D. I. Severiukhin, eds. *Samizdat Leningrada: 1950-e–1980-e: Literaturnaia entsiklopediia* [The samizdat of Leningrad: 1950s–1980s: A literary encyclopedia]. Moscow: Novoe literaturnoe obozrenie, 2003.

Donaldson, Gary, ed. *Modern America: A Documentary History of the Nation since 1945.* Armonk, NY: M. E. Sharpe, 2007.

Dragomoshchenko, Arkadii. "Accidia." In *25 Tverskoi bul'var: Golosa molodykh,* 216–21. Moscow: Sovetskii pisatel', 1990.

———. "Accidia (Voina)." *Text Only* 14 (2005). http://textonly.ru/self/?issue=14&article=32050.

———. *Description.* Translated by Lyn Hejinian and Elena Balashova. Los Angeles: Sun and Moon, 1990.

———. *Fosfor* [Phosphor]. St. Petersburg: Severo-Zapad, 1994. Available online at http://www.vavilon.ru/texts/dragomot1.html.

———. "I(s)." Translated by Lyn Hejinian and Elena Balashova. *Poetics Journal* 9 (1991): 127–37. Translation of "Ia v(') Ia." In Dragomoshchenko, *Fosfor,* 129–40.

———. "Kraplenaia pamiat'" [Marked memory]. *GF—Novaia literaturnaia gazeta* 6 (1994): 2–3.

———. *Ksenii.* St. Petersburg: Borei, 1994. Available online at http://vavilon.ru/texts/dragomot3.html. Translated as Dragomoshchenko, *Xenia.*

———. "Nasturtsiia kak real'nost'" [Nasturtium as reality]. *Mitin zhurnal* 13 (1987). Available online at http://kolonna.mitin.com/archive.php?address=http://kolonna.mitin.com/archive/mj13/drag.shtml.

———. "Nebo sootvetstvii" [Sky of correspondences]. *Mitin zhurnal* 7 (1986). Available online at http://kolonna.mitin.com/archive.php?address=http://kolonna.mitin.com/archive/mj07/dragom.shtml.

———. *Nebo sootvetstvii* [Sky of correspondences]. Leningrad: Sovetskii pisatel', 1990.

———. "O iazyke piva, postmodernizma i bashmakov" [About the language of beer, postmodernism, and shoes]. Interview. *Peterburgskii knizhnyi vestnik* 2, no. 5 (1999).

———. *Opisanie* [Description]. St. Petersburg: Gumanitarnaia akademiia, 2000. Available online at http://vavilon.ru/texts/dragomot4.html.

———. "Primechaniia / Footnotes." Translated by Lyn Hejinian and Elena Balashova. In *In the Grip of Strange Thoughts: Russian Poetry in a New Era*, edited by J. Kates, 268–71. Brookline, MA: Zephyr Press, 1999.

———. "The Shadow of Reading." Translated by Lyn Hejinian and Mikhail Hazin. In *Re-Entering the Sign: Articulating New Russian Culture*, edited by Ellen E. Berry and Anesa Miller-Pogacar, 227–44. Ann Arbor: University of Michigan, 1995.

———. "Uzhin s privetlivymi bogami" [A supper with affable gods]. *Mitin zhurnal* 1 (January–February 1985): 3–54.

———. *Xenia*. Translated by Lyn Hejinian and Elena Balashova. Los Angeles: Sun and Moon, 1993. Translation of Dragomoshchenko, *Ksenii.*

Dragomoshchenko, Arkadii, and Margarita Meklina. *Pop3: Epistoliarnyi roman* [Pop3: An epistolary novel]. USA: Franc-Tireur, 2010.

Drichel, Simone. "Regarding the Other: Postcolonial Violations and Ethical Resistance in Margaret Atwood's *Bodily Harm*." *Modern Fiction Studies* 54, no. 1 (2008): 20–49.

Duoduo 多多. *Duoduo shi xuan* 多多诗选 [Selected poems of Duoduo]. Guangzhou: Hua cheng, 2005.

———. "Gaobie" 告别 [Farewell]. In *Xin shi chao shi ji* 新诗潮诗集, edited by Lao Mu 老木, 386–87. Beijing: Beijing Daxue Wusi wenxue she, 1985.

Dworkin, Craig. "The Fate of Echo." In *Against Expression: An Anthology of Conceptual Writing*, edited by Craig Dworkin and Kenneth Goldsmith, xxiii–liv. Evanston, IL: Northwestern University Press, 2011.

———. "Penelope Reworking the Twill: Patchwork, Writing, and Lyn Hejinian's *My Life*." *Contemporary Literature* 36, no. 1 (1995): 58–81.

———, ed. *The UbuWeb Anthology of Conceptual Poetry*. http://ubu.com/concept.

———. "Zero Kerning." *Open Letter* 12, no. 7 (2005): 10–20.

Eaglestone, Robert. "Levinas, Translation, and Ethics." In *Nation, Language, and the Ethics of Translation*, edited by Sandra Bermann and Michael Wood, 127–38. Princeton, NJ: Princeton University Press, 2005.

Eagleton, Terry. *Walter Benjamin; or, Towards a Revolutionary Criticism.* London: Verso, 1981.

Eco, Umberto. *The Role of the Reader: Explorations in the Semiotics of Texts.* Bloomington: Indiana University Press, 1979.

Edmond, Jacob. "Beyond Binaries: Rereading Yang Lian's 'Norlang' and 'Banpo.'" *Journal of Modern Literature in Chinese* 6, no. 1 (2005): 152–69.

———. "The Closures of the Open Text: Lyn Hejinian's 'Paradise Found.'" *Contemporary Literature* 50, no. 2 (2009): 240–72.

———. "Dissidence and Accommodation: The Publishing History of Yang Lian from *Today* to Today." *China Quarterly* 185 (2006): 111–27.

———. "Locating Global Resistance: The Landscape Poetics of Arkadii Dragomoshchenko, Lyn Hejinian and Yang Lian." *AUMLA: Journal of the Australasian Universities Language and Literature Association* 101 (2004): 71–98.

———. "'A Meaning Alliance': Arkady Dragomoshchenko and Lyn Hejinian's Poetics of Translation." *Slavic and East European Journal* 46, no. 3 (2002): 551–63.

———. "Revistas, antologías y clubs: La cultura poética samizdat en la década de los setenta y ochenta" [Journals, anthologies, and clubs: Samizdat poetic culture in the 1970s and 1980s]. *Nerter* 13–14 (Summer–Fall 2009): 14–23.

Edmond, Jacob, and Hilary Chung. "Yang Lian, Auckland and the Poetics of Exile." In *Unreal City: A Chinese Poet in Auckland*, by Yang Lian, 1–23. Auckland: Auckland University Press, 2006.

Eisenstadt, Oona. "Levinas versus Levinas: Hebrew, Greek, and Linguistic Justice." *Philosophy and Rhetoric* 38, no. 2 (2005): 145–58.

Enright, D. J. "Fading or Blooming." Review of *Waves*, by Bei Dao, translated by Bonnie S. McDougall and Susette Ternent Cooke. *Times Literary Supplement*, 29 January 1988, 101.

Epstein, Mikhail. *After the Future: The Paradoxes of Postmodernism and Contemporary Russian Culture.* Translated by Anesa Miller-Pogacar. Amherst: University of Massachusetts Press, 1995.

———. *Postmodern v Rossii: Literatura i teorii* [The postmodern in Russia: Literature and theory]. Moscow: R. Elinina, 2000.

Erlich, Viktor. *Russian Formalism: History-Doctrine.* The Hague: Mouton, 1955.

Espmark, Kjell. "The Nobel Prize in Literature." In *The Nobel Prize: The First 100 Years*, edited by Agneta Wallin Levinovitz and Nils Ringertz, 137–52. London: Imperial College Press, 2001.

Faithfull, Marianne. *Broken English.* London: Island, 1979, 33⅓ rpm.

Felski, Rita. "After Suspicion." *Profession* (2009): 28–35.

———. *Doing Time: Feminist Theory and Postmodern Culture*. New York: New York University Press, 2000.

———. Introduction to "Everyday Life." Special issue, *New Literary History* 33 (2002): 607–22.

———. *Uses of Literature*. Malden, MA: Blackwell, 2008.

Ffrench, Patrick. *After Bataille: Sacrifice, Exposure, Community*. London: Legenda, 2007.

Filreis, Alan. *Counter-Revolution of the Word: The Conservative Attack on Modern Poetry, 1945–1960*. Chapel Hill: University of North Carolina Press, 2008.

Foucault, Michel. "Of Other Spaces." Translated by Jay Miskowiec. *Diacritics* 16, no. 1 (1986): 22–27.

———. *The Order of Things: An Archaeology of the Human Sciences*. London: Tavistock, 1970. Originally published as *Les mots et les choses* (Paris: Éditions Gallimard, 1966).

Fredman, Stephen. "Lyn Hejinian's Inquiry into the Relationship between Language and the Person." *West Coast Line* 36 (2001): 60–72.

Friedlander, Eli. "The Measure of the Contingent: Walter Benjamin's Dialectical Image." *Boundary* 2 35, no. 3 (2008): 1–26.

Friedman, Susan Stanford. "Periodizing Modernism: Postcolonial Modernities and the Space/Time Borders of Modernist Studies." *Modernism/Modernity* 13, no. 3 (2006): 425–43.

———. "Planetarity: Musing Modernist Studies." *Modernism/Modernity* 17, no. 3 (2010): 471–99.

Fukuyama, Francis. "The End of History?" *The National Interest* 16 (Summer 1989): 3–18.

Glad, John. Preface to *Literature in Exile*, edited by John Glad, vii–xiii. Durham, NC: Duke University Press, 1990.

Gleber, Anke. *The Art of Taking a Walk: Flanerie, Literature, and Film in Weimar Culture*. Princeton, NJ: Princeton University Press, 1999.

Gluck, Mary. "The *Flâneur* and the Aesthetic Appropriation of Urban Culture in Mid-19th-Century Paris." *Theory, Culture and Society* 20, no. 5 (2003): 53–80.

Goebel, Rolf J. "Benjamin's *Flâneur* in Japan: Urban Modernity and Conceptual Relocation." *The German Quarterly* 71, no. 4 (1998): 377–91.

Goldsmith, Kenneth. "Conceptual Poetics." *Harriet the Blog*. The Poetry Foundation. 22 January 2007. http://www.poetryfoundation.org/harriet/2007/01/journal-day-one.

———. "Kenneth Goldsmith on Uncreative Writing." Interview by R. J.

Thomson. *The Skinny*, 20 June 2008. http://www.theskinny.co.uk/books
/features/43069-kenneth_goldsmith_uncreative_writing.

———. "Uncreativity as a Creative Process." *Drunken Boat* 5 (Winter 2002–
3). http://www.drunkenboat.com/db5/goldsmith/uncreativity.html.

Golynko-Vol'fson, Dmitrii. "Chitaia Prigova: Neodnoznachnoe i neochevi-
dnoe." *Novoe literaturnoe obozrenie* 87 (2007). http://magazines.russ.ru
/nlo/2007/87/go20.html.

———. "Ot pustoty real'nosti k polnote metafory: 'Metarealizm' i karto-
grafiia russkoi poezii 1980–1990-kh godov." *Novoe literaturnoe obozre-
nie* 62 (2003): 286–304.

Golynko[-Vol'fson], Dmitry, and Evgeny Pavlov. "A Poetics of Intense Preci-
sion." *Landfall* 213 (2007): 52–59.

Groys, Boris. "Ekzistentsial'nye predposylki kontseptual'nogo iskusstva"
[The existentialist preconditions of conceptual art]. 37 12 (1977). Re-
printed in *Moskovskii kontseptualizm*, edited by Ekaterina Degot' and
Vadim Zakharov, 332–42. Moscow: World Art Muzei, 2005. A transcrip-
tion is also available at http://plucer.livejournal.com/71212.html.

———. "Moskovskii romanticheskii kontseptualizm / Moscow Romantic
Conceptualism." *A-Ya* 1 (1979): 3–11.

———. *The Total Art of Stalinism: Avant-Garde, Aesthetic Dictatorship,
and Beyond*. Translated by Charles Rougle. Princeton, NJ: Princeton Uni-
versity Press, 1992.

Gysin, Brion. "Cut Ups: A Project for Disastrous Success." 1964. In *Back in
No Time: The Brion Gysin Reader*, edited by Jason Weiss, 125–32. Mid-
dletown, CT: Wesleyan University Press, 2001.

Hart, Matthew. "Taking the Unity out of Community." *Mantis* 1 (2000).
http://mantisjournal.stanford.edu/M1/Texts/UnityCommunity.html.

Hayot, Eric. "The Asian Turns." *PMLA* 124, no. 3 (2009): 906–17.

———. "Bertrand Russell's Chinese Eyes." *Modern Chinese Literature and
Culture* 18, no. 1 (2006): 120–54.

———. *Chinese Dreams: Pound, Brecht, Tel Quel*. Ann Arbor: University of
Michigan Press, 2004.

———. *The Hypothetical Mandarin: Sympathy, Modernity, and Chinese
Pain*. Oxford: Oxford University Press, 2009.

———. Introduction to "Modernisms' Chinas." Special issue, *Modern Chi-
nese Literature and Culture* 18, no. 1 (2006): 1–7.

———. Review of *Allegoresis: Reading Canonical Literature East and West*,
by Zhang Longxi. *Comparative Literature Studies* 45, no. 1 (2008):
122–26.

Hejinian, Lyn. Afterword to *Third Factory*, by Viktor Shklovsky, 99–106.
Translated by Richard Sheldon. Chicago: Dalkey Archive, 2002.

———. *The Cell*. Los Angeles: Sun and Moon, 1992.

———. *The Cold of Poetry*. Los Angeles: Sun and Moon, 1994.

———. *The Guard*. 1984. In Hejinian, *Cold of Poetry*, 11–37.

———. *The Language of Inquiry*. Berkeley: University of California Press, 2000.

———. Lyn Hejinian Papers. MSS 74. Mandeville Special Collections Library, University of California, San Diego.

———. *My Life*. Providence, RI: Burning Deck, 1980.

———. *My Life*. 1987 ed. Los Angeles: Green Integer, 2002.

———. "On *Oxota: A Short Russian Novel*." *Pequod* 31, no. 1 (1990): 67–68.

———. *Oxota: A Short Russian Novel*. Great Barrington, MA: Figures, 1991.

———. "The Person." In Hejinian, *Cold of Poetry*, 143–96.

———. "Roughly Stapled." Interview by Craig Dworkin. *Idiom* 3 (1995). Available from the Electronic Poetry Center. http://www.epc.buffalo.edu /authors/hejinian/roughly.html.

———. *Writing Is an Aid to Memory*. Great Barrington, MA: Figures, 1978.

Hendershot, Cyndy. "Paranoia and the Delusion of the Total System." *American Imago* 54, no. 1 (1997): 15–37.

Herd, David. "'From Him Only Will the Old State-Secret Come': What Charles Olson Imagined." *English* 59, no. 227 (2010): 375–95.

Hicks, Robert. Review of *Girly Man*, by Charles Bernstein. *Kansas City Star*, 31 December 2006.

Hirt, Günter, and Sascha Wonders. "Dmitri A. Prigov: Textual Manipulator." In Prigov, *Grazhdane!*, 140–48.

Hodgson, Peter. "Viktor Shklovsky and the Formalist Legacy: Imitation/ Stylization in Narrative Fiction." In *Russian Formalism: A Retrospective Glance*, edited by Robert Louis Jackson and Stephen Rudy, 195–212. New Haven, CT: Yale Center for International and Area Studies, 1985.

Howe, Susan. *That This*. New York: New Directions, 2010.

Huang, Yunte. *Transpacific Displacement: Ethnography, Translation, and Intertextual Travel in Twentieth-Century American Literature*. Berkeley: University of California Press, 2002.

———. *Transpacific Imaginations: History, Literature, Counterpoetics*. Cambridge, MA: Harvard University Press, 2008.

Huggan, Graham. *The Postcolonial Exotic: Marketing the Margins*. London: Routledge, 2001.

Hughes, Ted. *Selected Translations*. Edited by Daniel Weissbort. London: Faber and Faber, 2006.

Huk, Romana, ed. *Assembling Alternatives: Reading Postmodern Poetries Transnationally*. Middletown, CT: Wesleyan University Press, 2003.

———. "A New Global Poetics?" *Literature Compass* 6, no. 3 (2009): 758–84. doi: 10.1111/j.1741-4113.2009.00624.x.

Iampolski, Mikhail. "Poetika kasaniia" [The poetics of touch]. In Dragomoshchenko, *Opisanie*, 357–78.

Inaga, Shigemi. "The Making of Hokusai's Reputation in the Context of Japonisme." *Japan Review* 15 (2003): 77–100.

Ink Spots. "I Don't Want to Set the World on Fire." Decca, 1941, 78 rpm.

Ioffe, Dennis. "Arkady Dragomoshchenko's Photography: A New Visuality and a Poetics of Metaphysical Inebriation." *Slavic and East European Journal*. 55, no. 4 (2011): 583–613.

Ivanov, Boris I. "V bytnost' Peterburga Leningradom: O leningradskom samizdate" [When Petersburg was Leningrad: On the Leningrad samizdat]. *Novoe literaturnoe obozrenie* 14 (1995): 188–99.

Izenberg, Oren. "Language Poetry and Collective Life." *Critical Inquiry* 30 (2003): 132–59.

Jackson, Matthew Jesse. *The Experimental Group: Ilya Kabakov, Moscow Conceptualism, Soviet Avant-Gardes*. Chicago: University of Chicago Press, 2010.

Jameson, Fredric. "Cognitive Mapping." In *Marxism and the Interpretation of Culture*, edited by Cary Nelson and Lawrence Grossberg, 347–60. Urbana: University of Illinois Press, 1988.

———. *The Geopolitical Aesthetic: Cinema and Space in the World System*. Bloomington: Indiana University Press, 1992.

———. "Postmodernism, or the Cultural Logic of Late Capitalism." *New Left Review* 146 (July–August 1984): 53–92.

———. *Postmodernism; or, The Cultural Logic of Late Capitalism*. London: Verso, 1991.

———. *The Prison-House of Language: A Critical Account of Structuralism and Russian Formalism*. Princeton, NJ: Princeton University Press, 1972.

———. *The Seeds of Time*. New York: Columbia University Press, 1994.

———. "Third-World Literature in the Era of Multinational Capitalism." *Social Text* 15 (1986): 65–88.

Janecek, Gerald. "Dmitry Prigov." Unpublished manuscript, 2010.

———. "Lin Khedzhinian perevodit Arkadiia Dragomoshchenko" [Lyn Hejinian translates Arkadii Dragomoshchenko]. In *Po materialam mezhdunarodnoi konferentsii-festivalia "Poeticheskii iazyk rubezha XX–XXI vekov i sovremennye literaturnye strategii,"* 293–301. Moscow: Institut russkogo iazyka im. V. V. Vinogradova, 2004.

———. "Seriality in Prigov: The Alphabet Poems." Unpublished manuscript, 2008.

———. "Seriinost' v tvorchestve D. A. Prigova." In *Nekanonicheskii klassik: Dmitrii Aleksandrovich Prigov*, edited by E. Dobrenko, M. Lipovetskii, I. Kukulin, and M. Maiofis, 501–12. Moscow: Novoe literaturnoe obozrenie, 2010.

Jarman, Derek, dir. *Broken English: Three Songs by Marianne Faithfull.* 1979. Super-8 and 16mm.

Jintian bianjibu «今天»编辑部 [*Jintian* Editorial Board]. "Zhi duzhe" 致读者 [To the reader]. *Jintian* 今天 1 (1978): 1–2.

Johnson, Kent. "Bernstein's 'Enough!'" *Vert Poetry Magazine* 8 (March 2003). http://epc.buffalo.edu/mags/vert/Vert_issue_8/poeticsofform.html.

———. *Homage to the Last Avant-Garde.* Exeter, UK: Shearsman Books, 2008.

———. *Lyric Poetry after Auschwitz: Eleven Submissions to the War.* Austin, TX: Effing Press, 2005.

Jones, Andrew F. "Chinese Literature in the 'World' Economy." *Modern Chinese Literature* 8 (1994): 171–216.

Judt, Tony. *Postwar: A History of Europe since 1945.* London: Heinemann, 2005.

———. "What Have We Learned, If Anything?" *New York Review of Books,* 1 May 2008, 16–20.

Kadir, Djelal. "Comparative Literature in an Age of Terrorism." In *Comparative Literature in an Age of Globalization*, edited by Haun Saussy, 68–77. Baltimore: Johns Hopkins University Press, 2006.

Kahn, Andrew. "Causework: The Poet's Authority in the Age of Utopia." *Times Literary Supplement,* 10 September 2010, 14–15.

Klein, Lucas. "Foreign Echoes and Discerning the Soil: Dual Translation, Historiography, and World Literature in Chinese Poetry." PhD diss., Yale University, 2010.

Komar, Vitaly. "The Conceptualism No One Noticed." Paper presented at the American Association for the Advancement of Slavic Studies 40th National Convention, Philadelphia, 22 November 2008.

Komaromi, Ann. "The Material Existence of Soviet Samizdat." *Slavic Review* 63, no. 3 (2004): 597–618.

———. "The Unofficial Field of Late Soviet Culture." *Slavic Review* 66, no. 4 (2007): 605–29.

Krishnaswamy, Revathi. "The Criticism of Culture and the Culture of Criticism: At the Intersection of Postcolonialism and Globalization Theory." *Diacritics* 32, no. 2 (2002): 106–26.

Kulik, Oleg. *Reservoir Dog*. Performance art. Kunsthaus, Zurich, Switzerland, 30 March 1995.

Küpper, Stephan. *Autorstrategien im Moskauer Konzeptualismus: Il'ja Kabakov, Lev Rubinštejn, Dmitrij A. Prigov*. Frankfurt: Peter Lang, 2000.

Kuritsyn, Viacheslav. *Russkii literaturnyi postmodernizm* [Russian literary postmodernism]. Moscow: OGI, 2000.

Kushner, Tony. *Angels in America: A Gay Fantasia on National Themes*. New York: Theatre Communications Group, 1993.

Kuz'min, D. V. "Literaturnyi periodicheskii samizdat rubezha 80–90-kh godov" [Samizdat literary periodicals at the boundary between the 1980s and 1990s]. In *Voprosy ontologicheskoi poetiki: Potaennaia literatura; Issledovaniia i materialy*, edited by L. P. Bykov, 208–14. Ivanovo: Ivanovskii gosudarstvennyi universitet, 1998.

Latour, Bruno. *We Have Never Been Modern*. Translated by Catherine Porter. Cambridge, MA: Harvard University Press, 1993.

Lee, Gregory. *Dai Wangshu: The Life and Poetry of a Chinese Modernist*. Hong Kong: Chinese University Press, 1989.

———. *Troubadours, Trumpeters, Troubled Makers: Lyricism, Nationalism and Hybridity in China and Its Others*. Durham, NC: Duke University Press, 1996.

Lee, Leo Ou-fan 李欧梵. "Huli dong shihua" 狐狸洞诗话 [Ramblings on poetry from the "Studio of a Fox"]. *Jintian* 今天 1 (1992): 201–4.

———. "On the Margins of Chinese Discourse: Some Personal Thoughts on the Cultural Meaning of the Periphery." In *The Living Tree: The Changing Meaning of Being Chinese Today*, edited by Tu Wei-ming, 221–38. Stanford, CA: Stanford University Press, 1994.

———. *Shanghai Modern: The Flowering of a New Urban Culture in China, 1930–1945*. Cambridge, MA: Harvard University Press, 1999.

Lefebvre, Henri. *The Production of Space*. Translated by Donald Nicholson-Smith. Oxford: Blackwell, 1991.

Leffler, Melvyn P. "Dreams of Freedom, Temptations of Power." In *The Fall of the Berlin Wall: The Revolutionary Legacy of 1989*, edited by Jeffrey A. Engel, 132–69. Oxford: Oxford University Press, 2009.

Levinas, Emmanuel. "Dialogue with Emmanuel Levinas." Interview by Richard Kearney. In *Face to Face with Levinas*, edited by Richard A. Cohen, 13–33. Albany: State University of New York Press, 1986.

———. "Ethics as First Philosophy." Translated by Seán Hand and Michael Temple. In *The Levinas Reader*, edited by Seán Hand, 75–87. Oxford: Blackwell, 1989.

———. "Prayer without Demand." Translated by Sarah Richmond. In *The Levinas Reader*, edited by Seán Hand, 227–34. Oxford: Blackwell, 1989.

Levinson, Marc. *The Box: How the Shipping Container Made the World Smaller and the World Economy Bigger*. Princeton, NJ: Princeton University Press, 2008.

Li, Dian. *The Chinese Poetry of Bei Dao, 1978–2000: Resistance and Exile*. Lewiston, NY: Edward Mellen, 2006.

Lionnet, Françoise, and Shu-mei Shih. Introduction to *Minor Transnationalism*, edited by Françoise Lionnet and Shu-mei Shih, 1–23. Durham, NC: Duke University Press, 2005.

Lo Kwai-Cheung. "Writing the Otherness of Nature: Chinese Misty Poetry and the Alternative Modernist Practice." *Tamkang Review* 29, no. 2 (1998): 87–117.

Lovell, Julia. *The Politics of Cultural Capital: China's Quest for a Nobel Prize in Literature*. Honolulu: University of Hawai'i Press, 2006.

Lutzkanova-Vassileva, Albena. "Reference, History, and Memory in Russian Conceptualist Poetry." *Symposium* 59, no. 1 (2005): 43–55.

Lyon, Janet. *Manifestoes: Provocations of the Modern*. Ithaca, NY: Cornell University Press, 1999.

McDougall, Bonnie. "Anxiety of Out-fluence." In *Inside Out: Modernism and Postmodernism in Chinese Literary Culture*, edited by Wendy Larson and Anne Wedell-Wedellsborg, 99–112. Aarhus, Denmark: Aarhus University Press, 1993.

———. "Bei Dao's Poetry: Revelation and Communication." *Modern Chinese Literature* 1, no. 2 (Spring 1985): 225–52.

———. Introduction to *The August Sleepwalker*, by Bei Dao, 9–14. New York: New Directions, 1990.

———. "Literary Translation: The Pleasure Principle." *Zhongguo fanyi: Chinese Translators Journal* 28, no. 5 (2007): 22–26.

———. "A Poetry of Shadows: An Introduction to Bei Dao's Poems." In *Notes from the City of the Sun: Poems by Bei Dao*, edited and translated by Bonnie S. McDougall, 1–29. Ithaca, NY: China-Japan Program, Cornell University, 1983.

———. "Problems and Possibilities in Translating Contemporary Chinese Literature." *Australian Journal of Chinese Affairs* 25 (1991): 37–67.

———. *Translation Zones in Modern China: Authoritarian Command versus Gift Exchange*. Amherst, NY: Cambria, 2011.

———. "Zhao Zhenkai's Fiction: A Study in Cultural Alienation." *Modern Chinese Literature* 1, no. 1 (1984): 103–30.

McDougall, Bonnie, and Kam Louie. *The Literature of China in the Twentieth Century*. London: Hurst, 1997.

McGuirk, Kevin. "'Rough Trades': Charles Bernstein and the Currency of Poetry." *Canadian Review of American Studies* 27, no. 3 (1997): 205–14.

McHale, Brian. "Telling Stories Again: On the Replenishment of Narrative in the Postmodernist Long Poem." *Yearbook of English Studies* 30 (2000): 250–62.

———. "Weak Narrativity: The Case of Avant-Garde Narrative Poetry." *Narrative* 9, no. 2 (2001): 161–67.

———. "What Was Postmodernism? or, The Last of the Angels." In *The Shock of the Other: Situating Alterities*, edited by Silke Horstkotte and Esther Peeren, 39–56. Amsterdam: Rodopi, 2007.

Mamin, Iurii, dir. *Okno v Parizh* [Window to Paris]. St. Petersburg: Fontaine; Paris: La Sept Cinéma, Le centre national de la cinématographie, 1993. Motion picture.

Matejka, Ladislav. "The Formal Method and Linguistics." In *Readings in Russian Poetics: Formalist and Structuralist Views*, edited by Ladislav Matejka and Krystyna Pomorska, 281–95. Ann Arbor: Michigan Slavic Publications, 1978.

Mao, Douglas, and Rebecca L. Walkowitz. "The New Modernist Studies." *PMLA* 123, no. 3 (2008): 737–48.

Mayakovsky, Vladimir. *The Bedbug and Selected Poetry*. Edited by Patricia Blake. Translated by Max Hayward and George Reavey. London: Weidenfeld and Nicolson, 1961.

Mayhew, Jonathan. *Apocryphal Lorca: Translation, Parody, Kitsch*. Chicago: University of Chicago Press, 2009.

Melas, Natalie. *All the Difference in the World: Postcoloniality and the Ends of Comparison*. Stanford, CA: Stanford University Press, 2007.

Middleton, Peter. "The Transitive Poetics of Rothenberg's Transnational Anthologies." *West Coast Line* 34, no. 2 (2000): 90–104.

Mikhailichenko, B. "Sbornik *Krug*" [The collection *Krug*]. Endnote 2 to Zolotonosov, "*Krug* i vokrug," 236–41.

Molnar, Michael. "The Vagaries of Description: The Poetry of Arkadii Dragomoshchenko." *Essays in Poetics: The Journal of the British Neo-Formalist Circle* 14, no. 1 (1989): 76–98.

Monroe, Jonathan. "Avant-Garde Poetries after the Wall." *Poetics Today* 21, no. 1 (2000): 95–128.

Moretti, Franco. "Conjectures on World Literature." *New Left Review*, n.s., 1 (January–February 2000): 54–68.

Nathanson, Tenney. "Collage and Pulverization in Contemporary American Poetry: Charles Bernstein's *Controlling Interests*." *Contemporary Literature* 33, no. 2 (Summer 1992): 302–18.

Nelson, Deborah. *Pursuing Privacy in Cold War America*. New York: Columbia University Press, 2002.

Ngai, Sianne. "Bad Timing (A Sequel): Paranoia, Feminism, and Poetry." *Differences: A Journal of Feminist Cultural Studies* 12, no. 2 (2001): 1–46.

Nicholas, Mary A. "Dmitrij Prigov and the Russian Avant-Garde, Then and Now." *Russian Literature* 39 (1996): 13–34.

Nicholls, Peter. *Modernisms: A Literary Guide.* Berkeley: University of California Press, 1995.

———. "Phenomenal Poetics: Reading Lyn Hejinian." In *Postwar American Poetry: The Mechanics of the Mirage*, edited by Christine Pagnoulle and Michel Delville, 241–52. Liège: University of Liège, 2000.

Nienhauser, William H. *The Indiana Companion to Traditional Chinese Literature.* Vol. 1. Bloomington: Indiana University Press, 1986.

Noland, Carrie, and Barrett Watten, eds. *Diasporic Avant-Gardes: Experimental Poetics and Cultural Displacement.* New York: Palgrave, 2009.

North, Michael. *The Dialect of Modernism: Race, Language, and Twentieth-Century Literature.* New York: Oxford University Press, 1994.

Obermayr, Brigitte. "P-rigov wie P-uškin: Zur Demystifikation der Autorfunktion bei Dmitrij A. Prigov." In *Mystifikation—Autorschaft—Original*, edited by Susi Frank, Renate Lachmann, Sylvia Sasse, Schamma Schahadat, and Caroline Schramm, 283–311. Tübingen: Gunter Narr Verlag, 2001.

———. "Tod und Zahl: Transitive und intransitive Operationen bei V. Chlebnikov und D. A. Prigov." *Wiener Slawistischer Almanach* 56 (2005): 209–85.

Olson, Charles. *The Collected Poems of Charles Olson: Excluding "The Maximus Poems."* Edited by George F. Butterick. Berkeley: University of California Press, 1997.

———. *Mayan Letters.* 1953. London: Jonathan Cape, 1968.

Ostanin, Boris. "Byt' vmesto imet'" [To be instead of to have]. *Toronto Slavic Quarterly* 2 (2002). http://www.utoronto.ca/tsq/02/ostanin2.shtml.

Ostanin, Boris, and Aleksandr Kobak. "Molniia i raduga: Puti kul'tury 60–80-kh godov (Opyt emblemnogo analiza)" [Lightning and rainbow: The paths of culture from the 1960s to the 1980s (An experiment in symbolic analysis)]. 1986. In *Molniia i raduga: Literaturno-kriticheskie stat'i 1980-kh godov*, 9–37. St. Petersburg: N. I. Novikova, 2003.

Owen, Stephen. "Stepping Forward and Back: Issues and Possibilities for 'World' Poetry." *Modern Philology* 100, no. 4 (2003): 532–48.

———. "What Is World Poetry? The Anxiety of Global Influence." *The New Republic*, 19 November 1990, 28–32.

Pavlov, Evgeny. Translator's preface to "What We Talk about When We

Talk about Poetry: A Recent View from St. Petersburg," by Arka-
dii Dragomoshchenko, translated by Evgeny Pavlov. *Postmodern Cul-
ture* 9, no. 1 (1998). http://muse.jhu.edu/journals/postmodern_culture
/voo9/9.1pavlov.html.

———. "'Poetry' vs. 'Literature': Dragomoshchenko's Tautologies." *Slavic
and East European Journal* 55, no. 4 (2011): 553–70.

Pensky, Max. "Method and Time: Benjamin's Dialectical Images." In *The
Cambridge Companion to Walter Benjamin*, edited by David S. Ferris,
177–98. Cambridge: Cambridge University Press, 2004.

Pepeliaev, Aleksandr, dir. *Al'fa-Chaika* [The alpha seagull]. Proekt fabrika
(now also known as Aktovyi zal), Moscow, premiered July 2006.

Perelman, Bob. "Polemic Greeting to the Inhabitants of Utopia." In Huk, *As-
sembling Alternatives*, 375–83.

———. *Primer.* Berkeley, CA: This Press, 1981.

Perloff, Marjorie. "Avant-Garde Tradition and the Individual Talent: The
Case of Language Poetry." *Revue française d'études américaines* 103
(2005): 117–41.

———. *The Dance of the Intellect: Studies in the Poetry of the Pound Tradi-
tion.* Cambridge: Cambridge University Press, 1985.

———. *The Futurist Moment: Avant-Garde, Avant Guerre, and the Lan-
guage of Rupture.* Chicago: University of Chicago Press, 1986.

———. "How Russian Is It?" *Parnassus: Poetry in Review* 18, no. 1 (1992):
186–209.

———. *Poetry on and off the Page: Essays for Emergent Occasions.* Evan-
ston, IL: Northwestern University Press, 1998.

———. *Radical Artifice: Writing Poetry in the Age of Media.* Chicago: Uni-
versity of Chicago Press, 1991.

———. Review of *Leningrad: American Writers in the Soviet Union*, by Mi-
chael Davidson, Lyn Hejinian, Ron Silliman, and Barrett Watten. *Sulfur*
29 (1991): 216–21.

———. "Russian Postmodernism: An Oxymoron?" *Postmodern Culture* 3, no.
2 (1993). http://muse.jhu.edu/journals/postmodern_culture/voo3/3.2perloff
.html.

———. "'The Sweet Aftertaste of Artichokes. The Lobes of Autobiography':
Lyn Hejinian's *My Life.*" *Denver Quarterly: A Journal of Modern Cul-
ture* 25, no. 4 (1991): 116–28.

———. *21st-Century Modernism: The "New" Poetics.* Malden, MA: Black-
well, 2002.

———. *Unoriginal Genius: Poetry by Other Means in the New Century.*
Chicago: University of Chicago Press, 2010.

————. "Unoriginal Genius: Walter Benjamin's *Arcades* as Paradigm for the New Poetics." *Études Anglaises* 61, no. 2 (2008): 229–52.

Peterson, Tim. "Either You're with Us and against Us: Charles Bernstein's *Girly Man*, 9–11, and the Brechtian Figure of the Reader." *Electronic Book Review*, 9 March 2008. http://www.electronicbookreview.com /thread/electropoetics/reflective.

Pollard, Charles W. *New World Modernisms: T. S. Eliot, Derek Walcott, and Kamau Brathwaite*. Charlottesville: University of Virginia Press, 2004.

Pollard, David E. "The Controversy over Modernism, 1979–84." *China Quarterly* 104 (1985): 641–56.

————. Preface to *The Chinese Essay*, edited and translated by David E. Pollard, 11–15. Hong Kong: Research Centre for Translation, Chinese University of Hong Kong, 1999.

Pozzana, Claudia. "Distances of Poetry: An Introduction to Bei Dao." *Positions: Asia Critique* 15, no. 1 (2007): 91–111.

Pratt, Mary Louise. *Imperial Eyes: Travel Writing and Transculturation*. 2nd ed. New York: Routledge, 2008.

Prigov, Dmitri. *Azbuki* [Alphabets]. http://www.prigov.ru/bukva/index.php.

————. "Conceptualism and the West." Interview by Alexei Alexeyev [Aleksandr Sidorov]. Translated by Michael Molnar. "Elsewhere." Special issue, *Poetics Journal* 8 (June 1989): 12–16.

————. "Dmitry Prigov / Dmitrii Prigov." *A-Ya* 1 (1979): 52.

————. "Everything You Ever Wanted to Know about Moscow Conceptualism." Translated by Jessy Kamer. In *Novostroika / New Structures: Culture in the Soviet Union Today*, edited by Lisa Appignanesi, 27. London: Institute of Contemporary Arts, 1989. Published in conjunction with a projected season on contemporary Soviet culture at the ICA in London, 1989.

————. *Faksimil'noe vosproizvedenie samodel'noi knigi Dmitriia Aleksandrovicha Prigova 'Evgenii Onegin Pushkina' s risunkami na poliach raboty Aleksandra Florenskogo* [Facsimile reproduction of Dmitrii Aleksandrovich Prigov's self-made book "Pushkin's *Eugene Onegin*" with drawings on the margins of the work by Aleksandr Florenskii]. St. Petersburg: Mit'kilibris; Krasnyi matros, 1998.

————. *Grazhdane! Ne zabyvaites', pozhaluista! Raboty na bumage, installiatsiia, kniga, performans, opera i deklamatsiia / Citizens! Please mind yourselves! Works on Paper, Installations, Books, Readings, Performance, and Opera*. Edited by Ekaterina Degot'. Moscow: Moscow Museum of Modern Art, 2008. Published in conjunction with the exhibition shown at the Moskovskii muzei sovremennogo iskusstva / Moscow Museum of Modern Art, 13 May–15 June 2008.

———. *Iavlenie stikha posle ego smerti* [The appearance of verse after its death]. Moscow: Tekst, 1995.

———. *Ischisleniia i ustanovleniia: Stratifikatsionnye i konvertatsionnye teksty* [Calculations and determinations: Stratified and converted texts]. Moscow: Novoe literaturnoe obozrenie, 2001.

———. "Iskusstvo predposlednich istin: Beseda s Dmitriem Prigovym" [The art of penultimate truths: A conversation with Dmitri Prigov]. *Al'manach Panorama*, 17–24 February 1989, 16–18.

———. "Kniga kak sposob nechitaniia" [The book as a means of not reading]. In *Tochka zreniia: Vizual'naia poeziia, 90-e gody*, edited by Dmitrii Bulatov, 61–62. Kaliningrad: Simplitsii, 1998.

———. "Mantra vysokoi russkoi kul'tury" [Mantra of Russian high culture]. "Vtoraia mezhregional'naia konferentsiia v ramkakh isledovatel'skogo proekta 'Lokal'nye istorii,'" Norilsk, 2–5 November 2005. YouTube video, 11:00. Posted by "djbabyboom," 27 July 2007. http://www.youtube .com/watch?v=y2my8S_dwZA.

———. *Piat'desiat kapelek krovi*. Moscow: Tekst, 1993. Translated by Christopher Mattison as *Fifty Drops of Blood in an Absorbent Medium* (New York: Ugly Duckling, 2004).

———. "Preduvedomlenie avtora k publikatsii tsikla rabot" [Author's foreword to the publication of a cycle of works]. Unpublished manuscript. Dmitrii Prigov Papers, A-Ya Archive, O-71.001.028.01.

———. "Prigov kak Pushkin." Interview by Andrei Zorin. In *Podobrannyi Prigov*, 233–52. Moscow: Rossiiskii gosudarstvennyi gumanitarnyi universitet, 1997.

———. "From *Reagan's Image in Soviet Literature*." In *Third Wave: The New Russian Poetry*, edited by Kent Johnson and Stephen M. Ashby, 104–6. Ann Arbor: University of Michigan Press, 1992.

———. *Sbornik preduvedomlenii k raznoobraznym veshcham* [A collection of forewords to various things]. Moscow: Ad Marginem, 1996.

———. *Slezy geral'dicheskoi dushi* [Tears of a heraldic spirit]. Moscow: Moskovskii robochii, 1990.

———. *Sobranie stikhov* [Collected poems]. Edited by Brigitte Obermayr. 5 vols. Vienna: Gesellschaft zur Förderung slawistischer Studien, 1996–2009.

———. *Sovetskie teksty, 1979–84* [Soviet texts, 1979–84]. St. Petersburg: Ivan Limbakh, 1997.

———. *Stikhogrammy* [Poemographs]. Paris: A-Ya, 1985. A facsimile edition is available at http://www.vavilon.ru/texts/prigov5.html.

———. *Tol'ko moia Iaponiia* [Only my Japan]. Moscow: Novoe literaturnoe obozrenie, 2001.

———. "Uteshaet li nas eto ponimanie?" [Does this understanding give us comfort?] *Novoe literaturnoe obozrenie* 62 (2003). http://magazines.russ .ru/nlo/2003/62/prigov.html.

———. "What More Is There to Say?" In *Third Wave: The New Russian Poetry*, edited by Kent Johnson and Stephen M. Ashby, 101–3. Ann Arbor: University of Michigan Press, 1992.

Prigov, Dmitri, Natalia Mali, and Andrei Prigov (Prigov Family Group; later known as PMP Group). *PMP-pozitiv; ili, Rekonstruktsiia po kasatel'noi / PMP-Positive; or, Tangential Reconstruction*. Moscow: Gosudarstvennyi tsentr sovremennogo iskusstva / National Centre for Contemporary Arts, 2004. Published in conjunction with the exhibition shown at the National Centre for Contemporary Arts in Moscow, 27 May–6 June 2004.

Prigov, Dmitri, Rea Nikonova [Anna Tarshis], and Sergei Sigei [Sergei Sigov]. "Perepiska" [Correspondence]. *Novoe literaturnoe obozrenie* 32 (1998): 269–82.

Prigov, Dmitri, and Studiia Muzei Anna Termen [The Anna Theremin Museum Studio; Aleksandr Dolgin and Iraida Iusupova]. "Rossiia" [Russia]. 2004. YouTube video, 6:14. Posted by "AnnaThereminMuseum," 25 February 2010. http://www.youtube.com/watch?v=p28B67twgwg.

Pushkin, A. S. *Polnoe sobranie sochinenii v desiatykh tomakh* [Complete collected works in ten volumes]. Edited by B. V. Tomashevksii. Leningrad: Nauka, 1977–1979.

Ramazani, Jahan. *The Hybrid Muse: Postcolonial Poetry in English*. Chicago: University of Chicago Press, 2001.

———. *A Transnational Poetics*. Chicago: University of Chicago Press, 2009.

Raser, Timothy. "Barthes and Riffaterre: The Dilemmas of Realism in the Light of Baudelaire's 'Le Soleil.'" *French Review* 59, no. 1 (1985): 58–64.

Robbins, Bruce. *Feeling Global: Internationalism in Distress*. New York: New York University Press, 1999.

———. "Uses of World Literature." In *The Routledge Companion to World Literature*, edited by Theo D'haen, David Damrosch, and Djelal Kadir, 383–92. Abingdon, UK; New York: Routledge, 2012.

Robertson, Graeme B. "Managing Society: Protest, Civil Society, and Regime in Putin's Russia." *Slavic Review* 68, no. 3 (2009): 528–47.

Robinson, Douglas. *Estrangement and the Somatics of Literature*. Baltimore: Johns Hopkins University Press, 2008.

Rogers, John, dir. *Saxophone Diplomacy*. First aired in the summer of 1984 on KQED in San Francisco and then nationally on the PBS network. Berkeley, CA: Ideas in Motion, 1984. Videocassette (VHS), 28 mins.

Rony, Fatimah Tobing. *The Third Eye: Race, Cinema, and Ethnographic Spectacle.* Durham, NC: Duke University Press, 1996.

Rothenberg, Jerome. "Pre-face (1967)." In *Technicians of the Sacred: A Range of Poetries from Africa, America, Asia, Europe and Oceania,* edited by Jerome Rothenberg, xxv–xxxiii. 2nd ed. Berkeley: University of California Press, 1985.

———, ed. *Shaking the Pumpkin: Traditional Poetry of the Indian North Americas.* Garden City, NY: Doubleday, 1972.

———, ed. *Technicians of the Sacred: A Range of Poetries from Africa, America, Asia, Europe and Oceania.* Garden City, NY: Doubleday, 1968.

Rothenberg, Jerome, and Pierre Joris. *Poems for the Millennium: The University of California Book of Modern and Postmodern Poetry.* Berkeley: University of California Press, 1995–2009.

Rova Saxophone Quartet. *Saxophone Diplomacy.* Basel: Hat Hut Records, 1985, 33⅓ rpm.

Rubinshtein, Lev. "Professiia: Prigov" [Profession: Prigov]. In *Podobrannyi Prigov,* by Dmitri Prigov, 230–32. Moscow: Rossiiskii gosudarstvennyi gumanitarnyi universitet, 1997.

Said, Edward. *Orientalism.* New York: Pantheon Books, 1978.

Sakina, M. "Dragomoshchenko, Arkadii Trofimovich." Endnote 3 to Zolotonosov, "*Krug* i vokrug," 241–42.

Samuels, Lisa. "Eight Justifications for Canonizing Lyn Hejinian's *My Life.*" *Modern Language Studies* 27, no. 2 (1997): 103–19.

Sandler, Stephanie. "Arkadii Dragomoshchenko, Lyn Hejinian, and the Persistence of Romanticism." *Contemporary Literature* 46, no. 1 (2005): 18–45.

———. *Commemorating Pushkin: Russia's Myth of a National Poet.* Stanford, CA: Stanford University Press, 2004.

Sarotte, Mary Elise. *1989: The Struggle to Create Post–Cold War Europe.* Princeton, NJ: Princeton University Press, 2009.

Saussy, Haun. "Bei Dao and His Audiences." Introduction to a presentation by Bei Dao. Stanford Presidential Lectures in the Humanities and Arts. 29 November 1999. Available online at http://prelectur.stanford.edu/lecturers /dao/daoaudience.html.

———. ed, *Comparative Literature in an Age of Globalization.* Baltimore: Johns Hopkins University Press, 2006.

———. "Death and Translation." *Representations* 94 (2006): 112–30.

———. *Great Walls of Discourse and Other Adventures in Cultural China.* Cambridge, MA: Harvard University Press, 2001.

———. "Mei Lanfang in Moscow, 1935: Familiar, Unfamiliar, Defamiliar." *Modern Chinese Literature and Culture* 18, no. 1 (Spring 2006): 8–29.

Savitskii, Stanislav. *Andegraund: Istoriia i mify leningradskoi neofitsial'noi literatury* [Underground: The history and myths of Leningrad's unofficial literature]. Moscow: Novoe literaturnoe obozrenie, 2002.

Schultz, Susan M. *A Poetics of Impasse in Modern and Contemporary American Poetry.* Tuscaloosa: University of Alabama Press, 2005.

Seiler, Eddie, Sol Marcus, Bennie Benjemen, and Eddie Durham. "I Don't Want to Set the World on Fire." New York: Cherio Music Publishers, 1941.

Shelkovsky, Igor. "Zametki iz drugogo tysiacheletiia" [Notes from another millennium]. Sakharov Museum. http://www.sakharov-center.ru /museum/exhibitionhall/a-ya/2008.php. Published online in conjunction with the exhibition *Zhurnal na podokonnike: Istoriia izdaniia "A-Ia,"* shown at the Sakharov Museum, Moscow, 2008.

Shields, Rob. "Fancy Footwork: Walter Benjamin's Notes on *Flânerie.*" In *The Flâneur,* edited by Keith Tester, 61–80. London: Routledge, 1994.

Shih, Shu-mei. *The Lure of the Modern: Writing Modernism in Semicolonial China, 1917–1937.* Berkeley: University of California Press, 2001.

Shklovsky, Viktor. "Art as Technique." In *Russian Formalist Criticism: Four Essays,* translated by Lee T. Lemon and Marion J. Reis, 3–24. Lincoln: University of Nebraska Press, 1965.

———. "Iskusstvo, kak priem" [Art as device]. 1917. In *O teorii prozy,* 7–23. Moscow: Federatsiia, 1929.

———. *Theory of Prose.* Translated by Benjamin Sher. Elmwood Park, IL: Dalkey Archive, 1990.

———. *Third Factory.* 1926. Translated by Richard Sheldon. Ann Arbor, MI: Ardis, 1977.

Shoptaw, John. "Hejinian Meditations: Lives of *The Cell.*" *Journal X: A Biannual Journal of Culture and Criticism* 1, no. 1 (1996): 57–83.

Silliman, Ron, ed. "The Dwelling Place: 9 Poets." *Alcheringa* 1, no. 2 (1975): 104–20.

———. "The Task of the Collaborator: Watten's *Leningrad.*" *Aerial* 8 (1995): 141–68.

Skidan, Aleksandr. "Poetry in the Age of Total Communication." Translated by Thomas H. Campbell. First published in the online journal *Nypoesi* (November 2007). http://www.nypoesi.net (site discontinued). Republished in the "Pre-print" section of *Translit: Literaturno-kriticheskii al'manakh.* http://www.trans-lit.info/trans.htm.

———. Review of *Opisanie,* by Arkadii Dragomoshchenko. *Novaia russkaia kniga* 6 (2000). http://www.guelman.ru/slava/nrk/nrk6/8.html.

Sloan, De Villo. "'Crude Mechanical Access' or 'Crude Personism': A Chronicle of One San Francisco Bay Area Poetry War." *Sagetrieb* 4 (1985): 241–54.

Smith, Gerald S. *Contemporary Russian Poetry: A Bilingual Anthology.* Bloomington: Indiana University Press, 1993.

Solovyov, Vladimir, and Elena Klepikova. *Yuri Andropov: A Secret Passage into the Kremlin.* Translated by Guy Daniels. New York: Macmillan, 1983.

Song Yongyi 宋永毅. "A Glance at the Underground Reading Movement during the Cultural Revolution." *Journal of Contemporary China* 16, no. 51 (2007): 325–33.

———. "Wenge zhong de huangpi shu he huipi shu" 文革中的黄皮书和灰皮书 [Yellow books and grey books in the Cultural Revolution]. *Ershiyi shiji* 二十一世纪 42 (1997): 59–64.

Soong, Stephen C., and John Minford, eds. *Trees on the Mountain: An Anthology of New Chinese Writing.* Hong Kong: Chinese University Press, 1984.

Spahr, Juliana. "Connected Disconnection and Localized Globalism in Pacific Multilingual Literature." *Boundary 2* 31, no. 3 (2004): 75–100.

Spivak, Gayatri Chakravorty. *Death of a Discipline.* New York: Columbia University Press, 2003.

———. *In Other Worlds: Essays in Cultural Politics.* New York: Routledge, 1988.

———. "Translation as Culture." *Parallax* 6, no. 1 (2000): 13–24.

Stein, Gertrude. *Writings, 1932–1946.* Edited by Catharine R. Stimpson and Harriet Chessman. New York: Library of America, 1998.

Steiner, Peter. *Russian Formalism: A Metapoetics.* Ithaca, NY: Cornell University Press, 1984.

Stewart, Susan. *Poetry and the Fate of the Senses.* Chicago: University of Chicago Press, 2002.

Striedter, Jurij. *Literary Structure, Evolution, and Value: Russian Formalism and Czech Structuralism Reconsidered.* Cambridge, MA: Harvard University Press, 1989.

Suzuki-Morris, Tessa. "In Interesting Times: Northeast Asia's Tipping-Point and Its Implications for the Southern Hemisphere." In *Recentring Asia: Histories, Encounters, Identities*, edited by Jacob Edmond, Henry Johnson, and Jacqueline Leckie, 33–53. Leiden: Brill / Global Oriental, 2011.

Swedenborg, Emanuel. *Arcana Cœlestia.* Vol. 4. London: Swedenborg Society, 1879.

Tamburello, Giuseppa (Zhu Xi 朱西). "Ershi shiji houqi Zhongguo shiren yu xiyang shi" 二十世纪后期中国诗人与西洋诗 [Late twentieth-century Chinese poets and Western poetry]. In *A Century of Modern Chinese Poetry: An International Conference, Collected Papers vol. 1*, n.p. Beijing: Peking University and Capital Normal University, 2005.

Tapper, Gordon. "Technocrats of the Mind." Review of *Girly Man*, by Charles Bernstein. *Brooklyn Rail*, March 2007. http://brooklynrail .org/2007/03/books/nonfiction-technocrats-of-the-mind.

Tarasov, Vladimir, Kerry Shawn Keys, Dmitri Prigov, Yang Lian, and Sigitas Geda. *Sonatina for Percussion and Four Poets*. Vilnius, Lithuania: Prior Records, 2006, compact disc.

Tchouboukov-Pianca, Florence. *Die Konzeptualisierung der Graphomanie in der russischsprachigen postmodernen Literatur*. Munich: Otto Sagner, 1995.

Thomas-Glass, Dan. "Accessibility of Obscurity." *Jacket* 33 (July 2007). Archived by the National Library of Australia. http://nla.gov.au/nla.arc -10059-20071027-0238-jacketmagazine.com/33/thomas-glass-bernstein .html.

Todorov, Tzvetan. "Three Conceptions of Poetic Language." In *Russian Formalism: A Retrospective Glance*, edited by Robert Louis Jackson and Stephen Rudy, 130–47. New Haven, CT: Yale Center for International and Area Studies, 1985.

Tupitsyn, Margarita. "About Early Soviet Conceptualism." In *Global Conceptualism: Points of Origin, 1950s–1980s*, edited by Philomena Mariani, 99–107. New York: Queens Museum of Art, 1999.

Tynianov, Iu. N. "O literaturnoi evoliutsii" [On literary evolution]. In *Poetika. Istoriia literatury. Kino*, 270–81. Moscow: Nauka, 1977.

Van Crevel, Maghiel. *Chinese Poetry in Times of Mind, Mayhem and Money*. Leiden: Brill, 2008.

———. *Language Shattered: Contemporary Chinese Poetry and Duoduo*. Leiden: Research School CNWS, 1996.

———. "Unofficial Poetry Journals from the People's Republic of China: A Research Note and an Annotated Bibliography." A *Modern Chinese Literature and Culture* Resource Center Publication, February 2007. http:// mclc.osu.edu/rc/pubs/vancrevel2.html.

Volchek, Dmitrii. "Interv'iu s Viktorom Krivulinym" [An interview with Viktor Krivulin]. *Mitin zhurnal* 6 (1985). http://kolonna.mitin.com /archive.php?address=http://kolonna.mitin.com/archive/mj06/krivulin .shtml.

Von Hallberg, Robert. "Poetry, Politics, and Intellectuals." In *The Cambridge History of American Literature*. Vol. 8, *Poetry and Criticism, 1940–1995*, edited by Sacvan Bercovitch, 9–259. Cambridge: Cambridge University Press, 1996.

Wadleigh, Michael, dir. *Woodstock: Three Days of Peace and Music*. New York: Wadleigh-Maurice, 1970. Motion picture.

Wang, David Der-Wei. Introduction to *Chinese Literature in the Second Half of a Modern Century*, edited by Pang-Yuan Chi and David Der-Wei Wang, xiii–xliii. Bloomington: Indiana University Press, 2000.

Wang, Jing. *High Culture Fever: Politics, Aesthetics, and Ideology in Deng's China*. Berkeley: University of California Press, 1996.

Wang, Yiyan. "Venturing into Shanghai: The *Flâneur* in Two of Shi Zhecun's Short Stories." *Modern Chinese Literature and Culture* 19, no. 2 (Fall 2007): 34–70.

Watten, Barrett. *The Constructivist Moment: From Material Text to Cultural Poetics*. Middletown, CT: Wesleyan University Press, 2003.

———. "Post-Soviet Subjectivity in Arkadii Dragomoshchenko and Ilya Kabakov." *Postmodern Culture* 3, no. 2 (1993). http://muse.jhu.edu /journals/postmodern_culture/v003/3.2watten.html.

———. *Total Syntax*. Carbondale: Southern Illinois University Press, 1985.

———. "The Turn to Language and the 1960s." *Critical Inquiry* 29, no. 1 (Fall 2002): 139–83.

Wenders, Wim. *Der Himmel über Berlin* [English title: *Wings of Desire*]. Berlin: Road Movies; Paris: Argos, 1987. Motion picture.

Wesling, Donald. Review of *Redo*, by Lyn Hejinian. *Archive Newsletter* [Mandeville Department of Special Collections, University of California, San Diego], Fall 1986, 23.

Wilson, Elizabeth. "The Invisible Flâneur." *New Left Review* 191 (1992): 90–110.

Witte, Georg. "Katalogkatastrophen—Das Alphabet in der russischen Literatur." In *Zeichen zwischen Klartext und Arabeske*, edited by Susi Kotzinger and Gabriele Rippl, 35–55. Amsterdam: Rodopi, 1994.

Wittgenstein, Ludwig. *Philosophical Investigations*. Translated by G. E. M. Anscombe, P. M. S. Hacker, and Joachim Schulte. 4th ed. Chichester, UK; Malden, MA: Wiley-Blackwell, 2009.

Wolin, Richard. *The Wind from the East: French Intellectuals, the Cultural Revolution, and the Legacy of the 1960s*. Princeton, NJ: Princeton University Press, 2010.

Yang Lian 杨炼. *Concentric Circles*. Translated by Brian Holton and Agnes Hung-Chong Chan. Tarset, UK: Bloodaxe, 2005.

———. *Dahai tingzhi zhi chu: Yang Lian zuopin 1982–1997; shige juan* 大海停止之处: 杨炼作品 1982–1997; 诗歌卷 [Where the sea stands still: Works by Yang Lian, 1982–1997; Poetry volume]. Shanghai: Shanghai wenyi, 1998.

———. *The Dead in Exile*. Translated by Mabel Lee. Canberra: Tiananmen, 1990.

———. *Guihua; Zhili de kongjian: Yang Lian zuopin 1982–1997: Sanwen; wenlun juan* 鬼话·智力的空间: 杨炼作品 1982–1997: 散文·文论卷 [Ghost speech/lies; Intellectual space: Works by Yang Lian, 1982–1997: Short prose and essays volume]. Shanghai: Shanghai wenyi, 1998.

———. "To Touch the Border and Cross It: An Interview with Yang Lian." Interview by Sabrina Merolla, conducted 24 June 2004. Published on Yang Lian's website. http://yanglian.net/yanglian_en/talk/talk02.html.

———. *Unreal City: A Chinese Poet in Auckland*. Edited by Jacob Edmond and Hilary Chung. Translated by Hilary Chung and Jacob Edmond, with Brian Holton. Auckland: Auckland University Press, 2006.

———. "Wode wenxue xiezuo: Yang Lian wangzhan 'Zuopin' lan yinyan" 我的文学写作: 杨炼网站"作品"栏引言 [My literary writings: Foreword to the "Works" section of Yang Lian's website]. In *Yi zuo xiang xia xiujian de ta* 一座向下修建的塔, 161–64. Beijing: Fenghuang, 2009. First published as "Yinyan" 引言 [Foreword] to Yang Lian's website, 24 November 2005. http://www.yanglian.net/yanglian/produce.html.

———. "Zhuixun zuowei liuwang yuanxing de shi" 追寻作为流亡原型的诗 [In search of poetry as the prototype of exile]. In *Yan dui wo shuo* 雁对我说, 279–86. Hong Kong: Ming bao yuekan; Singapore: Xinjiapo qingnian, 2010. Available on Yang Lian's website. http://yanglian.net/yanglian/pensee/pen_wenlun_02.html.

Yeh, Michelle. "Chayi de youlü—yige huixiang" 差异的忧虑——一个回响. *Jintian* 今天 1 (1991): 94–96. Translated by Michelle Yeh as "The Anxiety of Difference: A Rejoinder." Unpublished manuscript. Private collection.

Young, Robert. *Colonial Desire: Hybridity in Theory, Culture, and Race*. London: Routledge, 1995.

———. *The Idea of English Ethnicity*. Oxford: Blackwell, 2008.

Yu, Timothy. *Race and the Avant-Garde: Experimental and Asian American Poetry since 1965*. Stanford, CA: Stanford University Press, 2009.

Zhang Longxi. *Allegoresis: Reading Canonical Literature East and West*. Ithaca, NY: Cornell University Press, 2005.

———. "Out of the Cultural Ghetto: Theory, Politics, and the Study of Chinese Literature." *Modern China* 19, no. 1 (1993): 71–101.

Zhang Ming 章明. "Ling ren qimen de 'menglong'" 令人气闷的"朦胧" [The "obscurity" that makes one brood]. *Shi kan* 诗刊 8 (1980): 53–54.

Zhang, Xudong. *Chinese Modernism in the Era of Reforms: Cultural Fever, Avant-Garde Fiction, and the New Chinese Cinema*. Durham, NC: Duke University Press, 1997.

Zhang, Yingjin. *The City in Modern Chinese Literature and Film: Configu-

rations of Space, Time, and Gender. Stanford, CA: Stanford University Press, 2006.

Zolotonosov, M., ed. "*Krug* i vokrug; ili, K istorii odnoi krugovoi poruki: Lamentatsiia tsenzora s kommentariiami" [*Krug* and around; or, Toward a history of one mutual dependence: A censor's lamentation with commentary]. *Novoe literaturnoe obozrenie* 14 (1995): 234–51.

Zorin, Andrei. "'Al'manakh'—vzgliad iz zala" ["Al'manakh"—a view from the audience]. In *Lichnoe delo No_: Literaturno-khudozhestvennyi al'manakh*, edited by Lev Rubinshtein, 246–71. Moscow: Soiuzteatr, 1991.

———. "Chtoby zhizn' vnizu tekla: Dmitrii Aleksandrovich Prigov i sovetskaia deistvitel'nost'" [So that life would flow on down: Dmitri Aleksandrovich Prigov and Soviet reality]. In Prigov, *Sovetskie teksty*, 10–17.

INDEX

Page numbers in italics refer to figures.

37 (samizdat journal), 134, 138

affect: global comparison, 165, 178–79,
191–92; hermeneutics of suspicion,
171, 173–74; lyric, 179–81, 183–84,
186–90
Alcheringa (journal), 167. *See also*
Rothenberg, Jerome
Alexandre, Vincente, 102–3
allegory: in Baudelaire's poetry, 21–22,
28–29; in Bei Dao's poetry, 105–9,
113–17, 119–20, 123; of cross-
cultural reading (Dragomoshchenko),
64; and the flâneur, 17, 204n15; and
ideology, 221n41; and iteration, 196;
national and global, 13, 95–101, 103,
110–12, 124
Allen, Donald (*The New American
Poetry, 1945–1960*), 166
Americanness. *See* Westernness and
Americanness, notion of
Anderson, Laurie (*Strange Angels*), 194
Andrews, Bruce, 184
Anti–Bourgeois Liberalization Campaign
(1987), 26, 111–12, 222n53
Anti–Spiritual Pollution Campaign (1983),
26, 111–12
Anvil Poetry Press, 112, 222n53
April 5, 1976, incident, 106
artworks: Bee's *Fleurs du mal*, 185–
86, *186*; Chinese and Russian
conceptual, 125–126, 150, 223n3;
Ostap Dragomoshchenko's *This Time
We Are Both*, 87, 92, 218n66; Kulik's
Reservoir Dog, 226n49; and poetry,
130, 132–34, 161–62; samizdat texts
as, 13, 138–44, 151–54. *See also*
conceptualism; *and specific titles
under* Prigov, Dmitri, works
Auckland, as a literary topos, 11, 26–30,
34–41, *35*, 41–42, 196–98
Auschwitz. *See* Holocaust
automatization, 74, 76, 93–94, 191. *See
also* estrangement; Shklovsky, Viktor

avant-garde poetry and art: conceptual
writing, 162; debates within, 170,
190; and estrangement, 8–10, 13, 72,
74; and the flâneur, 16; response to
Russian tradition of, 136, 147–48;
response to US tradition of, 166, 168,
184–85; transnationalism of, 2–8,
79, 130, 175, 198, 201n22, 202n31.
See also conceptualism; Language
writers; *and names of individual
poets*
A-Ya (art journal), 138–46, 150, 224n3,
226n44

Bakhtin, Mikhail, 129–30
Baptiste-Chirot, David, 190
Barthes, Roland, 49–50, 172, 191
Baudelaire, Charles: Chinese translations
of, 19–20, 101, 205n23, 205n31,
205n34; correspondences, 45, 47, 60,
64, 210n11; and Duoduo, 20–21,
24–25, 197, 206n48; echo, iteration,
and rhyme, 47–50, 54, 198; exile,
28–29; flâneur, 11–12, 16–17, 19, 98,
119, 203n12, 204n21; objectification
of women, 18, 185; poetic prose, 31,
207n86; pun on "vers," 21–23, 38,
41; reading Chinese poetry through,
27, 42; temporality of modernity,
31–33, 36, 39
– WORKS: "L'albatros," 207n77; "À
une mendiante rousse" ("To
a Red-Haired Beggar Girl"),
185; "À une passante" ("To a
Passerby"), 17, 39, 49, 204n17,
204n21; "Une charogne,"
205n34; "Correspondances"
("Correspondences"), 12, 44, 45,
47–48, 54, 60, 64, 209n11; "Le
crépuscule du matin" ("Dawn"),
20, 33, 205n31; "Le cygne" ("The
Swan"), 28–29, 32–33; *Les fleurs
du mal (The Flowers of Evil)*, 19–
20; "The Painter of Modern Life,"